Reviewers Praise...

"If you want to inspire your children's heart energy and heart intelligence, devour this book and utilize every tool it teaches."

Mark Victor Hansen
author of *Chicken Soup for the Soul*

"Exceptional...no matter what the activity, there is a correlation to love and development of a child's emotional skills."

Hudson Valley Parent

"Very much worthwhile...positive ways to invoke family communication and understanding. Shows what makes the world go 'round!"

Nashville Parent Magazine

"Tools for...a new generation of humans capable of handling anything and everything."

Moving Words

"Valuable for parents, teachers, and, of course, kids."

NAPRA ReVIEW

"A must for all parents, educators and childcare providers!"

Leading Edge Review

"Ideal for family night activities...essential reading for any parent...helping their child to grow up happy and loving."

Wisconsin Bookwatch

Teaching Children to Love

80 Games & Fun Activities for Raising Balanced Children in Unbalanced Times

by
Doc Lew Childre

Edited by Sara Hatch Paddison

Contributing Editors:
Deborah Rozman, Ph.D., Psychology
Jeffrey Goelitz, M.Ed.

Field-Test Editor:
Wanda Wortman

PLANETARY PUBLICATIONS
Boulder Creek, California

Published in the United States of America by:

Planetary Publications

P.O. Box 66, Boulder Creek, California 95006

(800) 372-3100 (408) 338-2161 Fax (408) 338-9861

hrtmath@netcom.com

http://www.planetarypub.com

Manufactured in the United States by BookCrafters

First Printing 1996
Second Printing 1996
Third Printing 1997

Cover Design by Sandy Royall

Library of Congress Cataloging-in-Publication Data

Childre, Doc Lew, 1945-
        Teaching children to love : 80 games & fun activities for raising balanced children
in unbalanced times / by Doc Lew Childre ; edited by Sara Hatch Paddison.
                p.   cm.
        ISBN 1-879052-26-1
        1. Child rearing. 2. Creative activities and seat work. 3. Games. 4. Love.
I. Paddison, Sara, 1953-   . II. Title.
HQ769.C482   1996
649'.1--dc20
                                                                            96-12013
                                                                            CIP

10 9 8 7 6 5 4 3

OTHER BOOKS AND MUSIC
by
Doc Lew Childre

A Parenting Manual:
Heart Hope for the Family

The How to Book of Teen Self Discovery

CUT-THRU:
Achieve Total Security and Maximum Energy

CUT-THRU Audiobook

FREEZE-FRAME:
Fast Action Stress Relief;
A Scientifically Proven Technique

FREEZE-FRAME Audiobook

Self Empowerment:
The Heart Approach to Stress Management

Women Lead With Their Hearts:
The New Paradigm and New Solution for the 21st Century
—A White Paper—

Heart Zones (cassette and CD)

Speed of Balance (cassette and CD)

Buddy Bubbles cassette

DEDICATION

This book is dedicated to all parents, teachers, childcare providers, counselors, relatives, families, and everyone who is responsible for loving, educating, and caring for the children of our world. It is my sincere hope that the games, activities, and understanding of love presented in *Teaching Children to Love* will help adults and children everywhere discover the intelligence, joy, and power of love required to raise balanced children in today's unbalanced times.

Acknowledgments

Many parents, teachers, counselors, and children from different geographical regions and socio-economic strata helped contribute to this book by field testing these activities. Their willingness to explore these new concepts and share their comments and evaluations afterwards were invaluable in refining the activities and making them more suitable for everyone.

We appreciate the following parents who took time to play these activities with their children: Diana Govan, Naomi Hamamoto, Josefina Viramontes, Carmela Diaz, James Beach, Judie DePesa, Carol Nahod, Barbara Benson, Jane Shuman, Mary Felice, Byron Vineyard, Linda Davine, Kay Steinfeld, Cate McCaughan, Christy Barrera, and Michele Pearson.

We appreciate the following teachers, counselors, childcare instructors, and coordinators for their help: Jim McCaughan, Johnette Picard, Bonita Grandal, Kay Lui, Martha Aines, Kerry Hunt, Marilyn Shaner, Jenny Day, Jan Blom, Ursula Thrush, Edie Fritz, Susan Timmer, Chris Brazil, Linda Jo White, Mikki Robert, Patrice Khan, Twila Christman, and Susan Polletts.

A special thanks to the photographers: JJ McCraty, Lena Goelitz, Mikki Robert, Bonita Grandal, Byron Vineyard, Naomi Hamomoto, Sheila Carrillo, Patrice Khan, and Susan Timmer.

Much appreciation goes to Joseph Chilton Pearce for writing the introduction, to Sandy Royall, the illustrator, whose artwork makes the games come alive, to Kathryn McArthur, for her fine technical proofing, and to JJ McCraty, for her production and artwork logistics.

Table of Contents

Introduction

For several years now, the Institute of HeartMath has presented a series of publications and seminars centering on the revolutionary discovery that our heart plays a critical role in brain function. This function has recently been labelled "emotional intelligence" — a popular adoption which has not as yet included the "heart intelligence" from which it springs. The heart-brain dynamic plays a profoundly important role in our intellectual and creative development, and determines the nature of our family and social life. Discovery of it offers a new perspective on the meaning of intelligence in general and should surely revolutionize our concept of the word "love." The Institute of HeartMath has, indeed, lifted heart intelligence and love "out of sentiment and into biology" through brilliant, innovative research. As importantly, Doc Lew Childre and his staff have worked out practical procedures, such as those found in this book, through which we can, as individuals, work with, develop, and enhance these natural endowments.

A recent and widely acclaimed book, *Descarte's Error: Emotion, Reason, and the Brain*, by Antonio R. Damasio, gave conclusive proof that emotions play not just a supportive role but the primary role in all human thinking, particularly reason, logic, analytical thought and all higher forms of intellect. Daniel Goleman's subsequent book, *Emotional Intelligence,* confirmed these observations and brought the matter to national attention. At stake is the classical ideal that has been held before us, particularly as students, of intelligence being an aloof, pure, cerebral activity not "contaminated" with emotions or feelings. We now know that this is a dangerously wrong myth.

Within our brain is a dramatically distinctive "emotional-cognitive" structure, which functions as a veritable command center for our mind-body system. It is this center of the brain which is connected to our heart through direct neural and hormonal connections, and is subject to a heart-centered electromagnetic field 40 to 60 times more powerful in amplitude than the brain's own electrical output. This heart-brain dynamic modulates and regulates every function of the body and brain, influences our endocrine glandular functions, immune system, capacity for body healing, all memory and learning, DNA activity, and of course, all relationships.

Our emotional center integrates and entrains the myriad parts of our brain into synchronous, efficient activity, though only to the extent that our emotional life is itself developed, centered, and stable. Such development is the purpose of the many exercises and games that follow here. Research shows that the moment we are "upset" emotionally, all neural action, learning, memory, cognition, problem solving, and so on, is adversely affected. Simply put, in a state of anxiety, anger, or fear, the brain cannot make an appropriate response. Our common word for anger is "mad," which means irrational, unwhole, or insane, a state in which we dwell far more often than we like to admit, and through which we make critical decisions that too often wreak havoc in our lives. Developing emotional intelligence, or teaching children to love, is critical to plain survival as well as creative intelligence.

A decade ago psychologists discovered "state specific learning" and the fact that our emotional state is an integral and permanent part of each learning experience. Whether it be our first hesitant steps as a toddler, or doing math at university, the emotional state that we are in at the moment the learning takes place is imprinted as part of that learning. When we later employ that learning, the same emotional state will tend to manifest and accompany that employment. For example, learning that two plus two equals four in a fearful atmosphere means that two plus two equals a fearful four later in life. Further, the emotional state we are in at the time of a learning influences the accessibility of that learning to willful recall or to associative thinking by which we accommodate to new information.

Though we are unaware of such action, our brain is highly selective and may even avoid learnings that were associated with pain or unhappiness, though such "memories" could be recognized as the most important single aspect of education. We have discovered that, for a true intelligence to unfold, children must be loved and learn to love in turn. Here, in *Teaching Children to Love*, we have a fun textbook to accomplish in our homes or classrooms that which is too often tragically ignored, teaching "emotional management." Maintaining a positive emotional state in the face of adversity is the way we make intelligent responses to our environmental needs. Too often we make "knee-jerk" fearful reactions that are self-defeating.

Our emotional brain has direct neural connections with the prefrontal lobes of our new-brain. This has great significance. The prefrontal lobes are the latest addition to our brain; and while the use or function of the prefrontals is largely unknown, since they haven't as yet been developed on any significant level, this latest addition is a critical part of the heart-brain connection. It appears to be associated with the "higher human virtues" such as love, charity, forgiveness, empathy, care, and so on. These "heart capacities," so absent in our current society, are the focus and issue addressed and fostered in the following pages.

Although the lowest strata of the prefrontal lobes are active from early in our life, and involved in all logical computations and "common sense," the higher prefrontal sections are the last parts of the brain to physically form. They begin serious development only after a "growth spurt" around age eight, are still "laying down their neural tracks" throughout late childhood and adolescence, and are not structurally complete and so not ready for full development until around age 21. This indicates that a large portion of our brain is designed for development throughout our mature years, whereas we previously thought the brain was fully myelinated and stable by late adolescence.

The heart is connected with the prefrontal lobes through the emotional brain, and a "higher heart frequency" is available through this connection, giving us access to a radically different form of intelligence at maturity (which seems to be nature's obvious intent in making such additions). Since this heart connection is only through the emotional brain, however, we can access this higher stage only if that emotional brain has itself been fully developed. Childhood and adolescence are the "stage-specific" times for that emotional development, which alone prepares us for a more advanced and mature intelligence later. Doc Lew Childre's *Teaching Children to Love* is the first and, so far as I know, the only specific guideline for such a teaching preparation.

Love proves to be our principal survival intelligence, but, like all intelligences, it must be developed. Not only is learning to love the cornerstone of all higher forms of intellect, but it is a learning we can undertake at any time of life. Ideally, a child learns to love through first being loved, but some of us were not so nurtured as children and have difficulty so nurturing our own children in turn. Fortunately, the following games and exercises will open our adult hearts as well as the hearts of the young. For only as we ourselves, as adults, actually move and have our being in the state of love, can we be appropriate models and guides for our children. What we *are* teaches the child far more than what we say, so we must be what we want our children to become. And, in this book, you will find a superb guideline to such becoming.

Finally, I would point out that body movement is also an integral part of emotional intelligence and learning, even in adults. Love is an action as well as a state, and the following games range from learning to listen quietly to energetic actions, so you will find something suitable to almost every situation and need. The parent or teacher desiring to sponsor a true intellectual-physical-emotional-spiritual unfolding, will find this work an invaluable asset, as well as an adventure of high play that is open-ended and ongoing, both for one's self and one's child.

Joseph Chilton Pearce

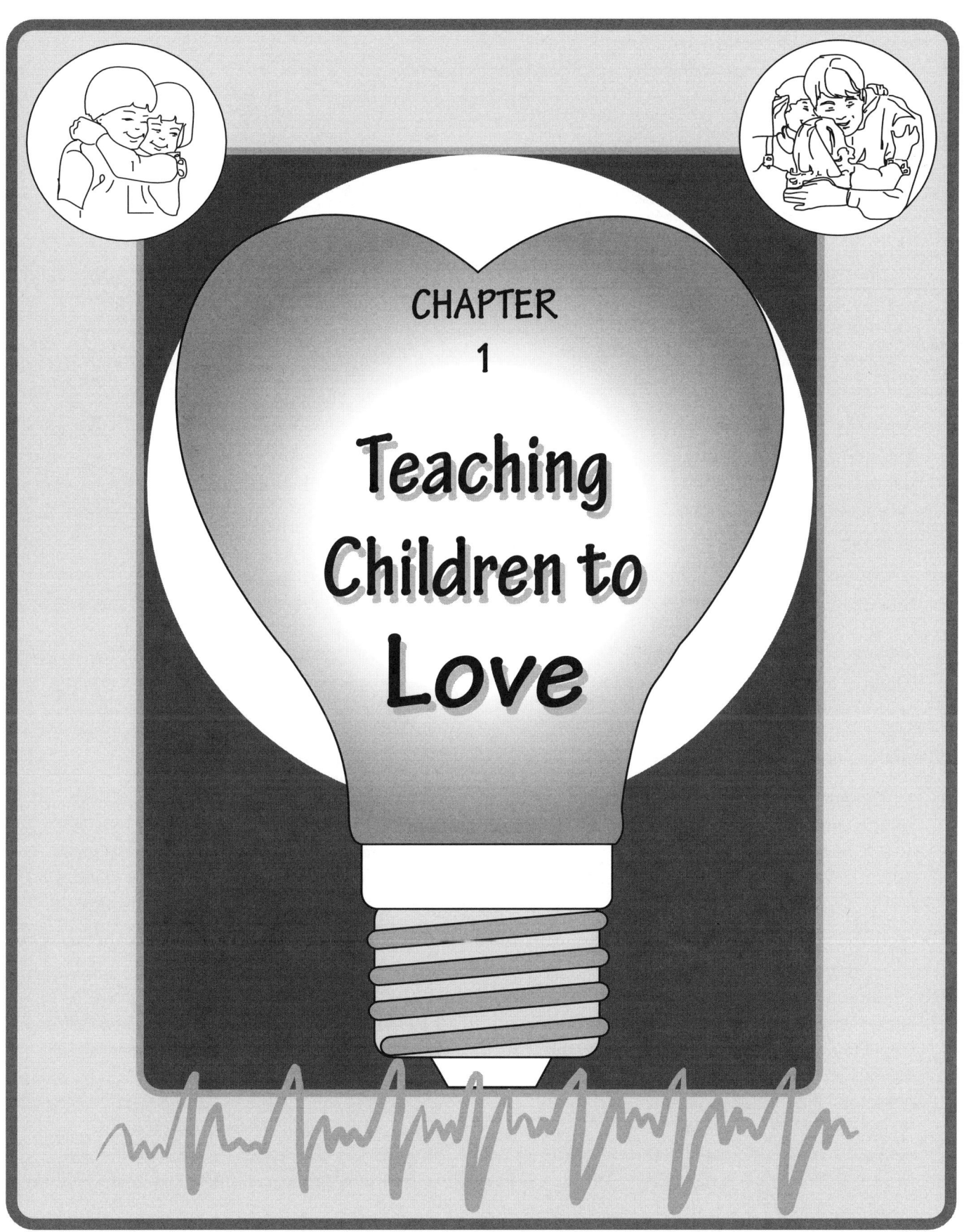

CHAPTER
1

Teaching Children to Love

Teaching Children to Love

Teaching Children to Love is about raising balanced children in today's fast paced, changing world. It goes to the heart of what's needed in teaching values, increasing intelligence, improving communication and family bonding, and raising happy, balanced children. Teaching children to love starts at birth and continues throughout life. Many parenting and activity books have been written in recent years on teaching children values, communication skills, increasing I.Q., and other popular subjects. Yet, today's children feel more unloved, more confused, afraid, and stressed than ever. Many have difficulty learning in school. The rate of depression among children is ten times the rate it was in the 1950s. Alcohol and drug abuse, crime, and violence among children are at an all-time high. There is a cry for a return to good old-fashioned family values. Parents and teachers make sincere efforts but have a hard time keeping up with the fast pace of life today.

Studies show that children who lack love have a harder time learning. In a nurturing and caring environment, children love learning. Practically speaking, adults know that love is important for security, health, and happiness. Yet fewer children now than in previous years have a loving home or school environment. Why is this? In spite of technological advances, very few of us were taught *how* to love. Learning how to love is important. It is the essence of values. Loving is a natural part of a child's fun and enjoyment in life. Love is necessary for feeling positive and hopeful about the future. The bottom line is this: Love is essential to balance the complexities of modern life.

Increasing your child's "know-how" to love is the purpose of this book. The tools, simple games, and fun activities will help your child keep her childlike spirit alive as she grows. Knowing how to love will help your child unfold a deeper love for life and address challenges optimistically, with a sense of responsibility and adventure. Children who learn how to love remain wholesome and balanced. They develop a more complete perspective of life. They are able to make wiser decisions, care for themselves and others, and pass the understanding of how to love onto their children.

In the book *A Parenting Manual: Heart Hope for the Family*, I explain how love imparts heart intelligence — increased perception and intuitive understanding. A favorite phrase quoted by parenting experts and educators from *A Parenting Manual* is: "Loving parents, by their very nature, provide children with a secure atmosphere in which to perceive life as a series of challenges that build confidence, rather than as a progression of unsolvable problems that destroy self-worth." When children don't feel loved and don't know how to love, their intelligence is restricted and so is their ability to select appropriate responses to challenges in life. *Teaching Children to Love* is a companion book to *A Parenting Manual*, providing fun games and creative activities to develop a child's heart intelligence.

What Is Intelligence?

Intelligence is commonly defined as the capacity for learning, reasoning, and understanding; aptitude in grasping truths, relationships, facts, meanings, etc. Intelligence is also the ability to discern effective and appropriate behavior. There has been much debate in recent years about whether intelligence is inherited or environmentally influenced. In *A Parenting Manual*, I explain that while DNA has coded within it the basic patterns for brain development, DNA does not determine all our neuronal connections. These form through experiences and environmental influence. When children lack love, are continuously over-stimulated, fearful, or worried, they become preoccupied with the internal stress. Their ability to adapt diminishes. As they become conditioned to stress, the brain's neuronal patterns are set in stress response patterns. According to Martin Seligman, Ph.D., author of *The Optimistic Child*, despite the emphasis on self-esteem and the abundance of child-rearing strategies, today's children have never been more depressed or pessimistic.[1] Children need love. They need to know how to keep alive or rekindle their childlike spirit. A playful, loving attitude is a key to lifelong learning.

Multiple Intelligences

Howard Gardner, author of the book *Frames of Mind*, proposes that the human system has multiple intelligences: linguistic, logical-mathematical, spatial, musical, bodily-kinesthetic, intrapersonal (knowing yourself), and interpersonal (knowing others). Children are generally stronger in one or two types than others.[2] In his book *Peak Learning*, Ronald Gross encourages adults and teachers to use a natural intelligence inclination to enhance other areas of intelligence.[3] Gross suggests, "Suppose you have a strong spatial intelligence and you're setting out on a study of philosophy. How might you link learning with your predilection for visual forms, shapes, and patterns?"

Having a strong spatial, logical-mathematical, or other isolated area of intelligence can serve as a tool or method for learning — but it is not necessarily "good" or altruistic in and of itself. Howard Gardner notes that while the word intelligence has a positive connotation in our culture, there is no reason to think that intelligence must be put to good purposes. In fact, one can use one's logical-mathematical, linguistic, or interpersonal intelligence for ill-motivated or corrupt purposes.

Learning to love and developing the intelligence of the heart enhances all other aspects of intelligence *for the good of the whole*. The heart intelligence always strives for a complete intelligence. It expands perception and imagination to transform any problem into a learning opportunity. Albert Einstein once stated, "The mere formulation of a problem is often far more essential than its solution, which may be a matter of mathematical or experimental skill. To raise new questions, new possibilities, to regard old problems from a new angle requires creative imagination and marks real advance in science." It was Einstein's passion for science and his love and care for humanity that allowed his heart intelligence to imagine, perceive, and explain so much to the world.

The games and activities in *Teaching Children to Love* incorporate the learning styles of each type of intelligence. However, the main theme — developing heart intelligence — is what will improve your child's learning in any area. Through heart intelligence it is possible to gain an understanding and appreciation of all types of intelligence. Whether or not children play music or paint well, through the heart they will be able to love and appreciate music and art. Whether or not they are strong in interpersonal skills and communication, the tools and games will develop interpersonal intelligence through enhancing the heart connection between the children and other people in their lives. If a child is learning disabled, practicing the HeartMath Heart Tools will enhance his ability to overcome that disability. As heart intelligence expands and develops, the brain's intelligence becomes more complete in actualizing its potential for fulfillment. Adults and children can become more intelligent in any area they choose. It starts with increasing your love, perception, and understanding.

The Physiology of Heart Intelligence

Central to our research at the Institute of HeartMath, and to this book, is the discovery that the heart is vital to effective learning on all levels — physically, mentally, and emotionally. The heart is an essential balancing organ. It helps balance the autonomic nervous system and produces a hormone, ANP, called "the balancing hormone," which has receptors in the brain.[4] Research at the Institute of HeartMath has shown that the higher perceptual faculties in the brain perform better when electrical rhythms produced by the heart are balanced and harmonious.[5] Positive feelings of love, care, appreciation, and compassion are what create balanced and harmonious heart rhythms.[6]

People feel love in the area of the heart. The physical heart responds to love and this can be measured in the ECG (electrocardiogram) and in HRV (heart rate variability) rhythms.[6] On the other hand, when a child or adult feels frustrated, angry, worried, fearful or stressed, their heart rhythms become unbalanced and disordered. Stress creates "cortical inhibition," a shutting down of the creative faculties which causes the brain to be less efficient in making choices. By learning to generate loving and appreciative feelings, heart rhythms come back into balance and regain their natural harmony. Adaptability and creative learning are reinstated. Whereas it usually takes adults hours or days to feel loving again after a stressful episode, children have a great ability to move from loving to frustrated and back to loving quickly. However, if stress remains unresolved and heart rhythms remain disordered, a child's natural adaptability and hopefulness diminishes.

Many Asian and native cultures have understood that the heart is much more than just a physical organ. In Japanese, the word "kokoro" describes the mind of the heart. It is this intelligence of the heart which is the key to learning and is activated by love. It is through *love* that the electrical rhythms of the brain synchronize with the harmonious electrical rhythms of the heart. When heart and brain are in sync, more power and intelligence become available to the brain. Perception increases. *Teaching Children to Love* shows children how to self-generate feelings of love, care, appreciation, and compassion to enhance perception and well-being. In addition to synchronizing heart and brain, loving feelings have been shown scientifically to have profound positive effects on the nervous, immune, and hormonal systems.

Dr. Karl Pribram is one of the pioneers of modern neuroscience and author of numerous books on brain function, including *Brain and Perception* which mathematically proves how the brain functions under holographic principles.[7] Dr. Pribram has commented, "The heart as an input system to the brain is very powerful. It can be studied in the way the visual or auditory system can be studied. The optic system can function, but without a lens you won't see anything. Add a lens to the optic system and you see. By focusing attention in the area of the heart and feeling love, it's like adding a lens to the heart's system. You've got to have eyes to see, you've got to have the heart to feel. The 'lens' of positive heart feelings like love, care, and appreciation bring intuitive perception. Love increases coherence and clarity. When you use tools like FREEZE-FRAME and CUT-THRU to stop all the nonsense (mental and emotional nonsense) for awhile, it's like focusing the lens of heart perception."

Dr. Pribram explains that the amygdala is the portion of the brain that specializes in strong emotional memories, such as fear. The amygdala compares what's *familiar* in memory with new information coming into the brain.[7] If fear has become familiar, a child may respond to new information with fear even if it's not the most intelligent response.

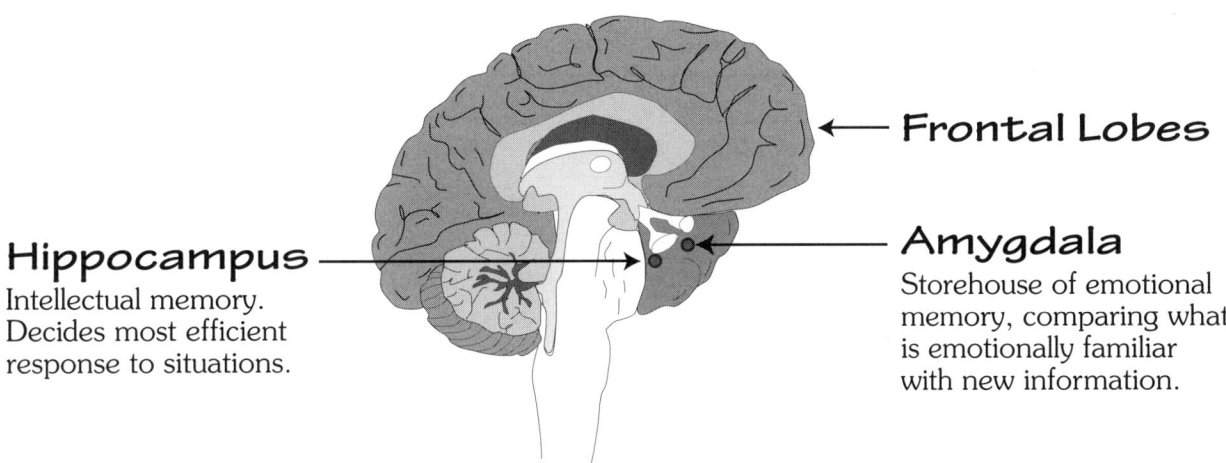

Hippocampus
Intellectual memory. Decides most efficient response to situations.

Frontal Lobes

Amygdala
Storehouse of emotional memory, comparing what is emotionally familiar with new information.

The amygdala communicates its response to the bottom part of the frontal lobe to determine what action would be *appropriate*. The frontal lobes take a long time to develop. At age nineteen, the frontal lobes are still maturing. That's why children and teens often feel and act before they think. They choose behavior based on what's familiar because they are not yet able to determine what's appropriate. If they do not learn appropriate behavior from adult role models, familiarized emotional reactions can continue into adulthood, overriding the potential of the frontal lobes.

People approach life from the viewpoint of familiarized emotional experiences and respond with familiarized behavior *in an attempt to feel secure*. For example, a child who lives in a house where there is frequent yelling, hitting, or other violence, may have feelings of insecurity and fear that have become familiarized. At school, if a peer raises his voice or looks questioningly at the child, the child may perceive from familiarized fear and hit the peer. This behavior is what the child deems appropriate in trying to feel secure. Without heart intelligence, the child cannot perceive that the peer is not threatening. Familiarized fear responses have become so common in schools today, that children are often afraid to even glance at other children in case they will be assaulted. Fear is beneficial if we are in real danger and need to react fast; but fear limits perception, communication, and learning if we are not in danger.

Children and adults need a foundation of balance and security to make appropriate choices throughout life. Daniel Goleman, in his groundbreaking book *Emotional Intelligence,* presents research on how the emotional lessons a child learns actually sculpt the brain's circuitry.[8] He also cites studies which show that people who excel in real life, whose relationships flourish, who become the stars in the workplace, are usually not the ones with the highest I.Q. scores. They are people who have learned emotional intelligence — a different way of being smart — which includes impulse-control, character and self-discipline, altruism, and compassion. According to Goleman, these are the indicators of success in life and the hallmarks of true intelligence. He points out, however, that the brain's circuitry can change and it's never too late to learn. It's through *heart intelligence* that we can acquire emotional maturity and heal the brain's circuitry.

While the amygdala deals with what's familiar, the intellectual memory of emotions is routed through another part of the brain called the hippocampus.[7] The hippocampus is involved in deciding what would be the most *efficient* response to a situation. However, research shows that high amounts of the stress hormone cortisol in the hippocampus indicate repeated episodes of anxiety. Perceptions of efficiency then become skewed by anxiety. The hippocampus communicates to the top part of the frontal lobe to determine the most *effective* response. For example, a child plans his day efficiently — going to school, playing with a friend, then doing homework — and an unexpected event occurs that triggers anxiety. If the hippocampus has laid down an intellectual memory of repeated anxiety, this will strongly influence what the child does next. The top part of the frontal lobe has to adapt and find an effective response based on the information it perceives. The middle frontal lobe is where top and bottom frontal lobe information comes together to choose a course of action. When unbalanced heart rhythms, frustration, fear, stress, or anxiety condition the perceptual process, the choice of what is most effective or appropriate is quite different than when balanced heart rhythms and perceptions of love, care, and security are conditioning the perceptual process. Feelings of love allow security to become familiar. Love increases a child's intuitive ability. The result is emotional perception that becomes more balanced in selecting appropriate behavior and creative thinking that becomes more efficient and effective.

The end result is what humanity has known intuitively for centuries — that the heart is a powerful agent for transforming perceptions, resolving challenges, and manifesting values that benefit the whole. What else would values be for if not for selecting efficient, effective, and appropriate behavior that would lead to increased harmony and fulfillment? Harmonizing heart and brain through love is what can establish a complete intelligence, a complete self, where a child can look at life and realize there are no dead ends, there are always possibilities. The greatest gift a parent can give a child during all the ups and downs of life is love.

The HeartMath Heart Tools provided in *A Parenting Manual* and in *Teaching Children to Love* give children and adults the gift of perceiving that there are always ways to work things out and the intelligence to see what to do.[9] The tools, based on extensive research and training programs with adults and with children, have been successfully taught to children in schools and workshops, and to adults in Fortune 500 companies, in governmental agencies, in doctor's offices, and in the military. Now the tools are offered here — through fun games and simple activities for the home, school, and childcare center. As children learn to balance the increasing stress of today's world through the intelligence of the heart, increased creativity and quality of life result. As a child's choices prove effective, a healthy and positive perspective of life is sustained.

How the Tools, Games, and Activities Work

Teaching Children to Love starts with teaching children how to focus "in the heart" and generate feelings of love, care, and appreciation that bring happiness. In the heart, we want to explore, learn, and be creative. When we are "out of the heart," frustration, anger, boredom, self-pity, or anxiety can take over. We perceive no way out of a problem. When children are "out of the heart" and upset, parents naturally try to calm, cajole, question, or distract them from the problem to get them back in the heart again. It's common sense that children are more responsive and listen better when they are in the heart. The Heart Tools help parents, teachers, or children shift back into the heart quickly. It's tremendously empowering for children (and adults) to realize that they can manage their emotions and discover new perspectives that help them feel happier, learn better, and help their friends and families, too.

A parent is a child's first role model of love. Since children absorb and follow their parents' perspectives, it is important for parents to walk in their child's shoes to see how their child is perceiving and modeling them. Parents can use the Heart Tools to help them love more intelligently. In using *Teaching Children to Love*, adults need to learn and practice the three basic tools, HEART LOCK-IN™, FREEZE-FRAME® and CUT-THRU®, to model what they are teaching. While the effectiveness of these tools has been well researched and documented through complex studies and analysis, the tools themselves are simple. Love is simple. The tools are designed to activate love. The more they are practiced, the easier it is to access heart intelligence.

I will present the basic steps of the tools in this chapter. An in-depth understanding of HEART LOCK-IN and FREEZE-FRAME and how to teach them to children of different ages is given in *A Parenting Manual: Heart Hope for the Family.* I have also written a book on *FREEZE-FRAME: Fast Action Stress Relief* and another on *CUT-THRU: A Scientifically Proven Insight on How to Care Without Becoming a Victim.*[10,11] Each book provides a chapter on the scientific research behind the tool, applications for the tool in personal, business, and family life, and in-depth explanations of the steps of the tools.* Listening to the tape *Heart Signals* is an excellent way for children ages 8-14 to learn the tools.

For the purpose of this book, adults can practice the basic HeartMath tools given and the suggestions for teaching them to children at different age levels. The games and activities incorporate creative and fun ways to teach the tools at home and in the classroom. Each chapter explores a different heart attitude or skill. The best way to use the book is to first learn the basic tools yourself, then start with Chapter 2, Discovering Love, and choose a game appropriate to your child's age. You can play additional games in Chapter 2 or go on to Chapter 3. While it is not necessary to explore the chapters or activities in any particular order, you may find it's easier and more fun to do so. Skills learned in earlier chapters can enhance the games and activities in later chapters. More importantly, however, is to select activities or variations that are appropriate to your situation. For some, the most appropriate order might be to teach the children the basic tools, then play team games in Chapter 10, listening games in Chapter 6, care games in Chapter 5, and so forth.

At the beginning of each game, the suggested ages, approximate time it will take to actually play the game, number of players, suggested location, and equipment needed are given. Suggested variations are added at the end of the game. The time it will take to play the game can vary

---

A Parenting Manual, FREEZE-FRAME, CUT-THRU and *Heart Signals* are available in bookstores or can be ordered direct from Planetary Publications.

depending upon the number of players and their attention span. The approximate time given does not include preparation time. Under "number of players," it is noted whether an adult is needed to play the game. If the word "adult" is not listed, then the adult can give instructions and supervise as the children play. If number of players is "one or more," this means that the activity can be played in the classroom or with a group of children. Equipment needed for the activity is listed with a black arrow (➡). Additional equipment needed for the variations is listed with a white arrow (⇨). It's best to read the activity, estimate the preparation time needed, then decide when to play the game. The activities are presented largely according to age level, with those for younger children first. In a few chapters, the first activity is a game that teaches the basic tool featured in that chapter.

The HEART LOCK-IN™ Tool

1. Find a comfortable place to relax for five to fifteen minutes and close your eyes.

2. Shift your attention away from your mind or head, relax your thoughts, and focus in the area around your heart, that place where you have felt deep feelings of sincere love, care, or appreciation.

3. Remember a special experience you've had with your child, when the feeling of love, care, or appreciation was rewarding. Recall the feeling. If you're upset with your child, it may be harder to recall a special feeling. Try to remember when you felt a joy of delight, perhaps when your baby was in your arms or when the "little angel" was asleep.

4. Radiate that sincere feeling of love to your child now; this energizes the love fully and gives you a more complete understanding of your child.

5. If head thoughts come in, gently bring your focus of attention back to the heart area and radiate love from the heart. Just by sending heart, your questions will eventually be answered. Loving your child builds patience and brings understanding.

6. Now, radiate love to your child for five to fifteen minutes to deepen the Lock-In. Reflect on what you love about your child, then radiate that feeling of love. It does not require words. This "locks" you into a feeling of love in the heart, appreciation for your child, and gives access to intuitive information. As you listen to your heart intuition, it helps sustain feelings of love and fulfillment. The rewards of parenting come quickly with a little sincere effort.

If you are having a difficult time with your child and you can't immediately recall a feeling of love, care, or appreciation, or if you feel some pain in your heart, it's okay. Relax into the "soft heart" and stay with that softer feeling. With practice, the HEART LOCK-IN will increase positive feelings and release insecure, painful feelings stored in the unconscious to bring you a solid heart security. As love expands in quality, the old attitudes and feelings release in stages. View all feelings that arise during a HEART LOCK-IN as love that is growing, but that is perhaps not yet complete in its full quality.

Before communicating on matters of importance with your child, first do a HEART LOCK-IN and radiate love for your child. Radiating love helps the heart and brain synchronize, increasing intuitive perception and understanding. Sincere heart communication with your child, understanding, and care are what help a child respect a parent and a parent respect a child. You can also use the "Intuitive Listening Tool" from *A Parenting Manual* to understand your child's communications more deeply — at the word level, the feeling level, and the essence level.

In teaching HEART LOCK-IN to children, find a quiet place (hold younger children on your lap), and guide them through the steps, adapting the steps to their situation and age level. Ask the children to practice with you. Practicing together, even if it's only for a minute or two, and radiating heart to family and friends, is a wonderful, quality-time activity that can open the door to deeper communication. Teaching children to close their eyes during a HEART LOCK-IN helps shut out distractions. The eye receives a tremendous amount of stimulation from the outside world. While the human eye only perceives one trillionth of all the information it registers, the brain is able to piece together and interpret several hundred million visual fragments at the same time. This makes human perception unique. From this information, thoughts, feelings, and impressions are created. That's why it helps children to shut their eyes for a time span during the HEART LOCK-IN, so they can feel the heart inside. You might find that younger children can only shut their eyes and focus for thirty seconds. As they practice, they can do it longer. As children learn to contact their hearts, they enjoy feeling the love and finding the intuition hidden in the heart.

Children who learn the HEART LOCK-IN tool use it when they want solutions to troubling problems or whenever they want to feel better. Adults use it for the same purposes, and to balance nervous energy, lower blood pressure, improve heart rhythms, and health. Eight-year-old Josh says, *"When you Lock-In, you feel the love all inside you. What you feel is heart warmth through your whole loving body. When you're upset, that's a deficit. When you solve it, it's an asset. Don't worry, everyone makes one or more deficits everyday. But when you Lock-In and turn it into an asset you get more energy."*

The FREEZE-FRAME® Tool

The FREEZE-FRAME tool is designed to be used with eyes open when you're on the run, in the middle of activity or conversation, or when you don't have time to do a HEART LOCK-IN. Once you memorize the steps, you can use the tool very quickly to release stress, frustration, anger, come back to balance, and find new solutions, often in less than a minute. It's also an excellent tool to enhance creativity in writing, art, music, sports, math, or any subject.

The FREEZE-FRAME Tool

1. Recognize a stressful feeling, and FREEZE-FRAME it. Take a time out!

2. Make a sincere effort to shift your focus away from the racing mind or disturbed emotions to the area around your heart. Pretend you're breathing through your heart to help focus your energy in this area. Keep your focus there for ten seconds or more.

3. Recall a positive, fun feeling or time you've had in life and attempt to re-experience it.

4. Now, using your intuition, common sense, and sincerity — ask your heart — what would be a more efficient response to the situation, one that will minimize future stress?

5. Listen to what your heart says in answer to your question. (It's an effective way to put your reactive mind and emotions in check — and an "in-house" source of common-sense, intuitive solutions!)

A Parenting Manual has instructions on how to teach the FREEZE-FRAME tool to toddlers, four to six-year-olds, and seven to twelve-year-olds. Teenagers can learn the adult steps. If you don't have *A Parenting Manual*, use your own creativity in adapting and explaining the steps to children or use the games and activities in Chapter 4 to help them learn and apply the tool. FREEZE-FRAME assists children and adults with impulse control and problem-solving in the moment. As children become skilled in FREEZE-FRAME, they can access intuitive heart intelligence any time they need it.

The CUT-THRU® Tool

FREEZE-FRAME helps adults and children manage frustration and anger, get back in the heart quickly, and find new perspectives. CUT-THRU is a tool to release lingering feelings of worry, anxiety, insecurity, guilt, or fear, and find new insight and understanding. CUT-THRU helps you relate to situations with balanced care, not overcare. An example of overcare is a parent fretting and crying over a teenager who has stayed out past the parent's curfew. When the nurturing feeling of care turns into a disturbed feeling of worry, anxiety, and stacks of stress, it has become overcare. Overcare blocks us from perceiving solutions. In reality, children (and teens especially) recoil from overcaring adults who are forevermore worrying.

Children learn to overcare from the adults around them. A child tends to worry or feel anxious about parents, family problems, school, or peer pressure. Practicing CUT-THRU helps adults and children release overcare feelings, regain emotional balance, and see new perspectives. The CUT-THRU steps are progressive — meaning you use only the steps you need until you find emotional release and new insight — then go to step 5 and follow your heart intelligence. With little fears and anxieties, often Steps 1 and 2 are all that's needed to feel better again. (Of course, professional help should be sought for children with serious emotional problems.)

The CUT-THRU Tool

1. Recognize feelings and thoughts of overcare — Take an inner weather report. See if your inner weather is rain or sunshine. Then change your weather to prevent a flood. Choose the more hopeful perspective. Your inner weather is determined by how good you feel in your heart — or not. If you feel worried, anxious, disturbed, or drained, your inner weather is rainy or cloudy. Go to your heart to find and choose a more hopeful perspective to improve your inner weather.

2. Hold overcare thoughts or feelings in the heart. Remember, adapting stops the energy drain. Pretend you are floating on a raft or soaking in a heartwarming bath for a few moments. If the disturbed feelings won't release, or if your emotions are really revved up, homogenizing or blending the feelings in the heart helps the energy disperse so you can see a new perspective. Floating in the heart releases over-identification with overcare feelings and helps you adapt. Try to relax any current of discomfort, find peace, and float in a soft heart. The purpose of this step is not to repress uncomfortable feelings but to dissipate them. Most people have not been educated on how to release disturbed feelings and thoughts. Instead, they vent, analyze, or suppress them in the effort to get rid of them. None of these methods works in the long run. The stress still accumulates. Emotional venting is different from talking over a problem with someone, which your heart intuition may suggest you do.

3. Find your peace. As the current of discomfort dissipates, a new sense of peace and intuitive knowing can emerge. Hold to any feeling of peace. Then go to the "fair heart" to see and reflect clearly. To find your fair heart, hold your focus of attention in the area of the heart while asking yourself questions about the problem, being honest and fair as you challenge the assumptions behind your perceptions. As you focus energy in the area of the heart, the heart and brain align to assess a situation fairly and with increased clarity.

4. Find the reference point of care. Ask yourself, "Why did I originally care?" Recall those beginning feelings of care for a few moments. Then ask yourself, "How did my original care slowly leak away due to overcare and drain me?" Recognize how your care was taken to inefficient extremes. Recall the original care and find the higher heart perspective.

Appreciate that overcare always originates from care. Asking these questions will help you track overcare back to the original feeling of care and see the sequence of events. It's important to remind yourself to stay with the original feeling of care. This stops the overcare from returning. It takes practice to hold to balanced care, but it feels great and regenerates the entire system. You learn that following what feels good to your heart brings empowering results. If your overcare has stacked for a time, it's been sincerely hard on your feelings. Have compassion for yourself as you practice.

5. Follow your heart intelligence. In this last step, with clear perception and feelings of security coming back, listen to your heart to know what true care would now be in this situation. Follow your true care. That's caring for self and others. Your heart intelligence comes to you as new perceptions and hope. It's important to deeply listen to and follow even fleeting heart perceptions. If a perception is peaceful and feels good to you, that's your signal to follow it. The heart signal is often weaker than the mind at first, so you have to listen deeply. Follow the heart and watch life unfold into a smoother, happier flow.

After you do all five steps, if there is still some feeling residue of overcare, rise above it and appreciate the new perceptions that you have. As you appreciate and continue to follow your heart, life will unfold a more complete understanding. Eventually all you will need to remember to balance your emotions and your care are the key terms in the CUT-THRU steps shown on the following page.

Key Terms in the CUT-THRU Steps:

Step 1 - Check your inner weather, "Rain or Sunshine?"

Step 2 - Adapt to stop the energy drain.
"Float, soak, or blend" feelings in the heart.

Step 3 - Find "Fair Heart."

Step 4 - Recall "Original Care."

Step 5 - Follow your Heart Intelligence.

Balanced care nurtures and heals, spawning security and support for all involved. It helps waive the dislikes and annoyances adults have with children by providing deeper understanding. CUT-THRU aids adults and children with the knowledge of how to gather their feelings in the heart to make more effective choices. Before teaching CUT-THRU to children, it is important to first practice the tool yourself so you have a "feeling" for how it works. Then role model how to CUT-THRU overcares.

Teaching teenagers to CUT-THRU helps them see a different possible outcome and understand the consequences of feelings and actions. It enables teens to harness their energies and envision their future with optimism. They will see they do have a choice in how they feel and act. With teenagers, discuss and practice the adult steps as they are given here or in the book *CUT-THRU*.

To help younger children release anxiety or worry, take them through the first few steps of HEART LOCK-IN or FREEZE-FRAME to help them feel their heart. Then say, *"Let's do something different this time. Let's gently stir and blend the feelings in our heart."* Keep the speed slow and rhythmic. Say, *"The heart talks to everyone in their own special way. You might see or feel different colors or shapes or have new thoughts and ideas. As sad (worried, anxious, fearful) feelings come up, put them back into the heart, and stir them, like you are mixing paint or stirring chocolate in milk. Let's do this for a few moments. (Pause) ... Then, as you feel better, relax, and soak in your heart. Feel like you are soaking in peace, in a nice, heartwarming bath."* Ask the children if they feel better. Encourage them to discuss what their heart says. After they learn to do this, explore the other steps with them. Have them check their inner weather and identify different feelings. Then guide them to go to their heart to find a more hopeful perspective. As you practice and discuss each step together, children soon learn how to release overcares, assess perceptions from a fair heart, and find balanced care. The games and activities in Chapter 5 help children learn to care for their own feelings and other people's feelings and understand the difference between true care and overcare.

Other Tools

There are other tools for increasing heart perception used in the games and activities. The tool, "Oops, No Big Deal" helps us remember that when we make a mistake or feel anxious about performing a task, that it's no big deal. Children learn to have compassion instead of being judgmental of themselves or others. They tell themselves, "Oops, No Big Deal, let me get back in my heart and move on." One example is doing poorly in tests at school. The child may feel badly, worry about her parents' reaction, or judge herself. The stress can inhibit improvement. Learning to tell herself, "Oops, No Big Deal, let me get back to my heart and move on," doesn't mean she doesn't care. It releases the distress and empowers self-care so she can learn.

Heart Mapping® is a tool that helps older children or adults clearly see the difference between mind perception and heart perception. It brings in intuition to add wider perspectives to any topic, project, or issue. Heart Mapping is excellent for aligning values with action while planning projects, making major decisions, career planning, etc. The Heart Mapping activity (along with an example) can be found in Chapter 2. Playing this game with older children will accelerate their understanding of heart intelligence.

While *Teaching Children to Love* requires spending a little time planning and playing the games and activities, it's a worthwhile investment. If you stop to consider all the time that families and schools spend in less important activities, you will want to make time to give your children the highest quality of love that you can give them. What better gift could you give than an understanding of how to love that increases perception and intelligence, and tools to live a balanced and fulfilling life?

References

1. Seligman, M., *The Optimistic Child*, 1995, New York: Houghton Mifflin.
2. Gardner, H., *Frames of Mind. The Theory of Multiple Intelligences.* 1985, New York: Basic Books.
3. Gross, R., *Peak Learning.* 1991, Los Angeles: Jeremy Tarcher.
4. Cantin, M. and J. Genest, *The heart as an endocrine gland.* Clinical and Investigative Medicine, 1986. 9(4): p. 319-327.
5. McCraty, R., M. Atkinson, and W.A. Tiller, *New electrophysiological correlates associated with intentional heart focus.* Subtle Energies, 1995. 4(3): p. 251-268.
6. McCraty, R., et al., *The effects of emotions on short term heart rate variability using power spectrum analysis.* American Journal of Cardiology, 1995. p. 76.
7. Pribram, K.H., *Brain and Perception: Holonomy and Structure in Figural Processing.* 1991, Hillsdale, New Jersey: Lawrence Erlbaum Associates, Publishers.
8. Goleman, D., *Emotional Intelligence: Why it can matter more than IQ.* 1995, New York: Bantam Books.
9. Childre, D.L., *A Parenting Manual: Heart Hope for the Family.* 1995, Boulder Creek, California: Planetary Publications.
10. Childre, D.L., *FREEZE-FRAME®, Fast Action Stress Relief.* 1994, Boulder Creek, California: Planetary Publications.
11. Childre, D.L., *CUT-THRU®, Achieve Total Security and Maximum Energy.* 1995, Boulder Creek, California: Planetary Publications.

CHAPTER

2

Discovering

Love

HEART LOCK-IN™

PURPOSE

This activity helps children experience a feeling of security. By taking a few minutes to "Lock-In" to a positive feeling toward someone they care about or something they deeply appreciate, children learn how to connect with the power and strength of their own heart. Practicing "HEART LOCK-IN" also builds confidence in one's ability to meet the challenges of life.

AGES
3-10

TIME
5 minutes

PLAYERS
Adult and one or more children

LOCATION
Indoors or outdoors (Find a place where participants can sit in a relaxed manner. If they can't sit comfortably on the floor or ground, have chairs or cushions available.)

EQUIPMENT
➡ Tape or CD player
➡ Music of your choice that is fun and upbeat, yet relaxing. Musical pieces that are too slow or too relaxing can put children to sleep. The first and fourth songs on the <u>Heart Zones</u> album are excellent for this purpose. Children also enjoy Locking-In to the sixth, seventh, or eighth songs on the <u>Speed of Balance</u> album, which was designed to facilitate emotional balance. *
⇨ <u>Buddy Bubbles</u> tape

INSTRUCTIONS

1. Have everyone seated. Tell children that you are going to lead them in a HEART LOCK-IN to build the power of their heart. Explain that a "HEART LOCK-IN" is like putting a key into the lock of your heart and opening the door of your heart so more love can come in and so you can send more love out — to your parents, friends, animals, flowers, anyone. First, lead the children in a practice run.

2. Instruct them to imagine that there is a door in their heart with a lock on it. "By focusing on your heart, that place where you feel love and care (put your hand on your chest to demonstrate), then pretending that you are breathing through your heart, you can turn the key and unlock the door. Now, each time you breathe in, you can feel the door of your heart opening a little wider to let love and sunshine into your heart. Each time you breathe out, you can send your love and sunshine to someone you care about, perhaps your mom or dad." Demonstrate the breathing — close your mouth and put your hand on your chest. Gently breathe in and out and pretend that you are breathing through the heart area in your chest. (Don't breathe too hard or children will start huffing and puffing.)

3. Suggest that the children try it. Ask them to place their hand on their chest and pretend that they are breathing through their heart.

4. Now, ask them to get ready for the HEART LOCK-IN. Suggest that they might want to close their eyes, but don't make it an issue if they don't. Tell them that closing their eyes during a HEART LOCK-IN helps shut out distractions so you can focus more inside your heart.

*Heart Zones, Speed of Balance and Buddy Bubbles tapes are produced by Planetary. They are available in bookstores and record stores or can be ordered direct from the publisher.

5. Remind them that as they let love into the heart as they breathe in, the door opens a little wider to let more sunshine in. It might feel so good that it makes you want to smile. When they breathe out and send their sunshine and love to someone they care about, they might see the sunshine getting brighter, or see rainbow colors, or even see the sunshine in the hearts of the people receiving their love.

6. When everyone is quiet, start the music. Do a HEART LOCK-IN for two minutes or for one song of an album. You can increase the time as the attention span increases.

7. After the music is over, tell everyone to open their eyes. Ask if anyone would like to share their experience. Younger children especially will want to share.

One parent wrote, "The HEART LOCK-IN is my children's favorite game, next to the Family Appreciation Games. We do a HEART LOCK-IN every night before bed with our six and nine-year-olds."

VARIATIONS

1. Ask children to make a list of who they want to send their love to before the HEART LOCK-IN. It might be mom, dad, grandma, a family member who is sick or needs extra love, a pet, teddy bear, teacher — or anyone they care about.

2. If children have difficulty with the HEART LOCK-IN, ask them to find their "soft heart," that place inside that feels soft and gentle. They can pretend that there is a soft, furry bunny or soft, fluffy kitten in their heart to help them feel their soft heart. Have children ages two to eight listen to the tape *Buddy Bubbles: Magical Games for a Child's Heart** and play the "soft heart game" to help them understand and feel the soft heart.

3. As children become familiar with the HEART LOCK-IN, you can have them take short "LOCK-IN" breaks during the day, breathing love through the heart. This will help everyone sustain emotional balance.

Squeeze, Please
A Game For Infants

PURPOSE

This game encourages a child to connect with the feeling of love at an early age. Simply put, babies love to be cuddled and held close to a parent's heart. Babies learn that love comes from people and there are different feelings of love. Giving love is one feeling. Feeling loved is another feeling. Loving mommy feels different from loving daddy. As infants identify different feelings of love, they find a deeper heart connection with themselves and their family. Due to concerns about child protection, it is recommended that only parents play this game with their baby. Learning to send and receive love with parents will help create a truer heart connection with other people.

AGES
6-24 months

TIME
5 minutes or longer

PLAYERS
Parent and child

LOCATION
Indoors (in a comfortable place)

EQUIPMENT
A comfortable chair

INSTRUCTIONS

1. Always play "Squeeze, Please" when the baby is content or happy. Begin by holding the baby close to your heart for a few moments.

2. Then pull the baby closer and give him a gentle hug and squeeze, saying "Squeeze, please." Simple words or words that rhyme are easier for a young child to repeat.

3. After a short time, release the hug and relax. Your baby may be giggling with delight. Once the giggles have quieted down, add, "I love you."

4. Then, in a playful, cuddly way, pull the baby close to your heart again saying, "Squeeze, please." Feel love for your child as you squeeze, relax your hold, then add, "I love you."

5. Keep playing as long as you and your baby are having fun. Most babies love this simple game and as they learn to express themselves, may ask for "Squeeze, please."

6. With talking toddlers, you can develop a playful pattern: You squeeze, say the words, send out love, and release. Then wait for the child to ask, "Squeeze, please." Play the game for the duration of the child's attention span.

VARIATIONS

1. You can vary "Squeeze, please" by varying the squeeze from gentle to a big bear hug or by asking the child to give you a "Squeeze, please." You let the baby squeeze and love you. Tell him, "I can feel your love."

2. Sometimes it's fun for mom and dad to take turns playing the game. A baby will feel love from each and notice the different feelings of love. You can say, "mommy's love," then, "daddy's love." If the baby squeezes you back, say, "baby's love."

Heart Ball

PURPOSE

This game teaches young children how to send and receive love and that learning to love is fun and feels good to the heart. This game is also beneficial for getting children back in the heart and happy when they have been cranky or upset.

AGES
1-4

TIME
5 minutes or longer

PLAYERS
Adult and one to five children

LOCATION
Indoors (on the floor)

EQUIPMENT
Nerf™ Ball or other 4-5" (in diameter) ball

INSTRUCTIONS

1. Child and adult sit about six feet apart on the floor. Both child and adult spread their legs apart so that the ball can easily be caught when rolled back and forth.

2. The adult then instructs the child on how to play the game. Adult says, "I am going to roll the ball to you and as I do, I am going to send love to you."

3. Before rolling the ball to the child, hold the ball against your heart for a moment. Breathe in and out as though you are filling the ball with love. Then before rolling the ball, say, "Here it comes. It's full of love."

4. When the child catches the ball, the adult asks, " Did you get my love?" After the child responds, say, "Now you put love in the ball and roll it back to me." Keep the game going as long as the child shows interest.

5. With children as young as two and three years old, you can suggest sending love to dad, mom, grandma, etc., as you roll the ball back and forth. Let the child decide who to send love to. It can sometimes expand to loving the entire world.

EXAMPLE

A day-care center teacher played Heart Ball with four-year-old Tami, who was very angry with her parents for leaving her in the teacher's care. One of the other children and the teacher started playing Heart Ball and sending Tami their love. The four-year-old soon caught the spirit of sending love and joined the game. They all played for an hour. The teacher told the mother when she returned, "We started out sending love to her mom and dad and expanded to friends, grandparents, the world, the sun, moon, and stars. What started as a temper tantrum became a Heart Party!"

VARIATION

A small group can play Heart Ball together. Everyone sit in a circle with legs apart.

One person puts love in the ball and sends it across to another person. The person who receives the ball puts love into the ball and sends it to another person who has not yet received the ball. Keep sending the ball around, giving everyone a turn to play.

Love Throw

PURPOSE

This game is a young child's version of darts. However, instead of throwing darts, each child will be throwing bean bags filled with love. "Love Throw" promotes hand-eye coordination in young children while teaching them that love comes from the heart and can be actively felt and sent to others while they are playing.

AGES

2-8

TIME

15 minutes or longer

PLAYERS

Adult and one or more children

LOCATION

Indoors (on the floor)

EQUIPMENT

➡ *Large sheet of poster paper or a 3' square piece of plywood*
➡ *Crayons, paints, or markers*
➡ *Paper, pencil, and masking tape*
➡ *Several small bean bags or Heart Buddies (page 36) filled sparingly with beans or rice for throwing objects*

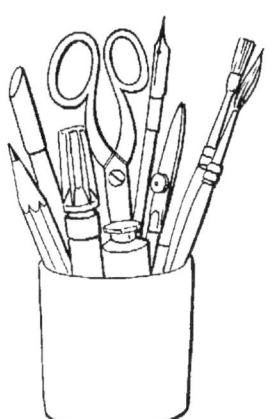

MAKING THE HEART TARGET

1. On the poster paper (or plywood) draw a heart approximately 20" high and 20" across. A smaller heart can be made for children over five with more developed skills.

2. Draw two concentric hearts inside the big heart. Write the number 5 in the outer heart, 10 in the middle heart, and 20 in the center heart.

3. Use your creativity to make the heart board as beautiful as possible using multiple colors with fun shapes and figures that surround the heart. Encourage the children to help.

INSTRUCTIONS

1. Place the heart target on the floor in an area large enough for the children to gather around.

2. Instruct the children to put love into the heart by filling their bean bag with love and then throwing it into the heart target. The leader first demonstrates by holding the bean bag close to his heart, breathing love into it, and throwing it into the heart target. Ask the children to think of someone they love and send that love while throwing the bean bag into the heart.

3. Have the children take turns and stand no more than 2' or 3' from the heart while throwing. Remind children to send love into the bean bag as they are throwing it.

4. Whenever a bean bag makes it into the circle, the leader speaks out, "Wow, there is more love going into the heart." With older children, the leader can use pencil and paper to add up the points for each child. To make the game more challenging for older children, have them stand farther away from the heart target. Create a boundary line with masking tape that they have to stand behind.

5. When the game is over, the leader should remind the children that they have put a lot of love into the heart and now they are going to send the love to each other. "Let's all send the love together at the count of three... One, two three, go." The leader first demonstrates "sending love" by placing his hand on his heart. This will also help the children calm down after the game.

VARIATION

Have the children take turns naming someone to send love to before each bean bag toss and all the children send love to that person.

Heart Buddy

PURPOSE

The "Heart Buddy" helps children stay focused in the heart. It can be quite distracting to try to have a serious talk with a child who is fidgeting or playing with something inappropriate. Many children need to hold something in their hands to stay focused during discussions. In addition to being something to hold, the "Heart Buddy" reminds children to stay in their hearts. Heart Buddies are soft and small. They are intended to be carried in a pocket at all times.

AGES

3 - 10

(If an adult does the sewing, children as young as 3 can help stuff the Heart Buddies and will enjoy playing with them)

TIME

30 minutes or longer

PLAYERS

Adult and one or more children

LOCATION

Indoors (where there is a table for cutting material and a comfortable place to sit while sewing)

EQUIPMENT

➜ Scissors
➜ 9" by 12" white felt squares (each square will make 2 Heart Buddies)
➜ Needle and thread for sewing
➜ Embroidery thread or indelible colored markers for making the face
➜ Cotton or foam for stuffing
➜ Heart Buddy pattern (next page)
⇨ <u>Buddy Bubbles</u> tape, tape recorder

INSTRUCTIONS

1. Fold the white felt pieces in half and lay the bottom point of the heart pattern on the fold so that you can cut both pieces at the same time. It isn't necessary to cut the two hearts apart completely.

2. Have the children first draw a face on one of the hearts with a pencil. Then have them either embroider the face or color it with indelible markers.

3. Turn the face inside out and prepare to sew the backs of the hearts together.

4. Sew around the entire edge as though you were making a pillow, but leave a hole large enough to turn the hearts inside out (so face is showing).

5. Stuff with cotton or foam, then finish sewing up.

6. Have children hold the completed Heart Buddy at their heart center (near the center of the chest). This will actually teach the child how to center and be more in the heart.

7. Everyone send one minute of love to their new Heart Buddy to help remind them to stay focused in the heart.

8. Have a discussion with the children while they hold their Heart Buddies. Remind them to send heart while they are talking and while they are listening.

EXAMPLES

One mother described how eight-year-old Jason and three-year-old Kara were so happy to have their Heart Buddies. "Jason named his 'Buster' and Kara named her's 'Bonnie.' Jason carries 'Buster' in his backpack all the time."

The mother added, "It's easy to forget the Heart Buddy when you get caught up in everyday activities. I noticed a big difference in my children when we didn't talk about their Heart Buddies for a week. I think it's important for parents to remind the children of their Heart Buddies and talk about them every day."

Another parent commented, "I always use the Heart Buddy when my son is not listening well. I ask him to go find his Heart Buddy so we can continue our conversation from the heart. At times, I also get my Heart Buddy. We both hold our Heart Buddies close to our hearts while we talk. This greatly improves my boy's listening."

Teachers report that the "Heart Buddy" enables them to have effective in-depth discussions with groups of children ages five to ten. Although younger children tend to lose focus more quickly, having their Heart Buddies to focus on keeps them attentive longer.

VARIATIONS

1. An excellent variation is to ask children to pet their Heart Buddy when they find themselves getting distracted. For high-strung children, gently squeezing the Heart Buddy as they listen can help them stay calm.

2. Have children listen to the tape *Buddy Bubbles: Magical Games for a Child's Heart* to see why their heart is their best buddy, then sing the "Buddy Heart Song" together.

HEART BUDDY PATTERN
(Actual Size)

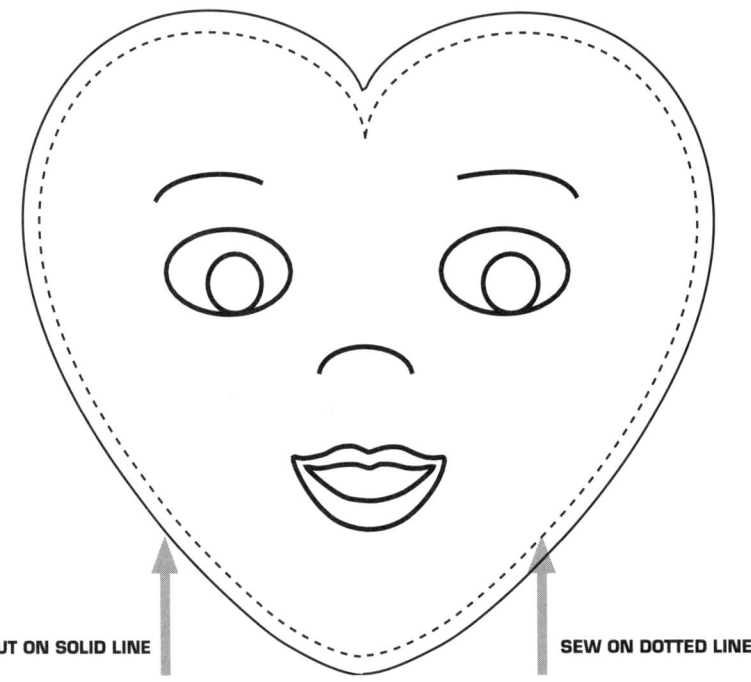

CUT ON SOLID LINE   SEW ON DOTTED LINE

Bubbles

PURPOSE

In teaching children to love, it's important for them to recognize what it feels like to be in their hearts and be loving while they play. This activity teaches little ones how to "be loving" while they blow bubbles. It's extremely helpful for both character development and building heart intelligence to frequently remind children to "be in the heart and be loving" as they participate in activities. To help them understand or remember what it feels like to "be in the heart and be loving," play the HEART LOCK-IN activity on page 28 right before playing this game.

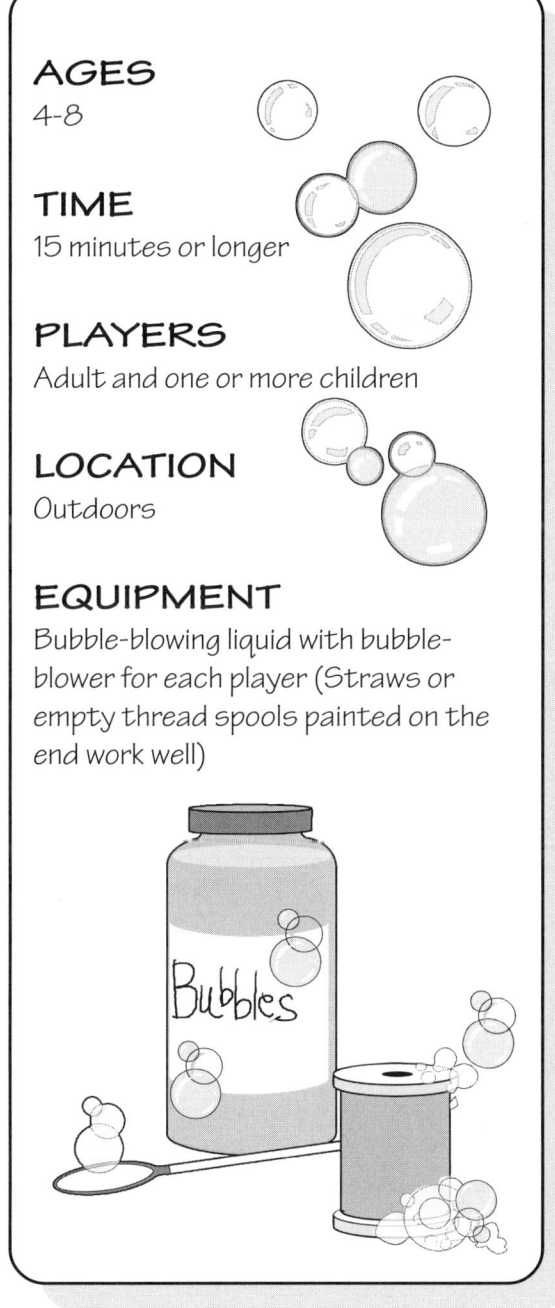

AGES
4-8

TIME
15 minutes or longer

PLAYERS
Adult and one or more children

LOCATION
Outdoors

EQUIPMENT
Bubble-blowing liquid with bubble-blower for each player (Straws or empty thread spools painted on the end work well)

INSTRUCTIONS

1. Prepare a bottle of bubbles for each player or create a fun activity where you make bubble liquid using containers of detergent and spools or straws for bubble blowers. (Spools work very well for young children. Caution them to blow through their bubble blowers but not inhale or drink the liquid.)

2. First demonstrate to the children how to blow bubbles.

3. Ask the children to play a game with you as they blow the bubbles. Instruct them to pretend that they are gently breathing love into each bubble, filling each bubble with love from the heart. Then when the bubbles float away and burst, all of their love will be spread out to everything in the area. As the bubbles float away, ask the children who or what is receiving their love. (People, flowers, trees, insects, the world, etc.)

Heart Pawn Game

PURPOSE

Here is a fun board game that has several purposes: 1) familiarize players with the Heart Tools, 2) remind them to stay in their hearts while playing a game with unpredictable outcomes, and 3) have a good time. The players are the pawns and they physically move around a large gameboard determined by the roll of dice. The end goal is to be the first to cross the finish line.

AGES

8-14

TIME

15 minutes or longer

PLAYERS

Two to six children

LOCATION

Indoors or outdoors (on concrete or linoleum)

EQUIPMENT

→ 1 pair of dice
→ 2 pieces of 8 1/2" x 11" cardstock cut into playing card size
→ Scissors, pencil or pen, tape, ruler
→ Chalk for drawing gameboard on concrete if outdoors, or 38 pieces of 8 1/2" x 11" cardstock to use as board squares if indoors. If you have a computer and printer, you can also type and print out gameboard squares and instruction cards
⇨ Table
⇨ Clear plastic
⇨ Buttons

INSTRUCTIONS

1. Draw your gameboard with chalk, following the gameboard diagram on page 42. The board will require an area approximately 5' by 7'. If you have room, make it large enough for two players to stand comfortably on the same square. Squares should be 12" to 18" wide, depending on available space. If two players land on the same square and the squares are too small, one player can stand outside the square. If you use cardstock to make squares, use two 8 1/2" by 11" pieces taped together per square.

2. Make your instruction cards. Use a pencil or pen to write instruction cards on cardstock, or photocopy template on pages 40-41 onto cardstock. Cut cardstock to playing card size. Use a ruler to make sure all cards are the same size.

3. Roll the dice to see who plays first, second, etc. Highest number is first.

4. First player rolls the dice and starting at square 1, moves a specific number of squares as indicated by the dice. If there are instructions in the square, player follows them. When the turn is complete, proceed to the next player.

5. Some of the board squares tell the player to draw a card from the deck of instruction cards placed in the middle of the gameboard area. When the player draws a card, he must follow the card's instructions before his turn is complete.

6. Players need to remember the number they land on, because they must move to the center of the gameboard to roll the dice and draw cards. The adult helps keep track of positions. If an argument results regarding what square a player is on, remind the players to use the Heart Tools to settle disputes.

7. The first player to make it to the finish (or Love square) is the winner. Prior to square 13, should the number a player rolls be greater than what's needed to reach the finish line, player must remain on that square and try again on his next turn to roll the exact number or a lessor one. After square 13, if the player rolls doubles that are greater than the number needed to finish, he automatically goes to the finish line.

Example: If someone is on square 13 and rolls 12 on the dice, he cannot finish unless dice both show 6 (doubles). If player lands on square 18, he must roll doubles to finish as it is impossible to roll a one with the dice.

VARIATION

The "Heart Pawn Game" can also be played on a table, using a photocopy of the gameboard template on page 42 protected under clear plastic, and using buttons as pawns.

MOVE BACK 3 SQUARES	MOVE TO APPRECIATION SQUARE	GO BACK TO SQUARE 1 HEART LOCK-IN
MOVE FORWARD 3 SQUARES	MOVE TO APPRECIATION Lose 1 Turn But Remember To APPRECIATE WHATEVER COMES YOUR WAY	YOU ARE A WINNER CROSS THE FINISH LINE INTO LOVE
GO BACK 5 SQUARES STAY IN YOUR HEART	MOVE FORWARD 2 SQUARES	You Just Won A HEART LOCK-IN GO BACK TO START DO NOT TAKE YOUR NEXT TURN But If You Remember To Lock-In Your Heart, All Will Be Well

MOVE
FORWARD
8
SQUARES

YOU
LOSE
YOUR NEXT
TURN

REMEMBER TO
SURRENDER
AND DON'T
CARE

ROLL THE
DICE AGAIN
AND TAKE
ANOTHER
TURN

MOVE TO
SQUARE
10
AND
APPRECIATE

MOVE
BACK
1
SQUARE

MOVE
FORWARD
2
SQUARES

MOVE
FORWARD
4
SQUARES
AND BACK
1
SQUARE

THIS CARD
CANCELS THE
LOSE A TURN CARD

After Using,
Return To
Bottom
of Deck

THIS CARD
CANCELS
SQUARE 14

SURRENDER
AND DON'T
CARE

After Using,
Return To
Bottom of Deck

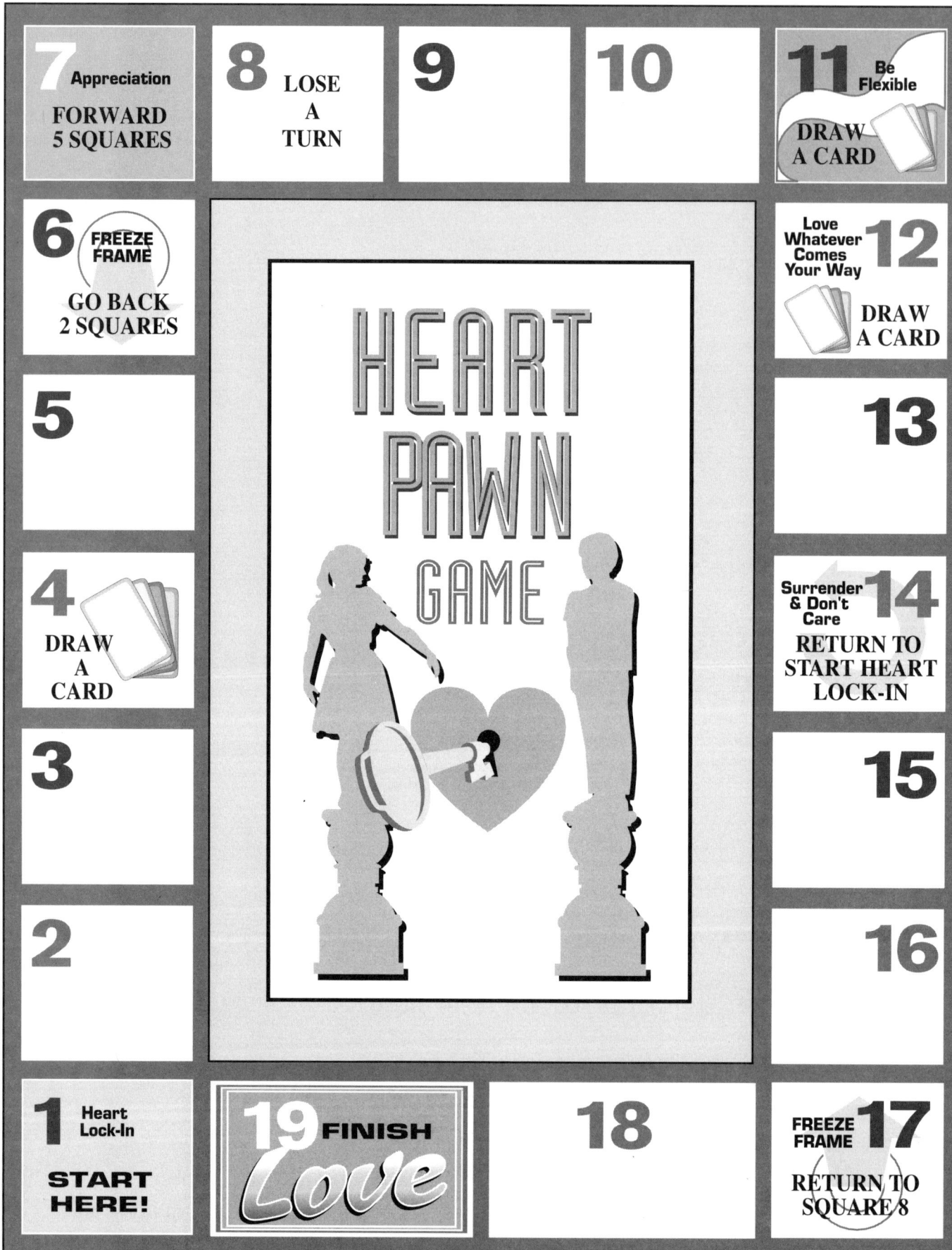

Heart Notes

PURPOSE

What most people understand about the heart, its function, and power, is like knowing about the tip of the iceberg. There is much more to the heart than just veins, arteries, and blood cells, although those physical attributes play a vital role in our health and survival. The heart's power and capacity for love, compassion, laughter, and intuition make it a source of positive feelings and intelligent choices. This activity introduces some notes, perceptions, and exercises that will provide a fun and instructive introduction to the heart.

AGES
10-19

TIME
30 minutes or longer

PLAYERS
Adult and two or more children

LOCATION
Indoors or outdoors

EQUIPMENT
➡ Heart Signals tape, tape recorder

INSTRUCTIONS

1. Begin by sharing some facts about the heart.*

   • The heart works without interruption for 70 or 80 years, without care or cleaning, without repair or replacement, day and night.

   • It beats 100,000 times per day, approximately 40 million times in a year, and within 70 years supplies the pumping capacity for nearly three billion cardiac pulsations.

   • It pumps two gallons of blood per minute and 100 gallons per hour, through a vascular system of about 60,000 miles in length — two and one-half times the circumference of the earth.*

   • The heart is the first sign of life in the uterus.

   • It starts and beats on its own and keeps working even after the brain dies.

   • In an adult, it is about the size of a closed fist.

Activity #1—Have each player open and close a fist repeatedly for two minutes. Compare the muscles of your heart to the muscles of your hand. Which is stronger? Why?

2. More notes about the heart.

   • The heart is the strongest electrical energy in the body, generating 40 to 60 times more electrical energy than the brain. When we go to the doctor's office, we can feel the pulse of our heart in our little toe but we can't feel the pulsations of the brain there.

*Facts are from Nutrition Plan for High Blood Pressure Problems, Birch-Benner

- Show the graphs below of the ECG electrical patterns of frustration and appreciation. With every heartbeat, electricity is generated and sent to *every* cell in your body. When we're frustrated, the electrical patterns of the heart become incoherent and scattered, causing the heart to work harder. When we feel appreciation or care, the heart patterns become coherent and harmonious.

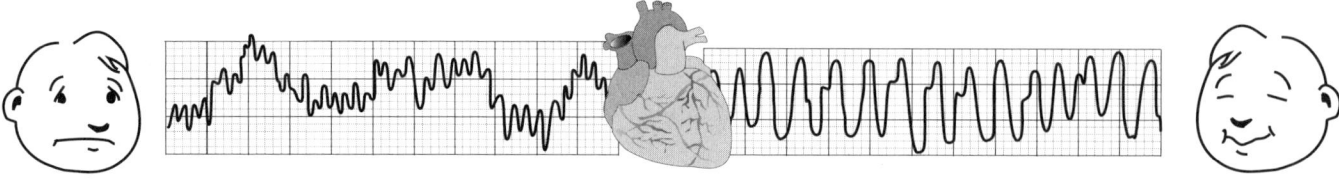

ECG ELECTRICAL PATTERNS

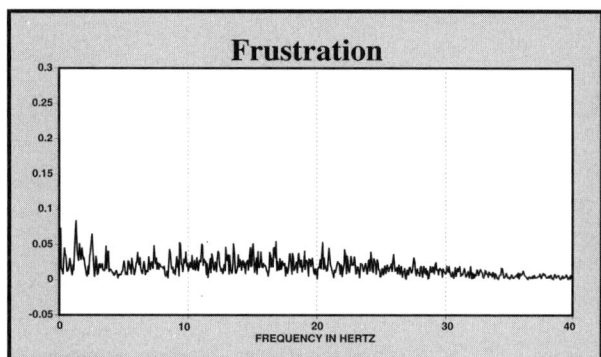

Emotional states like frustration create what are called incoherent spectra, meaning the power is scattered and disordered. This signal is transmitted to every cell in our body.

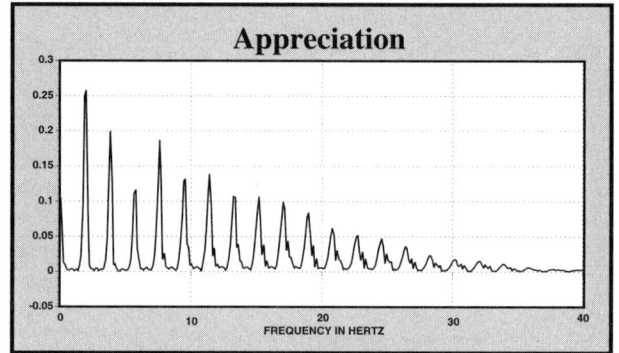

This person was feeling deep, sincere appreciation, which looks entirely different than the pattern of frustration. This is called a coherent spectra.

Activity #2— (5 or more children) Perform the "Wave" like people do at sporting events. Form a line of players and imitate a coherent or ordered electrical heart pattern of someone who is feeling appreciation or care. To do this, each row of players extends their hands up into the air in ordered sequence. Repeat this several times. Then shift the "Wave" pattern to a scattered and incoherent one where there is no sequence or order, representing someone who is frustrated. Repeat this several times.

Activity #3—Place your attention on your left big toe. Wiggle it for five seconds. Now place your attention on the area in the center of your heart. Pretend that you're breathing through your heart for about ten seconds. Recall a positive, fun feeling you have had recently or someone you care for or appreciate. Try to stay focused on that feeling in the heart for about one minute without jumping back and forth to the mind like an elevator.

3. With the brain, we think, read, memorize, do math, think of jokes, and acquire knowledge in school. With the heart, we feel care, love, appreciation, tune into people and what they're feeling, sense the difference between what is a good choice and a poor one, and experience a lot of fun. Can you imagine a mother saying to her little baby, "I love you with all my head?" Why not?

Activity #4—Draw out a list of heartfelt textures from the players, offering some of the following examples first: chocolate on your tongue, the smell of freshly-washed sheets, the warmth of a fireplace, feather-like raindrops falling on your hair and face, the sight of a new puppy, a summer breeze, etc.

Draw out lists from the following topics to further enrich the players' discussion and understanding of the heart:

- Places that speak to our hearts

- Common everyday phrases or words of wisdom relating to the heart

- Movies that stirred the heart

- Smells that moved the heart

- Books that moved the heart

- Activities that move us into the heart

- Music that move us into the heart

"Heart Notes" Participation from Two Fourteen-Year-Old Boys

Activity #4

Heart textures—Getting a back rub, hot shower on your back, seeing a good friend, scoring a 3 pointer in basketball, scratching an itch, when your home team wins a game, running in the ocean, putting on warm clothes just out of the dryer, hot chocolate on a cold day, seeing your dog when you come home, feeling good in the clothes you wear, speaking your truth, being proud of yourself

Places that speak to my heart—Basketball court, big mountain range, Disney World, being near a river, warm-climate place, discount department store, my house, deserted place with no people, the wind blowing

Phrases that speak to my heart—Just be myself, I should treat people the way I want to be treated

Movies that stirred the heart—*Little Princess, Legends of the Fall, Boys on the Side, Where the Day Takes You, Sandlot, Hoop Dreams*

Smells that moved the heart—Smell of a new basketball, new car, chocolate chip cookies right out of the oven, newly shampooed hair, wood

Books that moved the heart—*Lord of the Rings, Mathilda,* some of *Calvin and Hobbes* comics, *Belgerad*

Activities that move us into the heart—Playing basketball with a buddy, watching a movie with a friend, listening to music, seeing an old friend, riding in vehicles

Music that moves us into the heart—Beatles, Beach Boys, Al Green, some rap music, Classic Rock

Activity #5—Listen to the tape *Heart Signals* (ages 8-14) for more understanding of the power of the heart.

Pairs in the Heart

PURPOSE

Teenagers have a lot more in common than they often perceive. Without sincere communication and understanding from the heart, differences in appearance and social programming can block a teen's ability to see how much he or she does have in common with other teenagers. Perceiving only the differences causes much anxiety and unfair comparisons. This activity teaches teenagers to use their heart intelligence to understand other teenagers more deeply. It goes beneath surface perceptions to discover what is common and what is different between people.

AGES

12-18

TIME

15 minutes or longer

PLAYERS

Adult and four or more children

LOCATION

Indoors or outdoors (in a quiet location)

EQUIPMENT

➡ Pencils
➡ One copy of modified Venn diagram per pair (see template on page 48)

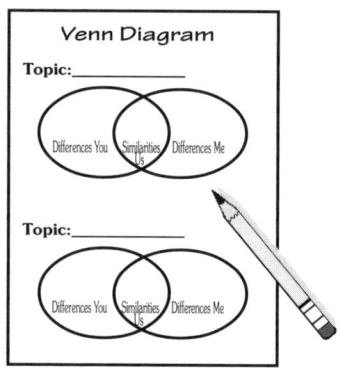

INSTRUCTIONS

1. Explain that the purpose of this activity is to understand what is different and what is common between pairs of players and in the larger group.

2. Have players pair up. Any odd numbered player left can pair up with the gamemaster.

3. Hand out a modified Venn diagram to each pair. Have each player reflect for one minute on what are five main things he appreciates and what are five main things he stresses over. Ask one player in each pair to be the scribe and write down all information shared. The scribe writes answers that are different from his partner's answers in the "Differences Me" section of the Venn diagram and writes his partner's different answers in the "Differences You" section. Any common answers are entered in the "Similarities Us" section.

4. The gamemaster provides examples before individual reflection starts.

Examples:
Things we appreciate: friends, movies, sports, parents, clothes, food, house, types of music, dancing
Things we stress over: schoolwork, parents, relationships, violence, clothes, adults, fitting in

5. As they play this game, ask the teens to notice their reactions to their partner's answers. Are they critical, questioning, or approving? Send heart or love to your partner to gain more understanding. After you both finish, talk about differences and similarities while continuing to send heart to each other.

6. When the conversation seems complete, the gamemaster gathers the Venn Diagrams, tallies up the most common things appreciated and stressed over, then tallies up the most common differences.

7. Share the results with the larger group. Ask the following questions to see what conclusions can be made. Were you surprised by the results in your pairs? in the larger group? Is there a common ground between teens? If so, what? Why do we emphasize differences so much? What do the differences indicate? How does sending heart or love help us understand each other better?

VARIATIONS

1. Have players pair up with teens they rarely talk to.

2. Play the same game introducing other topics: Care/Overcare, Fun/Not Fun, Happy/Sad, Angry/Peaceful, Head/Heart, etc.

3. Add a listening exercise to the pair's discussion, where each player has to intuitively listen, then feedback a) what was verbally said, and b) the feeling or emotion behind the words.

Venn Diagram

Topic:_____

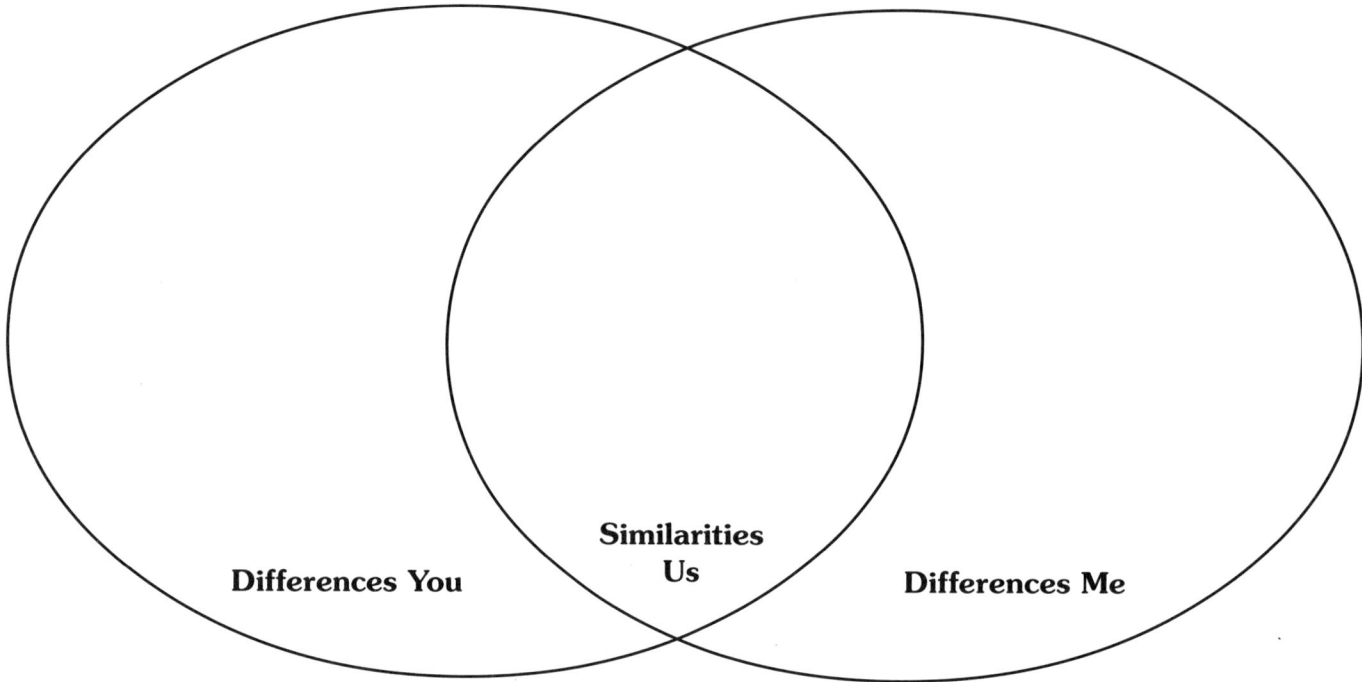

Topic:_____

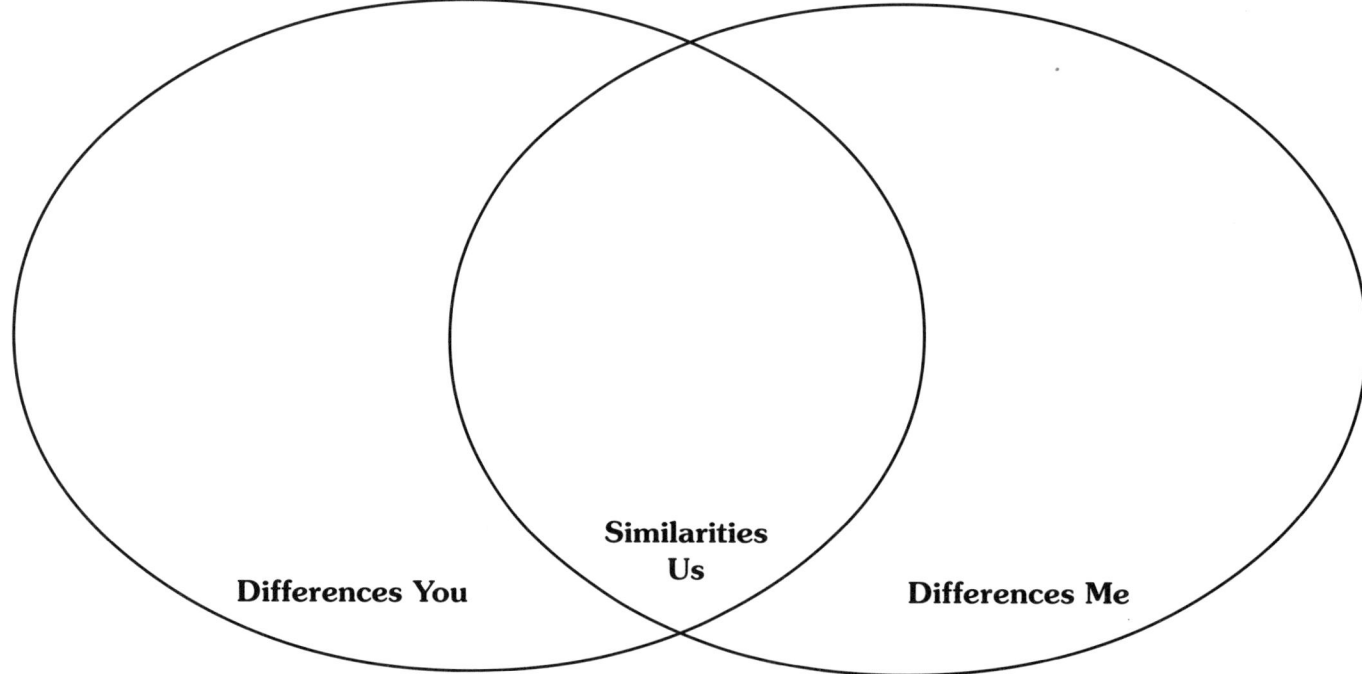

Heart Mapping®

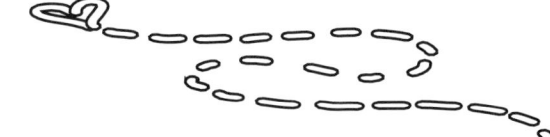

PURPOSE

Heart Mapping is a powerful tool that can demonstrate and unleash the power of the heart for teenagers and adults. Taught in corporations as a tool for problem-solving, project planning, and creativity, Heart Mapping also develops intuitive decision-making skills. Heart Mapping builds on Mind Mapping technology developed by educators for creative brainstorming and whole brain learning. Through the combination of head and heart intelligence, teenagers can use this tool to access greater potential in learning or choose a better course of action on any issue.

AGES
12-19

TIME
45 minutes or longer

PLAYERS
Adult and one or more children

LOCATION
Indoors

EQUIPMENT
➜ Flip chart, chalkboard, or greaseboard with appropriate markers
➜ 8¹/₂" x 11" plain white paper and pencils for each player
⇨ Colored markers for each player
⇨ Large poster paper for groups of players
⇨ <u>Heart Zones</u> tape, tape recorder

INSTRUCTIONS

1. Explain that the purpose of Heart Mapping is to find more intelligent and heartfelt perspectives on problems, issues, or projects. The process begins with a Mind Map, followed by a FREEZE-FRAME, then culminates with a Heart Map. This creates quality perceptions from both the head and heart. You can then create a conclusion or an action plan from the combined Mind and Heart Maps. (See example of a Mind Map/Heart Map done by a teenager on page 51 and his conclusion on page 50.)

2. Do a Mind Map as a group, using a flip chart, chalkboard, or greaseboard. Introduce a simple, fun topic that everyone can relate to, like planning a group outing or project. (Don't pick a problematic issue at first.) To create the Mind Map, draw a small circle in the center of the top half of the flip chart and write the topic title in the circle. Have players brainstorm (without editing) any and all ideas, concerns, issues, hopes, and challenges about the topic. Write each idea on a separate line branching out from the center of the circle like spokes of a wheel. Write sub-branches off main branch lines for ideas that further embellish a similar idea.

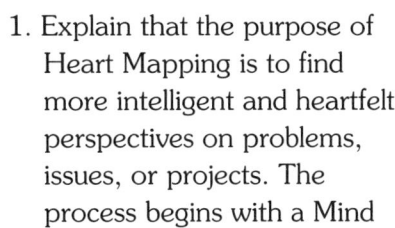

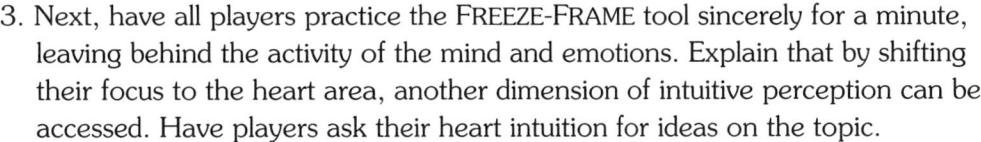

3. Next, have all players practice the FREEZE-FRAME tool sincerely for a minute, leaving behind the activity of the mind and emotions. Explain that by shifting their focus to the heart area, another dimension of intuitive perception can be accessed. Have players ask their heart intuition for ideas on the topic.

4. Draw a line across the middle of the flip chart. Begin the Heart Map process by drawing another small circle in the center of the bottom half of the flip chart and write the same topic in the middle of the circle. Ask players what thoughts and feelings came from their heart intuition after Freeze-Framing. Encourage the players not to edit their feelings but stay in touch with their heart and say what they feel and think. The heart intuition will always be positive, creative, and often surprisingly simple. Write down the players' heart perceptions. There might not be as many spokes on the Heart Map as on the Mind Map, but they will probably be significant, meaningful, and based on quality values.

5. Finally, compare the two maps. Note the differences or areas of overlap. Choose items from the Mind Map that support the Heart Map and connect them together by lines or circles.

6. List actions in order of priority, starting with Heart Map actions first. Add items from the Mind Map which support the Heart Map and are energy-efficient or practical.

7. Now ask players to select their own personal topic to Heart Map. Suggest they pick a personal project or problem. Discuss the example of the Heart Map on "computers" on the next page and the conclusion below.

8. Instruct players to draw two small circles on their piece of paper with the topic written in the middle of each circle, like you did on the flip chart. Ask them to first do a Mind Map, writing down all their ideas, concerns, hopes, fears, and challenges for seven minutes. Then everyone put their pencils down and FREEZE-FRAME together for one minute, asking their heart intuition for ideas on the topic. Finally, everyone do a Heart Map for seven minutes, writing down the feelings and ideas that came from the heart when they Freeze-Framed (again without editing them). Finally, ask them to turn the paper over and write a conclusion or action plan for seven minutes.

9. During the process, ask players who get stuck or need help to raise their hands and assist them until they understand the tool.

10. Discuss results.

EXAMPLE

The Heart Map on page 51 was done by a teenager. In his conclusion he wrote:

"The mind was more stimulated and getting frustrated because I wanted to learn so much in so little time, like staying up nights figuring things out. I was so set on computers only! The heart was true. To get obsessed is just an escape from dealing with my emotions. The real power is just to emotionally manage myself in balance and attitude."

VARIATIONS

1. Provide colored markers for players to create colorful visuals as they express their ideas.

2. Do a group Heart Map on a group problem.

3. Have groups of two or more players create a Heart Map together on projects or topics of common interest. Use large poster paper and place the final work and action plan on a bulletin board for others to see.

4. Play *Heart Zones* during the FREEZE-FRAME and in the background while the players are creating their Heart Maps.

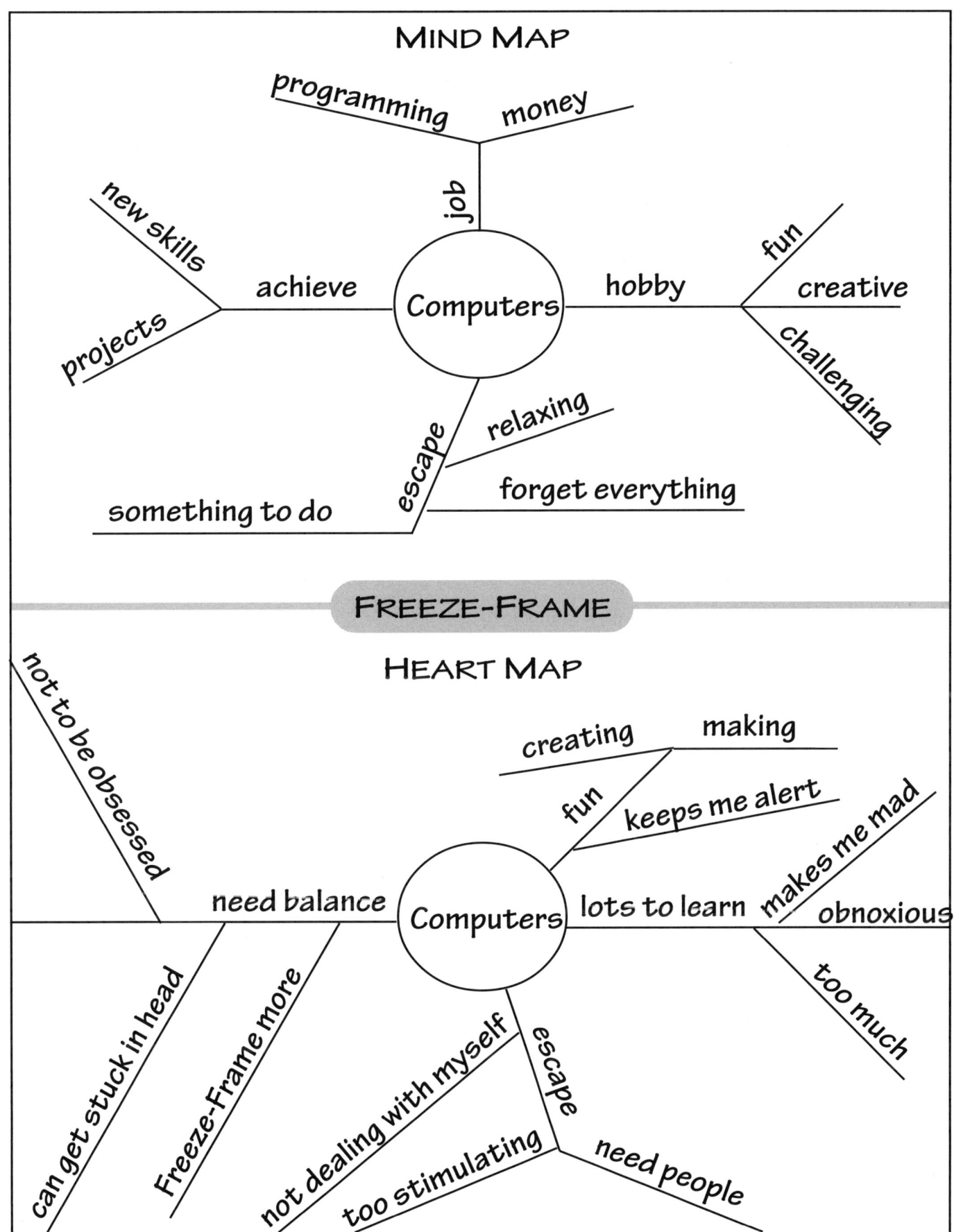

MIND MAP

programming
money
job
new skills
achieve
Computers
hobby
fun
creative
projects
challenging
escape
relaxing
something to do
forget everything

FREEZE-FRAME

HEART MAP

not to be obsessed
creating
making
fun
keeps me alert
makes me mad
need balance
Computers
lots to learn
obnoxious
can get stuck in head
Freeze-Frame more
not dealing with myself
escape
too much
too stimulating
need people

Journal of the Head And Heart

PURPOSE

A great way to help teens love themselves more and see the difference between the head and the heart is through journal writing. By recording a daily entry of feelings, events, and observations perceived from the head alongside a similar entry that emphasizes perceptions from the heart, a teen can find a secure place to express his or her innermost self. This can be a very meaningful activity as teens directly experience the heart as a source of intelligence and wider perspectives. In addition to writing sentences, teens can use phrases, poetry, metaphors, or drawings to express the difference between head and heart perspectives.

AGES
12 - 19

TIME
15 minutes or longer

PLAYERS
Adult and one or more children

LOCATION
Indoors or outdoors in a quiet location

EQUIPMENT
➡ A journal (preferably with a lock for privacy) or a notebook with lined or unlined paper for each participant
➡ Pen or pencil
⇨ Heart Zones or Speed of Balance tape, tape recorder

INSTRUCTIONS

1. Gather together the journals or notebooks and set aside a mutually convenient time for the journal writing process to begin. Hand out one journal or notebook to each teen and keep one for yourself. It is important that the adult participate so that the teen is supported and motivated by your effort and example.

Explain the goals of this activity:

• to learn to distinguish between the voices of your head and your heart

• to have fun exploring and expressing yourself

• to better handle stress

2. Explain how using the intelligence of the heart can make journal writing or keeping a diary more meaningful. *In the "head" part of the journal*, record the day's feelings, events, interactions, and observations that are worth entering. Include those that were enjoyable as well as those that were upsetting or stressful. Be honest and creative in recording the activities of the day. When the writing is completed from a head perspective, do a three-minute FREEZE-FRAME together, appreciating the good parts of your day. *During the latter part of the FREEZE-FRAME*, ask the teen what his heart intelligence has to say about what he wrote down. Is there anything his heart wishes to add or contribute? Are there events that you want to remember to go back to the heart and appreciate? Is there a better way of handling any stress or difficult situations? Add the heart's intuitive perspective to the journal entry.

3. If appropriate, discuss any differences between the head and heart perspectives. The adult can set an example and share first, but deeply respect each other's privacy if someone does not want to share.

EXAMPLE

A Head and Heart Journal
Entry from a 14-Year-Old Boy

Head Entry

Last night a buddy and I were hanging out doing a puzzle. My buddy was eating and drinking on the carpet where we were playing. I got hungry too, so I got something to eat while doing the puzzle. A good friend of my family was with us while my mom was away. She told us to move to the table in the living room from the little spot where we were hanging out so the carpet wouldn't get dirty. My buddy was eating only Chex Mix™ and that doesn't make all that much dirt. Then she said that we were too loud and that I knew better than to eat on the carpet. She was real tired and irritable.

Heart Entry

It was a hard day for her. Her foot was banged up. We used to be able to eat on the carpet but only certain things were OK, like water or nuts, but not grape juice. Stuff that stained the carpet we wouldn't do. Grownups sometimes don't communicate well so we get blamed when sometimes we really don't know. Last night I felt mad and a little hurt. I feel like I have to prove to the adults that I am self-sufficient and that I can handle myself, like take charge of "my games" and what has to be done. If I surrender to the adults and do what they tell me to do, that will help fix the situation. If I do something and it is wrong and I don't know it, if I let it go, they will see that I am trustworthy.

You always have feelings. They're there even if you aren't aware of them. It's your choice whether you want to relate to your feelings or forget about them. If I get too pissed, like last night, I should just let it go even though I think I am right. There might be a little feeling leftover but you can clarify it later with a parent. Sometimes there are thousands of feelings you have to deal with but there isn't time to deal with them. You try to clear most of them up and then the rest you hold in and try to forget. It is like a video game that you try to win.

"You always have feelings. They're there even if you aren't aware of them. It's your choice whether you want to relate to your feelings or forget about them."

VARIATION

Play *Heart Zones* or *Speed of Balance* during the FREEZE-FRAME and in the background while the teens are adding heart perspectives to their journals.

CHAPTER
3

The Importance of Appreciation

Family Appreciation Games

PURPOSE

We've all heard the expression, "Home is where the heart is." Practicing appreciation with family members increases family bonding and security while reinforcing family values. As children and teens become more absorbed with peer relationships and developing their own identities, their awareness and acknowledgment of day-to-day care from parents or family members often slips to the background. Reinforcing an attitude of appreciation, not just with parents and family but toward life in general, will boost morale and optimism and reduce tendencies toward pessimism, cynicism, or doubt. "Family Appreciation Games" will help all family members, and teens especially, widen their perspectives, feel more secure, and learn how to express their gratitude.

AGES

6-19 (invite younger children to participate if they can be quiet)

TIME

15 minutes or longer

PLAYERS

Adult and one or more children

LOCATION

Indoors (where there is a table to write or draw on)

EQUIPMENT

➡ Paper, note cards, or drawing paper

➡ Pencils, colored markers, or crayons

Game #1
Turning Pessimism into Optimism

1. Find a moment when you can talk about appreciation with the family and how it is a valuable tool. Discuss how cynical society can be at times, asking your teens to state what signs of cynicism they observe in their lives. Speak personally on how appreciation widens people's perspective of what is really important and valued.

2. Ask each family member to write a list of people, events, and things they appreciate. Request that no less than five items be written down. Help younger children write their lists.

3. Discuss some of the items on each person's list. Go deep in the heart and talk about how you can enhance your appreciation of the people, events, and things you listed. Help each other find creative ways to express appreciation.

4. Have each family member post their list in their bedroom to remind them of who and what they appreciate. Reviewing the list helps nurture creative ideas of how to express appreciation. It also gives people an energy boost whenever they feel down or pessimistic.

VARIATIONS

1. Everyone agree to post their lists in a central location. Reviewing each other's lists helps remind family members of what others appreciate, adds energy to their efforts to appreciate, and can spark creative ideas of how to help each other express appreciation.

2. Using the small note cards, write and/or illustrate an appreciation note card to someone on the list. Read and show the cards to each other. If someone wants to keep what they said private, that's fine. They can give it to the person being appreciated in private or just keep it for themselves as a reminder to appreciate that person.

3. Together write or draw a family note card of appreciation for people that deserve special thanks: parent, relative, friend, teacher, adult friend, etc.

4. Invite other relatives and close family friends to participate in a Family Appreciation Game.

Game #2
Appreciating Each Family Member

1. As a family unit, have each person list or draw five qualities they appreciate about another family member. To make sure that the entire family is included, the selection process for who appreciates who can be done in a variety of ways: oldest to youngest, youngest to oldest, those who have the nearest birthday dates, random number selection, etc.

2. Discuss the completed lists with all family members, identifying those qualities that were surprising to the recipient and those qualities that were predictable.

3. Post the completed lists in a central place.

4. In a week, switch each person's focus of appreciation to another family member and repeat the process.

VARIATIONS

1. Use the note cards to write about or illustrate two qualities you most appreciate about each family member. Create a card for each person. Go deep in the heart to truly express your appreciative feelings.

2. Read the cards in each other's presence. Place the cards that you receive by your bedside table to appreciate being appreciated.

3. Regularly post note cards of appreciation on each other's bedroom doors, bathroom mirror, or refrigerator.

4. Create an Appreciation Day for each family member. In addition to cards of appreciation, care for them in a special way. Consider fun events, like treating them to a series of special movies, breakfast in bed, a meal of their choice, a trip to their favorite clothing store, etc. The selected person chooses whatever food, form of entertainment, or schedule they want in their honor. Post note cards of appreciation around the house. In advance of the special day, gather together notes from other friends and relatives appreciating the selected person.

Game #3
Appreciating Yourself

1. Each family member write or draw five qualities that you appreciate about yourself. Compare your self-appreciation list to the previous lists created by other family members.

2. In a month's time, bring out all the appreciation lists and review. Add more qualities of appreciation that were not previously mentioned.

Fun With Please And Thank You

PURPOSE

Please and thank you are called "the magic words" because sincerity in asking or receiving creates a deeper heart connection between people. Many children, however, are taught to say "please" and "thank you" as a required courtesy rather than as a sincere request or expression of appreciation. To teach children the value of saying please and thank you, adults need to send a sincere feeling of love, kindness, or appreciation when they speak these words. Then when your children say please or thank you, they will also convey sincerity and respect with their words. Being consistent with this activity helps children feel and understand family values.

AGES
2-6

TIME
10 minutes or longer

PLAYERS
Adult and one or more children

LOCATION
Indoors or outdoors

EQUIPMENT
➡ Paper and pencil

⇨ Crayons or colored markers

⇨ Single hole punch, scissors

⇨ Paper cut into strips 2" x 11"

⇨ 2 loose leaf rings (from a stationery store)

INSTRUCTIONS

1. Start by being an example. Whenever you ask a child to do something for you, say "please" and send a feeling of appreciation, love, or kindness as you speak. Whenever a child does something nice for you, goes out of her way to help you, gives you a gift, etc., say "thank you" as you send a sincere feeling of appreciation. You can tell a toddler what you are doing by saying, "I am sending you a heart feeling of appreciation."

2. To illustrate for a toddler what a heart feeling is, place your hand on your heart and radiate love to the child. Explain that whenever you are being sincerely thankful, you are in your heart.

3. When a child says "thank you" or expresses appreciation for someone, you can remind her to add heart by saying, "Let's stop for a moment and send a feeling of love along with our thanks to (whomever the child is thanking)."

4. Explain that when someone makes us a gift, compliments us, or does something nice for us (like serves our dinner, cleans our room, picks up something we've dropped, shares their toy), it's because they care for us. When we say "thank you" from the heart, they will feel that we appreciate their care. Help your child make a list of examples of when to say thank you.

5. The same steps apply in teaching a child to say, "please." Explain that saying "please" is appreciating and respecting the person whose help you are asking. When we ask someone to go out of their way to do something for us, like bring us a glass of water, help button our shirt or tie our shoes, share a book, fix a toy, etc., saying "please" lets them know we care about them. And when they agree to help us, we feel cared for, too. Help your child write a list of examples of when to say please.

EXAMPLE

One mother played this game with her four and five-year-old daughters for weeks. They made their lists of when to say please and thank you and hung them up in the girls' bedroom. Each night before bed, they would look at their lists and see if any of those situations happened that day and whether they remembered to say please and thank you. Then they would recall other fun things that happened that day to appreciate and recall un-fun things that had happened to see if saying please and asking for help might have changed them.

VARIATIONS

1. Write the child's list of examples for saying thank you or please on a large piece of paper, leaving space under each example for a picture. Have the child draw a picture to illustrate each example.

2. Fold a piece of paper in half, then fold it once or twice again so the paper has four or eight equal spaces when unfolded. Have the child draw a picture of an example of when to say please or thank you in each space. When the child is finished drawing, ask her to say what each picture is showing. Print what she says under the picture.

3. For this variation, you will need a single hole punch, paper cut into strips about 2" x 11" and two loose leaf rings (from a stationery store). Hole punch the strips of paper on the left side. Write the child's "thank you" examples, putting one example on each strip of paper. Insert the strips of paper into one of the loose leaf rings. Do the same with examples for "please" and insert them into the second loose leaf ring. Children will love having their "please" and "thank you" examples on the rings and enjoy reviewing them each day. New examples can be added to the rings.

Appreciating Your Day

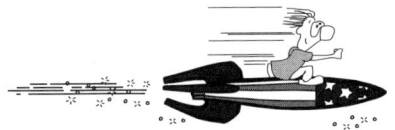

PURPOSE

Using the tool "appreciation" can be a rocket booster for a healthier outlook and attitude at the beginning of the day and a positive way to complete the day. Sharing different experiences and perceptions of appreciation with family members is contagious and creates a powerful momentum for deepening a heartfelt atmosphere in the home.

AGES

3-19

TIME

10 -15 minutes each day for one week

PLAYERS

Adult and one or more children

LOCATION

Kitchen, family room, or living room

EQUIPMENT

➡ Pens, pencils, crayons, or colored markers

➡ Blank white paper

➡ A flat writing or drawing surface

➡ A scrapbook or 3 hole punch and colored string to make a scrapbook

⇨ Scissors and glue

INSTRUCTIONS

1. At the end of the day, have everyone write, draw, or verbalize (for someone else to write) at least one thing they appreciated about the day. Next, ask everyone to write, draw, or verbalize one thing they want to appreciate about the upcoming day. Post everyone's papers in a central location.

2. Set a time to get together the next day to revisit the list.

3. Talk about how everyone did. Did you appreciate what you thought you would? Did you forget? Did you appreciate more things? What were they? Add the new things you appreciated to your paper.

4. Even when you are grumpy, making an effort to appreciate something can help offset feelings of upset or stress. Ask if this happened to anyone.

5. Repeat the process every day for one week. Save all the appreciation sheets.

6. Collect the week's appreciation sheets in a scrapbook. Bring out the scrapbook at the end of the week and review together. Use the scrapbook as a fun, family history of what was worth appreciating in the selected week.

7. Talk about what the game meant to each person. If the game has been fun, you might want to do it for a month and get together at the same time each week to update and review the scrapbook. Or you might want to do one of the Family Appreciation Games each week.

VARIATIONS

1. Do one or more of the Family Appreciation Games on pages 56-58 and add the family appreciation lists to the scrapbook.

2. Cut out pictures from magazines that convey objects or topics of appreciation. Have them available for family members to choose images that remind them to be appreciative. Glue the pictures on plain, white paper and post them in a central location.

Appreciation At Meal Time

PURPOSE

One of the best times to express appreciation is at meal times. The simple act of bringing the family together, eating together, and sharing what you appreciate together, deepens feelings of appreciation, love, and care for the whole family. Dinner time is also a great time for sincere communication. Playing this activity for a week will jump-start or increase positive family communication.

AGES

4 -19 (invite younger children to participate or quietly listen)

TIME

5 minutes or longer

PLAYERS

Adult and one or more children

LOCATION

Dinner table

EQUIPMENT

None

INSTRUCTIONS

1. Traditionally, grace is said prior to eating a meal. To make grace a deeper expression of appreciation, have everyone shut their eyes and send a feeling of appreciation from their heart for twenty to thirty seconds to each other, to the food, and to where the food comes from.

2. After serving the food and while eating, one person picks something about the family or household that he really appreciates, for example, the family dog, and says why he appreciates the dog.

3. Each person at the table adds something else that they appreciate about the dog.

4. At the next family meal, it's another person's turn to pick something to appreciate about the family or household and everyone adds to that.

Examples: a family member, grandpa visiting from another city, appreciating the heater that keeps us warm in the winter, the postman who delivers the mail every day, etc.

VARIATIONS

1. Invite the children to suggest different themes for appreciation and everyone add to the theme. For example, if a child picks food as the theme, we can appreciate mom for buying the food and always serving such good meals, appreciate the vegetable man at the store who picks out the nicest vegetables for us, appreciate how the food makes us healthy, etc.

2. Each person shares a problem they are having and everyone else states one thing about that problem that could be appreciated. Learning to find something to appreciate about tough situations or problems helps give a wider perspective on the problem and brings new solutions.

Appreciation Circle

PURPOSE

Appreciation is an essential tool for broadening a child's perspective of himself, others, and life. The "Appreciation Circle" broadens self-perception as peers or family discover and express each other's positive qualities. This information is very beneficial (not to mention a lot of fun) for a child to hear, as it can help change poor or narrow self-concepts.

AGES
7-14

TIME
30 minutes or longer

PLAYERS
Adult and two or more children

LOCATION
Indoors or outdoors (where there are no distractions)

EQUIPMENT
➡ Paper and pencil
➡ (Optional) Poster board and marker
⇨ Cards

INSTRUCTIONS

1. The group forms a circle, either sitting on chairs or on the ground. The adult states the purpose of the activity. Everyone will have the opportunity to sit in the center of the circle and hear the others, one at a time, describe some positive, heartfelt qualities they see in them. The person in the middle is the "receiver" and the person giving the comment is the "giver."

2. Before starting, draw out from the group several categories or areas that might trigger positive comments. Examples: communication skills, how they get along with others, attitude towards school, attitude when they lose a game, ability to have fun, be kind, funny, etc.

3. Ask for a volunteer to be a receiver in the Appreciation Circle. Tell the receiver that she is to be quiet while comments are being shared. Then ask the givers to go around the circle and share one or more qualities that they sincerely appreciate about the receiver. While statements about hair, clothing, and looks will come up (especially if a giver can't think of anything else), encourage deeper, more sincere efforts at finding comments. Record comments on paper so that they can be summarized on poster board later or handed out individually.

4. Continue with the process until everyone has had an opportunity to be a receiver. If time is limited, carry over activity to another day until everyone has had a turn. Then debrief about the experience. What was it like? Was it easy? Was it challenging? Was it easier to be on the receiving end or the giving end? Why? Did anyone hear any comments that they weren't expecting?

VARIATIONS

1. After all "giver" comments have been shared, ask the receiver to state what she appreciates about herself. Include those comments on the comment sheet.

2. Have a secret appreciation circle where participants send heartfelt appreciation for three minutes to either a) the person to their right or b) have all names written on cards and secretly send heart energy to the person each participant draws.

Everyone's A Winner

PURPOSE

"Everyone's A Winner" increases the value of each player's appreciation for friends, family, teachers, store clerks, firemen, and others. The object of the game is to place the name of one person, place, thing, or category (i.e. teachers, relatives, animals, rescue workers, etc.) that you appreciate on a gameboard square. Then place as many poker chips as qualities that you can sincerely appreciate about that subject on the square. The player with the most chips at the end of the game is the winner, although everyone ends up a winner from the sheer fun of the game and from sparking more appreciation.

AGES

7 - 15

TIME

30 minutes

PLAYERS

Adult and two to six children

LOCATION

Indoors or outdoors (on a table, floor, or ground)

EQUIPMENT

➡ A 2' by 3' grease board or 2'x 3' poster paper
➡ One die
➡ Poker chips (25 of one color per player)
➡ Greaseboard marker and paper towel for each player (small slips of paper and a pencil for each player if using poster paper)
➡ Watch with second hand or stopwatch
➡ Pencil and paper

INSTRUCTIONS

1. Divide the greaseboard or poster paper into six equal sections. Number the squares from one to six.

2. The adult is the gamemaster and decides how many rounds constitute a game. With three players, ten rounds can be completed in thirty minutes.

3. Give each player twenty-five poker chips.

4. Instruct players to pick a square. If you have three players, each player can have two squares. If you have two players, each can have three squares. If you have four, five, or six players, each has one square. Empty squares belong to the house. Players write the name of a different person, place, thing, or category they want to appreciate in each of their squares (or on slips of paper placed on the squares).

5. Each player goes to his heart and silently asks himself what he can appreciate about the name he has written in his square. He places as many chips as things he can think of to appreciate on the square. Suggest that players be sincere in finding qualities to appreciate and not place too many chips on one square.

6. The gamemaster rolls the die to begin the game. The number that comes up on the die indicates the square for that roll. Whoever wins the roll of the die has to state one quality that he appreciates about the subject named in the square for each chip in the square. If he can do this, he wins all the chips on the board.

Example: The gamemaster rolls the die and the number comes up six. Gary has three chips on square six and has written his brother's name in the square. In order to win the round and all of the chips on the board, he must sincerely express three qualities that he appreciates about his brother. If no one has chips on the number indicated by the die, the house wins that round and play resumes with a new round.

7. Don't let the game degenerate into superficial statements or sarcastic humor. The gamemaster can ask for a more sincere appreciation statement or refuse to pay if a statement is too superficial. While a player is expressing his appreciation, ask the other players to participate by sending a feeling of appreciation to the subject being appreciated.

8. After each round is over, players have twenty seconds to use their paper towels to erase the names in their squares, write in a new name, place, category, etc., and place their chips. The gamemaster keeps track of the time.

9. The gamemaster always rolls the die and also keeps track of the number of rounds played.

10. If a player runs out of chips, he may purchase five chips from the house by relating two things that he sincerely appreciated about his day or purchase ten chips by relating four things he appreciated about his day.

11. The winner is the player who had the opportunity to express the most appreciation and thus accumulate the most chips. Remind the players that *everyone* is a winner anytime they are appreciating.

EXAMPLE

Here's one teacher's experience of playing "Everyone's A Winner" with a new child in her class. "Johnny and Blake wanted to play, so they each got three squares on the greaseboard. After laying out the rules of the game, Johnny wrote his mother's name in one square and his two brothers' names in the other two squares. He placed three chips on his mom's square, three chips on one brother's square, and left the other brother's square empty. He sat for some time pondering the other brother. When I asked if he was ready to start, he informed me that he wasn't sure he wanted to leave Mike's name in his square. When I asked why, he replied that he couldn't think of anything at all to appreciate about Mike and that he didn't like him most of the time. I called a time out from the game and asked Johnny if he would like to try to find at least one thing he liked about Mike before the game began. After a long pause, he conceded that he did appreciate Mike for repairing his bike. I suggested that he place one chip on Mike's square, which he did. Johnny then paused again and said, 'He also helps me with my homework and sometimes makes milk shakes for me.' Johnny placed two more chips on Mike's square. All at once Mike had caught up (appreciation-wise) with his mother and other brother. It was fun to observe Johnny as the game progressed. Mike's name remained on the board for the entire hour we played and each time the die came up on Mike's name, Johnny found three more things to appreciate about him."

VARIATION

Have players pick names, places, or things all from the same category to write in their squares. The gamemaster calls out a different category for each round, e.g., family names, pets, favorite places they have gone on vacation, teachers, favorite foods, heroes, rescue workers, etc.

CHAPTER 4

Exploring the FREEZE-FRAME Tool

HEART LOCK-IN

Take 5 minutes in your day to go to your Heart

DEEP HEART LISTENING

Let your heart listen. That way you hear

FREEZE-FRAME

Stop! Put your thoughts on pause and go to your Heart.

Teaching FREEZE FRAME & Other HeartMath Tools

by Susan Timmer, Inner-City Elementary Teacher, and Edie Fritz, Counselor

Both children and teachers need tools to maintain emotional balance in today's classrooms. FREEZE-FRAME is an excellent tool to bring balance to the classroom and works quickly. Here are some tips for teaching FREEZE-FRAME in the classroom.

1. **Take your time when you begin.** First talk to children about the difference between the head and the heart. Teach FREEZE-FRAME after you have established rapport and a sense of safety and community in your classroom.

2. **Clearly establish ground rules.** As teachers, we can't make any child go to their heart, but we can ask them not to bother others. Insist on total respect for others. This means no touching others, whispering, or talking during FREEZE-FRAME. Go over any non-verbal signals that you will use to remove children who are creating a disturbance. Prepare quiet activities for them, like drawing or writing, if they do not want to participate.

3. **The key to a teacher staying in the heart is to do your personal HEART LOCK-IN before school** so you can focus on your students' needs during their heart time. Have a "needy" child sit next to you and send her extra heart. Ask your heart intelligence which child(ren) need extra heart during this time and send love to them. Remember, elementary children will fidget and wiggle sometimes, especially during the first month and even throughout the school year. The key is that they don't bother others.

4. **Include enough time so that the children can share their experiences after Freeze-Framing.** A teacher who is committed to reinforcing the heart must be prepared for deep personal sharing from her children. This is also an excellent way to elicit personal or narrative writing from children.

5. **Integrating FREEZE-FRAME and the other HeartMath tools with conflict resolution and peer mediation techniques** is an excellent way to help children with problem solving and conflicts at school. But do HeartMath first, then bring in the content of other programs. Look at HeartMath as a shot of steam that makes the other programs really work. After consistent daily practice, children will reach the point where they want to solve problems on the playground, at lunch recess, etc. Help them differentiate the head from the heart by pointing it out during the day. Do it on an individual basis to avoid embarrassment. Be sure to compliment children honestly. As a teacher or counselor, acknowledge when you are in your head and then model in front of children how to go to your heart. Remember, if children can come to school and recreate the feeling of a scary movie or TV show they have seen, they can just as easily recreate the feeling of a positive or joyful experience.

Letting the children listen to the *Heart Signals* tape (age 8-14) is helpful in teaching HeartMath tools. —Ed.

Freeze-Framing Happiness

PURPOSE

Young children can be upset one moment and back in their hearts, giggling, the next. One warm-hearted suggestion often turns an unhappy face into a joyous smile. As children grow older, they lose this natural flexibility. However, they can be taught to retain their heart ability to flex through life's ups and downs, develop resiliency — the ability to bounce back readily after suffering a loss — and gain personal control over their reactions. The purpose of this game is to teach young children a beginning version of the FREEZE-FRAME tool to build adaptability and find their heart power when they are unhappy.

AGES
3-7

TIME
20 minutes or longer

PLAYERS
Adult and one or more children

LOCATION
Indoors (at a table or on desks)

EQUIPMENT
➡ Brown paper bags for each participant (select size to fit comfortably over the head)
➡ Markers, crayons, and scissors

INSTRUCTIONS

1. Create a happy face on a brown paper bag with cut-out eyes and a cut-out smiling mouth and nose that can be used as a model for children to make their own. Twinkling eyes with fun eyelashes can be drawn. Place the model where children can see it.

2. Ask the children to recall a day when they had a lot of fun or were very happy. Ask them how they looked. Were they smiling? How did they feel? Help them remember the feeling.

3. Prepare children's bags by marking where eyes, nose, and mouth should be drawn (to be cut out later). Give each child a brown paper bag and ask them to draw a smiling, happy face, like the face they had on one of their happiest of days. (Cut holes for eyes and mouth for them.) Tell them that this is a mold of their happy face. When they are unhappy or out of their heart, they can put on their mold, FREEZE-FRAME, and go back to their heart, remembering how good they felt on that happy day in their life. Soon their face will mold back to the happy mask and in their privacy, they will feel a lot better.

4. Bring out the happy-face bag to help your child FREEZE-FRAME each time she is out of the heart. Once she is back in the heart, she can send appreciation for feeling happy again. Then take off the happy-face bag and put it away until needed for another "rainy day."

FREEZE-FRAME Pictures

PURPOSE

Every picture tells a story. In "FREEZE-FRAME Pictures," children draw a story about how to deal with a stressful event using FREEZE-FRAME (see page 21). For many children, visual learning and drawing enhances memory of the steps. Children also like drawing their feelings out on paper. FREEZE-FRAME is a great tool to build and reinforce resiliency, and once learned, children will have countless opportunities to apply the tool at home and at school.

AGES
5-14

TIME
20 minutes or longer

PLAYERS
Adult and one or more children

LOCATION
Indoors (at a table or on desks)

EQUIPMENT
➡ 8 ½" by 11" white paper
➡ Felt tip pen, pencils, crayons, or markers
➡ Ruler
⇨ Heart Zones or Speed of Balance tapes, tape recorder

INSTRUCTIONS

1. Using a ruler and felt tip pen, turn a piece of paper on its side and divide into three sections by drawing two lines down the long side of the paper, 3 $\frac{10}{16}$" from each edge. Hand out paper to each child along with a pencil and a set of markers or crayons.

2. Explain the activity. The children will be guided through a FREEZE-FRAME experience and draw their story. *The story has three parts requiring three drawings:* 1) something that made them feel bad which they need to FREEZE-FRAME; 2) an image of something or someone that evokes heartfelt feelings; and 3) a picture of how they can resolve the stressful situation. They may want to add fun, cartoon-like comments to each drawing.

3. Ask the children if they felt bad, upset, or stressed-out recently over some event or person — a problem they need to FREEZE-FRAME. Examples: Someone got mad at them, a toy broke, they got into a fight, last night's dinner tasted bad and they fussed about eating, etc. Have the children draw their answer in the first box.

4. Next, guide the children to recall a wonderful heartfelt experience, evoking images such as their love for a parent, friend, or pet, a favorite toy, or place to visit, etc. Suggest that the children close their eyes to help them focus in the heart and remember the feeling of the wonderful experience. Have the children draw their heart-inspired image in the middle section of the paper.

5. Complete the activity by asking the children to ask their heart what it says to do to help them deal with the stressful situation or bad feeling. Remind them that they are trying to make the situation better from a heart perspective. Examples: Does somebody need a hug, a kind word, forgiveness, should you forget about it and move on, etc.

6. Have the children explain each section of their FREEZE-FRAME pictures.

EXAMPLE

A mother of two wrote to say, "My six-year-old son Alex and I drew pictures of ourselves Freeze-Framing. Wow! It was a powerful learning tool. It really was the necessary element for me to teach the inner process taking place during FREEZE-FRAME. Thank you."

VARIATIONS

1. Write "FREEZE-FRAME Pictures" at the top of the sheet and write the following headings for the three drawings: Picture 1 - What is the stress? Picture 2 - What gets you into your heart? Picture 3 - What is your heart's response?

2. Play *Heart Zones* or *Speed of Balance* during the FREEZE-FRAME and in the background while the children are drawing their pictures.

FREEZE-FRAME Tag

PURPOSE

Games are a great way for children to play and express their natural desire to have fun. With games, however, come disagreements and even fights. "FREEZE-FRAME Tag" helps children understand the concept of FREEZE-FRAME (see page 21). As children FREEZE-FRAME to get back to their hearts and regain perspective, fun increases and they resolve disputes more quickly. Outlining the rules before the start of any game also helps prevent potential disagreements.

AGES
5-14

TIME
20 minutes or longer

PLAYERS
Adult and three to fifteen children per group (or more than one group)

LOCATION
Outdoors

EQUIPMENT
➡ Markers to designate boundaries

VARIATION

In the midst of the game (or in the midst of an argument), call out "Freeze," everyone goes to the heart and freezes their bodies in whatever position they're in. Ask everyone to place their attention on their heart and sincerely appreciate or feel care for each other. After an appropriate time, say "Everything is all right." This is the code to unfreeze and resume the activity in which they were previously engaged. Practicing spontaneous FREEZE-FRAMES helps children understand that they can experience their heart as quickly as the command "Freeze" is called out.

INSTRUCTIONS

The adult gamemaster leads a three to five-minute discussion on the rules of "FREEZE-FRAME Tag." Start by asking the following three questions and include the answers given here in the discussion.

Question 1: *Why are we playing this game? What do you want to achieve?*
• Fun, enjoyment, fairness, and excitement.

Question 2: *What are the rules of the game?*
• When you're tagged, you "Freeze" inside your heart. Then you "Freeze" your entire self and stay frozen.
• You can only be freed by another player tagging you.
• There are boundaries indicated by markers.
• The person "it" has to count to five before beginning to chase the other players.
• If the person "it" tags everybody and they're all frozen, then "it" wins that game and you start another game.
• If the person "it" doesn't win after five minutes (or other age appropriate time limit), then the gamemaster calls "FREEZE-FRAME" and everyone freezes. The gamemaster will choose a new "it" and start another game. The gamemaster decides when to stop playing.
• To decide who is "it," have a volunteer secretly choose a number between 1 and 50 and tell the gamemaster. Each player tries to guess the number and whoever comes closest is "it." (For small groups of four or less, consider drawing sticks (the shortest) or asking the players how they would like to choose who is "it.")

Question 3: *What if there's a disagreement?*
• If there is a disagreement and someone thinks they're right and the other person is wrong, play Surrender and Don't Care. This means we surrender to the other person's view, so it's no big deal, or surrender to the gamemaster's decision. If two people get into an argument or fight, call a team "Freeze," then start the game over again.

FREEZE-FRAME Treasure Chest

PURPOSE

FREEZE-FRAME is an excellent tool for children because it gives them a secure anchor to hold onto when faced with stressors or challenges. What facilitates the successful practice of FREEZE-FRAME (see page 21) is building a supply of positive images or assets that can be called-up on demand. "FREEZE-FRAME Treasure Chest" seeks to have children and adults identify a list of fun experiences, special relationships, or images that they sincerely appreciate or care about. With this reservoir, children are better prepared for Freeze-Framing unexpected stresses in day-to-day living.

AGES
6-12

TIME
30 minutes or longer

PLAYERS
Adult and one or more children

LOCATION
Indoors (at a table or desks)

EQUIPMENT
➡ 3"x 5" index cards
➡ Pencils
➡ Crayons or marking pens
➡ Scissors and white paper
➡ Paste or tape
➡ A box with a lid for each child
⇨ <u>Heart Zones</u> or <u>Speed of Balance</u> tapes, tape recorder

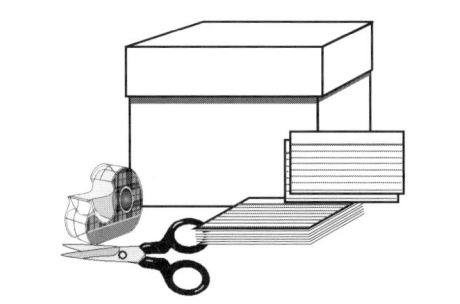

INSTRUCTIONS

1. Provide an example of an individual or group of people who are prepared for emergency action at a moment's notice.

   Example: firemen who are required to have fireproof clothing, equipment, fire trucks, working radio, maps, backup plans, and the attitude of being calm and professional. Explain to the children that just as a fireman will ask people in a burning building to remain calm as they exit, FREEZE-FRAME can help us calm our stresses in the moment. In order to be prepared, it is helpful to have a Treasure Chest of heartfelt images that can be called upon immediately.

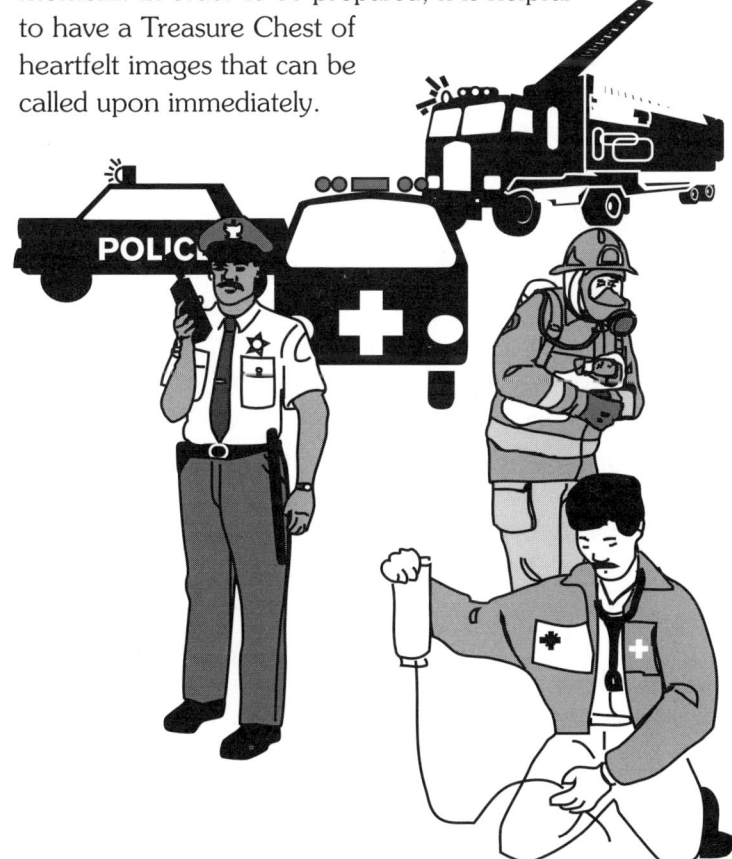

2. Ask children for more examples of individuals or groups who must be prepared for emergency action at a moment's notice.

   Examples: police, doctors and nurses, ambulance drivers, military personnel, teachers, rescue squad workers, and parents.

3. Have children practice FREEZE-FRAME with the intent of discovering things in their lives that they appreciate, care for, or help them have fun.

   Examples: parents, friends, relatives, pets, toys, house, clothes, favorite hobbies, vacation spots, etc. Suggest that each person come up with at least five things which they can place in reserve in their Treasure Chest.

4. Ask children to write or draw each thing that emerged from the FREEZE-FRAME on separate 3" x 5" index cards, then fold each card in half and save.

5. Making the Treasure Chest. Use crayons or marking pens to decorate your box and make it your own personal Treasure Chest. If the box already has writing on it, tape or paste white paper to the box, then decorate.

6. Put the folded index cards with your FREEZE-FRAME treasures written on them in your Treasure Chest. Afterwards, discuss some of the ideas in your Treasure Chest that you can call-up when you're faced with stress.

7. Set aside several mornings to open the Treasure Chest and choose one of the folded cards to be your special treasure for the day. Put it back in the box as your secret treasure or post it where you will see it as a reminder (refrigerator, mirror, bedroom door, notebook, etc.) Each time you want to FREEZE-FRAME, remember your special treasure for that day.

VARIATIONS

1. At the end of each day, ask children which treasure they used that day and how it helped them. Have children update the Treasure Chest from time to time, adding new heartfelt images.

2. Ask children to read all the treasures in the Treasure Chest each day and appreciate each one. When they need to FREEZE-FRAME, they will recall how much they have to appreciate.

3. Play *Heart Zones* or *Speed of Balance* during the FREEZE-FRAME and in the background while the children are drawing and creating their Treasure Chests.

The Heart Certificate

PURPOSE

Children enjoy having an achievable, positive goal to work toward. "The Heart Certificate" gives them an incentive to remember to apply the Heart Tools. When a child has remembered to stay in her heart or applied FREEZE-FRAME (see page 21) to get back in the heart (most of the time) for four out of five days, she is given a certificate with a blue seal. If extra efforts have been made during that time to sincerely use the tools when the need arose, a certificate with a gold seal is given, indicating that she has balanced her deficits and added more gold to her bank account.

AGES
7-12

TIME
10 minutes or longer

PLAYERS
Adult and one or more children

LOCATION
Indoors

EQUIPMENT
➡ Certificates
➡ Heart Chart
➡ Heart stickers
➡ Blue and Gold Notary Seals (found at any stationery or office supply store)

INSTRUCTIONS

1. Make certificates for all the children. If you have a computer, it's fun to make your own certificates. If not, you can copy the certificate on page 78.

2. Make Heart Charts (see page 77). You will place a heart sticker on each day the child makes sincere efforts to stay in the heart and use the tools. You will place a check next to the heart sticker if a child has stayed in her heart most of the day or made extra sincere efforts to use a tool quickly to get back to the heart. Because some children are more active than others and therefore may have more difficulty practicing the tools, take into consideration how much effort a child has put forth to earn a heart sticker or a check.

3. If a child earns a heart four out of five days, she receives a certificate with a blue seal. If she receives a heart with a check beside it four out of five days, she receives a certificate with a gold seal. The check marks indicate that the child put extra gold in her heart bank account. Children take pride in seeing their hearts and checks posted daily. It gives added incentive to do well the next day.

4. Next, tell the children your plan. Show them the chart, certificates, heart stickers and seals, then explain the game rules.

RULES

1. In order to receive a heart on the chart, you must make sincere efforts to be in your heart most of the time that day. If you get out of your heart, you remember to use a Heart Tool to get back. (Everyone gets out of their heart at times. It is how quickly you can get back that counts toward earning a gold seal on your certificate. FREEZE-FRAME is a quick way back to your heart.)

2. You do not receive a check on a day that you have had "Time-Out" or "Wall-Time." Explain "Time-Out" and "Wall-Time" to the children. Having to take a "Time-Out" indicates that you were out of your heart for a while and did not make efforts to use a tool to help you get back in your heart. "Wall-Time" is given if you are still out of your heart after the "Time-Out." You can still get a heart for the day if you use the "Time-Out" or "Wall-Time" to sincerely go back to a soft heart. Let your heart help you understand where you need to adjust your attitude so that you don't have the same "out of the heart" experience again.

Time-Out

"Time-Out" is used when a child has been out of the heart and needs help to get back to balance. You ask the child to stop playing the group activity and sit quietly until he is calm and back in the heart. "Time-Out" is usually from two to ten minutes.

FREEZE FRAME & FIND YOUR SOFT HEART

Wall-Time

"Wall-Time" is used when a child has not responded to "Time-Out" and needs a longer period of time to herself to get back in the heart. A child stands facing a wall in a quiet place for a specific length of time set by the adult (usually five to twenty minutes). Younger children sit on a chair facing the wall. "Wall-Time" gives a child undistracted time to slow down and really ponder the rule she has broken. First talk to the child, speaking your truth from the heart, so she understands why she's being put on the wall. Then ask her to spend the wall time pondering from the heart what she did. Ask her to practice FREEZE-FRAME to gain a deeper understanding. During "Wall-Time," no one speaks to the child nor is the child allowed to talk. When "Wall-Time" is over, have a calm, heart-to-heart talk with the child. Ask her what she has learned about the situation.

EXAMPLE

One mother commented, "This "Heart Certificate" game works! The combination of behavior modification and going to the heart is very powerful. It helped both my eight-year-old daughter and myself focus in and stick to a program."

Heart Chart

How Well Were You In Your Heart Today?

WEEK OF: _____

NAME	MONDAY	TUESDAY	WEDNESDAY	THURSDAY	FRIDAY	SATURDAY	SUNDAY

Heart Certificate

This is to Certify

_____

**has made sincere efforts
to stay in the heart and to use
the Heart Tools when needed.**

During the week of_____

Supervisor:_____

Heart Slip Reminders

PURPOSE

This activity helps children learn to see when an emotional drain (or deficit) begins to occur and gives them an immediate means of turning it into an asset. When a child is "out of the heart," different types of misbehavior accompany it. There is what is referred to as "Happy Head," which is loud, boisterous, sometimes silly behavior that depletes the child's energy. There is non-listening and interrupting or distracting others. Sometimes being "out of the heart" is expressed through anger, too much analyzing and arguing over communications, or trying to find loopholes in the rules and regulations. The list could go on. Misbehavior not only creates an emotional drain for the child, but requires an added output of energy that can result in an emotional drain (a deficit) for the adult if patience wears thin. Heart Slips do not get into the specifics of the infraction, but simply address the fact that the child is "out of the heart" and instruct the child how to correct it. By requiring the child to FREEZE-FRAME (see page 21) and use a Heart Tool, you are giving the child an opportunity to slow down and get back "in the heart." The child's heart intelligence can then give him a deeper understanding of where he was out of line.

AGES
7-12

TIME
10 minutes or longer

PLAYERS
Adult and one or more children

LOCATION
Indoors or outdoors

EQUIPMENT
➜ Colored paper for photocopying
➜ Photocopies of the Heart Tools (pages 155-160) cut into slips

HEART LOCK-IN

Take 5 minutes in your day to go to your heart and feel love.

FREEZE-FRAME

Stop! Put your thoughts on pause and go to your heart.

DEEP HEART LISTENING

Let your heart listen. That way you hear a person's deeper heart and not just someone's words.

INSTRUCTIONS

1. Make two photocopies of the Heart Tools (pages 155-160) on colored paper and cut one copy into Heart Slips. Post the other copy where children can read it and become familiar with the Heart Tools. Alternatively, you can make your own Heart Tool slips, such as "FREEZE-FRAME and Listen More Deeply To What Is Being Said," "FREEZE-FRAME and Appreciate Others More," "FREEZE-FRAME and Find Your Soft Heart," etc.

2. Go over the rules and the Heart Slips each day for one week or until the children understand them. Give examples of the difference between "out of the heart" behavior and "in the heart" behavior. Explain how Freeze-Framing and using the Heart Tools helps you get back in the heart. Explain that Heart Slip Reminders will be given when you need extra help to get back to your heart. Tell the children, "If you are given a Heart Slip, I will ask you to FREEZE-FRAME and go to your heart, then do what the Heart Slip tells you for five minutes (ten minutes for older children). Keep your Heart Slip until you feel that you are back in the heart. When you are ready, you quietly give your Heart Slip back to me."

3. If you are a teacher, sending a copy of the rules and Heart Slips home for parents to read with their children familiarizes everyone with the program and gives parents an opportunity to participate.

VARIATION

1. Using Heart Slip Reminders along with "The Heart Certificate" activity on page 75 gives children tangible rewards for being in the heart and a goal to work toward. Tell the children that **if they receive one Heart Slip**, it will not affect their receiving a heart and a check on their Heart Chart that day.

If they receive two Heart Slips, it means that they didn't slow down and FREEZE-FRAME deeply enough when they received their first Heart Slip. Now they need to take a "Time-Out" to FREEZE-FRAME more deeply and practice the Heart Tool stated on the second Heart Slip. At the end of the "Time-Out," they give the Heart Slip back to you and tell you what they learned. They may still receive a heart on the Heart Chart, but they cannot receive a check beside the heart for that day.

If they get a third Heart Slip, that means they are still out of their heart. They now need to take a longer "Time-Out" (or "Wall-Time" if it's appropriate to your situation) to sincerely FREEZE-FRAME and make a better effort to do what it says on the Heart Slip. Tell the children that you will let them know when ten minutes is up and you will come get the Heart Slip and discuss what they learned from Freeze-Framing and using the Heart Tool. If you get a third Heart Slip, you cannot get a heart or a check on the Heart Chart for that day.

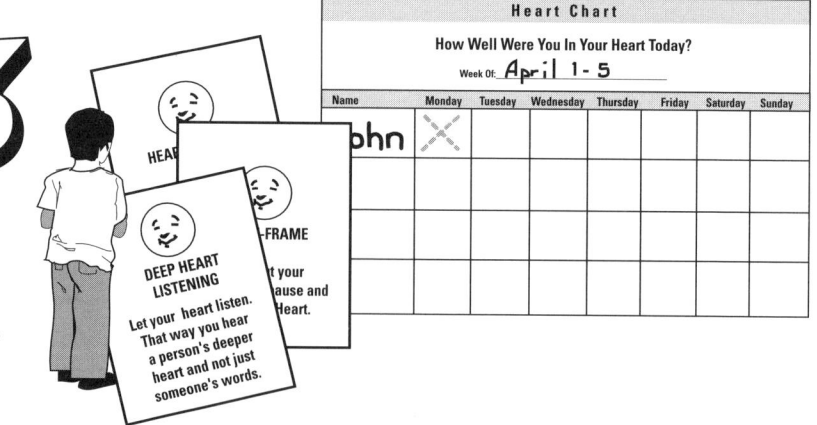

The Map To Heart Wonderland

PURPOSE

The goal of this game is to help children understand that the heart offers a higher intelligence and always knows what would bring you the most fun, peace, and the highest fulfillment. An analogy is that within the heart's intelligence is a map that shows you the shortest way to find your Heart Wonderland. We can try to find the map through the mind, but we usually get sidetracked either by the mind's negative traps that can keep us feeling unhappy for days or by emotional bogs that make us feel angry or sad and block the reception of all the heart's wonderful gifts. Through Freeze-Framing, we are able to go back to the heart and find our map back to our own personal Heart Wonderland.

AGES

8-14

TIME

10 minutes or longer

PLAYERS

Adult and two or more children

LOCATION

Indoors (on a table or floor)

EQUIPMENT

➡ Heart Wonderland gameboard (page 83) and cardstock or paper
➡ Flat buttons or dried butter beans to serve as markers. (Each player will need approximately 35 markers.)
➡ Paper bag for holding numbers
➡ Pencil and paper
⇨ Glue or laminate

OBJECTIVE

As in the game Bingo, each player tries to cover one of the three rows of numbers to complete their route to Heart Wonderland. All squares must be covered in the row, from the route's beginning to Heart Wonderland. As the caller calls out a number, the players place a marker on the matching number if their gameboard has that number. The first player to cover all squares in a row is the winner.

The shortest route is straight from the head to the heart. A player may wind around through the Gloomy Swamp of Emotions or through Mind Quick Sand to get there, but the players will see it's more fun and efficient to follow the map's shortest route. The last square, called Heart, is a free gift into Wonderland for all players. The free squares on the Heart Route represent those times you FREEZE-FRAME and "Get a Free Gift from your Heart" to help you arrive at Heart Wonderland.

MAKING THE GAMEBOARDS

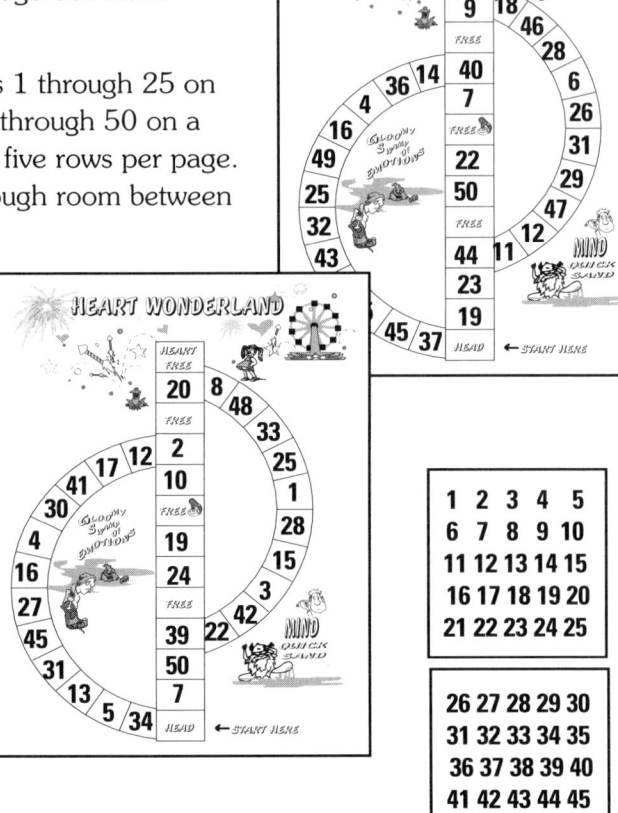

1. Prepare gameboards and call markers as follows:

   a. The Heart Wonderland gameboard is provided on page 83. Make copies for each player.

   b. Make call numbers by writing or typing the numbers 1 through 25 on one sheet of $8^{1}/_{2}$"x11" paper, and the numbers 26 through 50 on a second sheet of paper. Type five numbers per row, five rows per page. Space numbers evenly across the page, leaving enough room between numbers to cut each into approximately one inch squares. Cut up squares, fold each one in half, and place in a paper bag. Shake them up well.

   b. To create a different gameboard for each player, draw one number at a time from the paper bag and write the number in a different blank square on each gameboard. Continue the process until all squares are numbered with the exception of Free squares. You should now have a differently numbered Heart Wonderland gameboard for each player. Return numbers folded in half to the brown paper bag and shake well.

INSTRUCTIONS

1. The adult gamemaster is the "Caller" who distributes one gameboard and 35 markers to each player. Each player places one marker on all of the Free Squares. (The Head Square does not require a marker.)

2. Caller draws a number from the brown paper bag and calls it out several times. If a player has that number on their card, the player places a marker accordingly. Play continues in this manner until someone calls "Heart Wonderland" to signal that he has covered a complete route, with every square covered to the Free Heart Square.

VARIATION

To offset wear and tear, either copy Heart Wonderland gameboards onto cardstock, glue paper copies to cardboard, or laminate for sturdiness.

HEART WONDERLAND

HEART FREE

FREE

FREE

GLOOMY SWAMP OF EMOTIONS

FREE

FREE

MIND QUICK SAND

HEAD ← START HERE

Code Red: A Call To Action

PURPOSE

Teens want to feel secure and optimistic as they explore life. What interferes is stress. "Code Red: A Call to Action" is a fun, team-inspired mission (for both adult and teen) to plan out a stress-attack using the tool FREEZE-FRAME (see page 21). You learn to look out for and identify stress during the selected day and see what happens when you FREEZE-FRAME. Afterwards you debrief and discuss the success of the mission and celebrate accordingly.

AGES

12-18

TIME

20 minutes (two or more sessions)

PLAYERS

Adult and one or more children

LOCATION

Indoors or outdoors

EQUIPMENT

➡ Paper and pencils

➡ Small red stickers or rubber stamp and red ink purchased from a stationery store

⇨ Ribbons or certificates and gold stickers

⇨ Heart Zones tape, tape recorder

INSTRUCTIONS

1. Discuss as a team that you are going to be part of an important mission, "Code Red: A Call to Action." The purpose of this mission is to recognize and FREEZE-FRAME any stresses that arise over the next day or week. Begin by asking children what some of their typical, everyday stresses are. Draw out examples. Share some of your own typical adult stresses.

2. Discuss how the purpose of FREEZE-FRAME is to zap stress before it gets you and transform it into effective action.

Look at FREEZE-FRAME like a heart phaser to vaporize the stress.

Prepare for the mission by using FREEZE-FRAME on a recent stress. When you shift to the heart as the command station, the phaser locks-on to its stress target. As you listen to your heart directive, you activate the phaser. Write down a stress and how it's affecting you. FREEZE-FRAME it, then write down your heart directive. Only by acting on your heart directive can you vaporize the stress. Discuss the results.

3. Wish each other good luck and mention that the next time the team meets, everyone will report on the success of the mission. In other words, what stresses were experienced, how quick was each person in Freeze-Framing the stress, and following the heart's command? Remind each other to stay on alert by proactively testing FREEZE-FRAME, meaning get frequent FREEZE-FRAME read-outs before there is a stress attack. You do this when you FREEZE-FRAME, practice appreciation, and acknowledge what is important in life while stepping back from any activity. Then act on your heart intelligence. This will keep you alert and in shape for your mission.

4. Give everyone a code red sticker (or code red ink stamp) to put on their wrist to remind them of their mission. Any time they want to do a practice test or need to zap a real stress, they press the code red button to FREEZE-FRAME and activate the mission. If an emergency happens, push your code red button — **FREEZE-FRAME, FREEZE-FRAME, FREEZE-FRAME**, until the light comes on at heart command telling you what to do.

5. Discuss and document the results, strategize, and plan another "Code Red" day. See if the team can increase its success in preventing or vaporizing stresses.

VARIATIONS

1. If you are with others on the team when a stressor is present, anyone can call "Code Red" and each person activates FREEZE-FRAME. Follow your heart read-outs.

2. As a team, go out into a public place like a restaurant or store and observe, without judgment, situations and people that are stressed out and need to FREEZE-FRAME. Write down your observations, then discuss.

3. Continue the mission for a week or a month. At the end of the mission, have ribbons or certificates available for all who participated. For those who did especially well, add another colored ribbon or add a gold sticker to the certificate.

4. Play *Heart Zones* during the FREEZE-FRAME and in the background while writing down your heart directive.

CHAPTER 5

Because We Care

Captain CUT-THRU Cartoon Book

PURPOSE

Everyone loves a super hero. This activity helps children understand that by calming their thoughts and emotions and going to their heart, they can find better solutions to problems and often help others do the same. This is being super intelligent and a super hero. By visualizing and drawing pictures of their own super hero and creating stories about cutting through overcares, worries, and other problems with heart power, children learn to develop their heart intelligence. When a problem arises, they can ask themselves, "How would Captain CUT-THRU handle this?" The result is increased self-care and a lot of energy saved that would have been spent on unmanaged emotions.

AGES

8-14

TIME

30 minutes or longer

PLAYERS

Adult and one or more children

LOCATION

Indoors at a table or desks

EQUIPMENT

➡ Paper and pencils for each player

➡ Crayons or colored markers

⇨ Three hole punch, scissors & yarn

INSTRUCTIONS

1. Read a story line from the examples on the following pages. Ask children to draw pictures of the characters in the stories. Older participants who are artistically inclined may enjoy making a complete cartoon story. You can also make copies of the super hero characters in this book and have younger children color them.

2. Use daily for a week or even for a month until participants are thoroughly familiar with the idea of using the CUT-THRU tool. Keep the story lines short and simple. The less complicated, the easier it is for children to bring the examples to mind and recognize when they need to CUT-THRU.

VARIATIONS

1. Read the transcription of a discussion on Captain CUT-THRU on page 93 to the children. Discuss as you read.

2. Make up new story lines with the children. Ask them to recall times when they were caught in similar traps that the "villains" set. Then ask them how Captain CUT-THRU would handle the situation.

3. Have the children make their own Captain CUT-THRU Cartoon Book. Use a three hole punch and cut strips of yarn for ties. Suggest that they continue to add to their book as they come up with new ideas on how Captain CUT-THRU solves problems.

Captain CUT-THRU

Captain CUT-THRU, along with his sister, Crystal Clear CUT-THRU and invisible helper, Heart Buddy, have come to Earth on a mission to save the people from the Inefficient Thought Gang who are trying to take over the planet by implanting thoughts of fear, worry, and judgment in the minds of humanity. The Inefficient Thought Gang's plan is to create stress and chaos all over the world.

Lord Distortion is head of the Gang. Working directly under him are Generals Worry, Fear, and Judgment. Other officers are Major Dissatisfaction, Misperception, Hopelessness, and Unkindness. They undermine people by sending seemingly harmless representatives, such as Happy Head, Sarcastic Humor, and Miscommunication into people's minds.

Captain CUT-THRU and Crystal Clear CUT-THRU disguise themselves as the sixteen-year-old twins, Will Hope and Ima Hope, who are students at Freedom High School. Just like many teenagers, they are average students who enjoy having fun with their friends.

Will Hope and Ima Hope have an invisible helper, Heart Buddy, who is always traveling around the planet seeking out situations where Crystal Clear and Captain CUT-THRU's assistance is needed. When Heart Buddy sees someone in distress, he contacts Will and Ima Hope through their crystal heart radios. Then they know it is time for Captain CUT-THRU and Crystal Clear CUT-THRU to go into action.

When they hear their heart signal, Will and Ima drop all of their thoughts down into their hearts and go to neutral. They turn their heart blender on high to liquefy any remaining thoughts that could hamper their efficiency they become Captain CUT-THRU and Crystal Clear CUT-THRU. By dropping their thoughts into the heart blender, Will and Ima have protected themselves from any influence by Lord Distortion's Gang. The heart can now send thoughts of higher intelligence to the mind.

The Heart and Mind Working Together Create The Mighty, Empowered CUT-THRUs!

Captain CUT-THRU Story Lines

Helping A Friend

Will Hope and Ima Hope are attending a Freedom High football game. Will gets the following message from Heart Buddy on his crystal heart radio. Ima's friend, Dora Downheart, is trapped by General Judgment and Lieutenant Misperception. They have thrown a wall around her and she can't escape. She is at home, baby-sitting her younger brother, who is fussy and crying.

Will and Ima go to their car and use the CUT-THRU tool, dropping all thoughts into their heart and going to neutral. They turn their heart blender on high and Captain CUT-THRU and Crystal Clear CUT-THRU magically appear in Dora's room where she sits crying. Dora is surprised to see Captain CUT-THRU and Crystal Clear CUT-THRU. They ask her why she is so upset.

Dora: "I am so angry with my parents. They made me stay home and baby-sit, even though I was planning to go to the Freedom High football game and meet my friends there. The baby-sitter canceled and mom said this dinner was with a very important client of dad's and they really must attend. It isn't fair for me to have to sit here while they're out having fun. Bobby is their responsibility, not mine!"

Captain CUT-THRU: "Dora, you need to CUT-THRU. As long as you are angry, you will judge and not think clearly." Captain and Crystal Clear teach Dora the steps to CUT-THRU. Along with Heart Buddy, they send heart to Dora as she uses the tool.

Dora (wiping away her tears): "I am beginning to understand how important this dinner is to my dad. Without his clients, he would have no job and how would we get along with no money? It was wrong for me to be so selfish and judgmental. Gosh, I don't even know if they're having fun. They might have enjoyed being at home more."

Crystal Clear: "Not wrong Dora, just inefficient thinking." The wall put up by Major Misperception and General Judgment begins to disappear. The villains slink away...

Another Victory For Captain
And Crystal Clear CUT-THRU!

Wrongly Accused

Will Hope is having a lazy Saturday afternoon lying on his bed reading a book. Ima is out shopping with a friend. A call comes in from Heart Buddy on the crystal heart radio. Two boys are getting ready to fight on the corner of Elm and Madison Streets. General Judgment and Major Unkindness have thrown a net of Distortion over them. Will hops in his car and drives toward the scene of the conflict. A block away, he stops the car and does a CUT-THRU. He appears where the two boys are still quarreling.

"Wow, Captain CUT-THRU!" The boys are surprised but glad to see him.

Captain CUT-THRU: "What's the problem here?"

Bob (the larger boy): "Jerry is a liar. He said I stole his baseball cap."

Jerry: "You did too, you thief!"

Bob takes a swing at Jerry and Captain CUT-THRU intervenes: "Hey guys, you need to CUT-THRU. Both of you are out of your hearts." He then shows the boys how to go to the heart and use the CUT-THRU tool. Captain and Heart Buddy send heart as Bob and Jerry do CUT-THRU. Then Captain CUT-THRU asks the boys how they feel.

Jerry: "I shouldn't have accused Bob of stealing my cap. Just because he was wearing one exactly like mine, I assumed he had taken mine. If I had slowed down, I would have told him that my cap was missing. Then I would have realized that his cap is bigger than mine. It's possible that no one stole my cap. I could have misplaced it. I really like Bob and I hope he will forgive me."

Bob: "I got really angry when Jerry accused me of taking his hat. If I had been able to control my temper, I would have thought to show him that my hat is larger."

Captain CUT-THRU: "Remember to slow down and use a tool when you feel angry. Then you can CUT-THRU and listen to what your heart intelligence tells you."

Jerry (laughing): "I want to be friends with Bob."

Bob puts his arm around Jerry's shoulder and playfully punches him: "Okay, I'll forgive you, but don't push your luck, little guy. I could have hurt you." The boys laugh and walk away together.

Captain CUT-THRU tells General Judgment and Major Unkindness to pick up their net and move on. They go away scowling!

Foiled Again By Captain CUT-THRU!

Transcription of Discussion on Captain CUT-THRU with Blake

Wanda: Who can tell me who Captain CUT-THRU really is?

Blake: He is like part of your heart. He helps you CUT-THRU.

Wanda: That's good. He is like your real self. Right? Who can tell me who Crystal Clear CUT-THRU is?

Blake: She would be like the clear crystals in your heart.

Wanda: She is also like your real self. After you use the power of CUT-THRU, and go to neutral, your heart can relay higher intelligence to your mind. Your heart and mind working together give crystal clear information or higher intelligence.

Blake: Yeah, that's my real self.

Wanda: Right. Captain CUT-THRU is the power to CUT RIGHT THROUGH whatever is bothering you. It is the part of you that is empowered. When you become Captain CUT-THRU, you cut right through and zoom! The heart comes in with some clear understanding of what is going on.

Blake: Then you deep heart listen to what is going on. Your heart and head start working together and you aren't out of your heart any more.

Wanda: Who would Heart Buddy be?

Blake: Heart Buddy would be your heart.

Wanda: What would the crystal heart radio be?

Blake: It would be the radio that is the contact between your heart and your head, so that they can work together.

Wanda: Very good. And when there is crystal clear information going from the heart to the mind, you become highly intelligent and an empowered person. So each person can become Captain CUT-THRU or Crystal Clear CUT-THRU.

Wanda: Will and Ima are like our personalities. They use the tools. They are in their hearts. They are empowered, so they are Captain and Crystal Clear in disguise.

Blake: I hope to be able to stay in my heart all of the time and try to never get out of my heart.

Wanda: Who would you be then?

Blake: I would be Will and Ima Hope.

Wanda: And would you also be Captain CUT-THRU? When you can stay in your heart all the time, you are empowered and you get to be one of the super heroes that are helping other people do it too.

Captain CUT-THRU Blender Experiment

PURPOSE

This game helps children see how the CUT-THRU tool works. It helps them visualize how the heart has the power to take feelings and thoughts of worry or hurt and quickly turn them into better feelings and new understanding. When we turn our heart blender on high, we can liquefy feelings that trouble us, and that makes it easier to get back to the heart and care for ourselves and others. In the heart we find new solutions. A good time for this activity is when a child is out of the heart and having a hard time using the Heart Tools. Sometimes a visual image or science experiment helps people to better understand CUT-THRU.

AGES
8-14

TIME
10 minutes or longer

PLAYERS
Adult and one or more children

LOCATION
Kitchen near an electrical outlet ·

EQUIPMENT
➡ Blender
➡ Water
➡ Powdered laundry detergent
➡ Napkin or paper
⇨ Heart Signals tape, tape recorder

VARIATION

Teach children the CUT-THRU tool on page 22, adapting the words to their age (or listen to the tape *Heart Signals* (age 8-14). Have them pick a problem that gives them an uncomfortable feeling and use the tool. If they can't think of a problem, have them practice the tool anyway, so they'll know how to use it when they need it. Discuss the results.

INSTRUCTIONS

1. Put two cups of water in a blender.

2. Take a spoonful of powdered detergent and place it on a napkin or piece of paper. Ask the children to look at it and notice how dense it is. Explain dense versus liquid.

3. Tell the children, "When we are worried or upset, we create thoughts that are dense and heavy, making us feel unhappy or bad. Worry, fear, or feeling sorry for ourselves creates density. These thoughts and feelings feel heavy, dense, and they pull us down. Without help from the heart, they never bring helpful solutions. When we are in the heart, our thoughts and feelings are light, happy, and bubbly. When we use the CUT-THRU tool, we put the dense feelings and thoughts into the heart."

4. Sprinkle the detergent into the water in the blender.

5. Then tell the children, "Pretend that your heart is a blender. Put upset feelings and thoughts into it and turn the blender on high. The heart takes the density and negativity out and transforms your feelings and thoughts into more creative ideas and feelings."

6. Turn blender on long enough for the soap granules to turn into light, fluffy bubbles. (If possible, move the blender to a brightly lit spot where you can see rainbows in the bubbles.) Point out that the dense granules have been transformed into transparent, fluffy bubbles. And that is what your heart can do for negative thoughts, clearing them up and helping you feel good again.

7. Discuss examples of thoughts and feelings to put into our heart blender and CUT-THRU to find new solutions.

94

Turning Little Fears Into Fun

PURPOSE

Little fears can arise as toddlers encounter new experiences. You can prevent little fears from becoming traumatic events by helping children turn them into fun. This activity teaches children that overcoming little fears is a way to take care of themselves. Common early fears include being scared of dogs, having your photograph taken, large people talking to you, stepping into water at the pool or beach, and getting a haircut. This game is about turning the fear of a haircut into fun. If your child fusses about getting a haircut, this is a wonderful activity that few children will turn down. See the variations on how to adapt this activity to other fearful situations and help build your child's confidence.

AGES
2-6

TIME
10 minutes per day over three days

PLAYERS
Adult and child

LOCATION
Indoors and outdoors

EQUIPMENT
➡ Trimmings from a haircut
⇨ Compost bin

INSTRUCTIONS

1. Try to locate a bird's nest to illustrate to your child how birds use a variety of materials (bits of string, hair, etc.) to make nests. Alternatively, find a colorful picture of a bird's nest in a book or magazine. Discuss how birds use lots of things besides twigs and leaves to build nests, including remnants they find in the neighborhood. Your child will eagerly want to contribute his locks to the home of a feathered friend.

2. When the time arrives for a haircut, talk with your child about saving the hair clippings so the two of you can place them in a spot where birds can find them to make their nests soft.

3. Explore and find a place outside where a bird will feel safe enough to gather the hair. Suggest a viewing spot where you and your child might be able to observe the bird's activity.

4. Hopefully, you have diverted the attention from the misery of a haircut to caring for the birds.

5. Help your child place the hair trimmings in the designated spot on your return from the haircut.

VARIATIONS

1. Plan to use the hair trimmings to make a compost bin with your child to help replenish the soil in your garden and around trees and shrubs. Add other family member's hair to the bin as well.

2. If your child is afraid of dogs, make an appointment to visit someone with a safe, friendly dog where he can learn how to pet and relate to a dog. If your child is afraid of water, play games with splashing water before you take him to the beach or pool. If your child is afraid of large people or people of different color or different cultures, arrange to visit a day care center where he can get to know children and parents of different color or culture. Preparing fun activities related to any little fear can help prevent the fear from returning.

Example: A three-year-old was afraid of Santa Claus and screamed when visiting Santa in a department store. His mother bought a roll of newsprint and drew a large Santa on the paper. Then the boy and his mother had fun painting Santa's face, beard, hat, jacket, boots, and belt in bright red, black, and white paint. The mother hung Santa on the wall and they practiced talking to him.

The boy was happy to visit the "real" Santa the next time they went to the store.

Exploring The Feeling World

PURPOSE

Learning how to identify, communicate, and respond to feelings is an important skill for developing emotional intelligence and building self-esteem. "Exploring the Feeling World" is an activity that helps children understand their feelings and increases their ability to care for themselves, achieve success in relationships, and adapt to challenges with resiliency.

AGES
3-8

TIME
20 minutes, then 10 minutes each week

PLAYERS
Adult and one or more children

LOCATION
Indoors or outdoors

EQUIPMENT
➜ Construction paper and drawing paper
➜ Pencil, markers or crayons
➜ Yarn, scissors, a three-hole punch, glue
➜ Camera with film, magazine pictures (optional)
⇨ Different textured materials (e.g., rough rock, smooth stone, waxy leaf, fake fur, sponge, sandpaper, plastic, metal, velvet, velcro, clear plastic shipping bubbles)
⇨ Puppets

INSTRUCTIONS

1. Begin by discussing feelings that you experience and ask your child what types of feelings he often experiences. Write these on a piece of paper. Typically, children will share primary feelings like sadness, happiness, and anger. To add to the list, ask your child if he also experiences feelings like fear, joy, peace, surprise, jealousy, caring, worry, excitement, nervousness, and others. Try to create a list of at least five feelings that your child acknowledges feeling.

2. Put together a book of your child's feelings using twice as many pieces of paper as feelings the child named. Use construction paper for the cover and markers or crayons to decorate the cover. Three hole punch the cover and blank paper, cut yarn in three small strips to bind the book together, and tie in bows. Explore one feeling on each page. Use one or more of the following methods to explore your child's feelings with him: the child's drawing of a face expressing a particular feeling; camera shots of your child experiencing that feeling; a magazine cut out of someone expressing that feeling. Glue pictures in the book. Write the name of the feeling below the pictures, leaving space for additional comments.

3. Review the book one or more times per week, asking some of the following questions:

   • "Which feeling(s) did you experience this week?"

   • "What situation caused you to feel that feeling?"

   • "What does your heart have to say about the feeling(s)?" With stressful feelings, ask your child, "How might you respond differently next time so you won't feel so bad?"

   • "Do you know anyone else who experienced that feeling?"

   • "How did they respond?"

4. Record your child's comments in the book. As your child identifies new feelings, add pages to the book and repeat steps 2 and 3. Over time, the book will reveal a variety of feelings and your child will explore appropriate responses to feelings.

VARIATIONS

1. Have available different textures of material to touch. Ask the child to match a textured material with a different type of feeling. The child can tape the material to the appropriate feeling page in the book.

   Examples:
   • mad—rough rock or sandpaper
   • peaceful—velvet
   • excitement—clear plastic shipping bubbles

2. Role play or use puppets to dramatize situations that trigger different feelings.

   Examples of feeling situations for puppets to role play:
   • a hug from a parent
   • someone accidentally breaking your toy
   • laughing at a funny event
   • having fun with a friend
   • losing a game
   • getting into an argument

Try to illustrate resolution of any stressful situations by utilizing the power of the heart. Have the puppet practice the CUT-THRU tool steps on page 22, adapting the words to the children's age and find a new understanding.

Heart Animal Game

PURPOSE

The courage of a lion, the graceful galloping of a horse, the majesty of an eagle, and countless other wildlife images evoke care, wonder, and admiration from children. By naming animals that remind a child of herself or another person, the child is using intuitive intelligence to identify qualities that are fun and meaningful. The purpose of this game is to have each child ask their heart to help them caringly choose their own heart animal or choose an animal which reminds them of someone else.

AGES
4-12

TIME
10 minutes or longer

PLAYERS
Adult and one or more children

LOCATION
Indoors or outdoors

EQUIPMENT
⇨ Pencil and paper
⇨ Crayons or colored markers
⇨ Hand puppet
⇨ Clay or play dough

INSTRUCTIONS

1. Tell the children the purpose of the "Heart Animal Game" is to either identify an animal who has qualities that remind you of yourself or identify an animal that reminds you of someone else. For example, "Cindy, ask your heart what animal are you most like?" "Larry, what animal does your friend Joey remind you of?"

2. Before asking the children about their special animal, lead them through a one-minute exercise to help them get quiet and go deep in the heart.

    Leader: Now close your eyes and allow yourself to relax. Imagine a warm waterfall flowing down your head, arms and legs, making you very relaxed. Is everyone really relaxed? Good... Now ask your heart what kind of animal are you most like, or you can ask your heart what kind of animal does your friend, parent, brother, or sister remind you of. You can pretend to touch it or pick it up if you want to... Where does your animal live? In the woods, in a house?....

3. Complete the quiet exercise by asking, "Are you finished with choosing a heart animal?" Let's share what animal we chose. As each person shares, ask them to explain why they chose that animal for themselves or for another person.

Examples of children's heart animals:

Blake: Octopus, because it's always changing colors. And a human, that's an animal. I'm always changing and I'm also a human being.

Kristofer: Penguin diving off an iceberg. Penguins can swim and walk and float and they like to play.

Josh: A baby kitten, a baby jaguar, and a baby dolphin, and they were all hugging each other. I can be like all three at the same time, or sometimes I can just be a baby jaguar and have lots of power.

Elysia: A kitten with a big bow around its neck. Because it's sweet and cute and fun to play with.

VARIATIONS

1. Ask the other children why they think each child chose their particular animal. What positive qualities are in the child that they also see in the animal?

2. Have the children write a story or draw a picture of the animal they chose. If they chose the animal for another person, be sure to include that person in the story or the drawing.

3. Once a child has identified a heart animal for herself, consider buying a hand puppet that resembles the animal. With the hand puppet, the child can give voice and act out heartfelt thoughts and feelings. This addition can reinforce the positive behavior of a child.

4. Have the children create a clay or play dough model of their special animal.

Secret Care Buddies

PURPOSE

Care is a quality that sustains the loving spirit in families and schools, deepens the heart connection, and makes it easier to neutralize or overcome dislikes and disagreements. Simply said, care creates bonding. "Secret Care Buddies" increases care by having all family members participate in a fun game of secret care. Unknown to each family member, another family member has become their Secret Care Buddy and performs caring acts for them for one week. Whether big acts, like organizing their closet or buying them a nice present, or small acts, like writing an appreciation note or placing a flower on their bedside table or desk, all will profit from this delightful activity.

AGES
6-14

TIME
20 minutes

PLAYERS
Adult and two or more children

LOCATION
Indoors or outdoors

EQUIPMENT
→ Bowl
→ One uniform strip of paper per participant
→ Pen

INSTRUCTIONS

1. Bring everyone together and share the purpose of "Secret Care Buddies." Tell everyone that they will play the game for one week with the goal of performing one caring act per day for their secret buddy. Encourage each player not to leave behind any obvious hints.

2. On strips of paper of the same size, write the name of each participant. Fold up the papers and place in a bowl. Each family member picks one name, keeping the identity hidden from the receiver of their caring actions. (Before folding the slips, show younger children the slips to make sure they can read or identify all the names.)

3. Remind each other daily at the dinner table that we are playing the "Secret Care Buddy" game. In order to facilitate ideas, suggest that everyone ask their hearts in private what kind of caring actions would be possible. If younger children need help, tell them to ask a family member who is not their secret buddy. When the week is over, everyone tries to guess the identity of their secret buddy. When all names are revealed, discuss some of the secret strategies and the fun, caring acts everyone received.

VARIATION

Before picking names, have each family member state five caring acts they would like to receive.

Star Fleet Mission

PURPOSE

Many teachers have experienced the frustration of paper airplanes being thrown at inappropriate times. "Star Fleet Mission" is a structured opportunity for kids to create their paper airplane masterpieces and have some fun in an orderly and caring way. This activity encourages children to use creative imagination while caring about the earth and the environment. Playing a game of care and self-control helps children feel good and promotes self esteem.

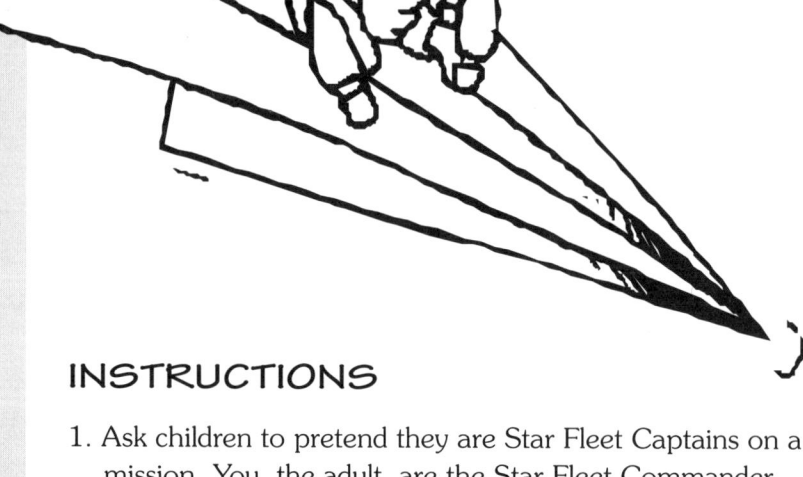

AGES
7-12

TIME
45 minutes

PLAYERS
Adult and three or more children

LOCATION
Indoors (at desks or in a circle on the floor) or outdoors (sitting in a circle to represent the world)

EQUIPMENT
➡ Two pieces of 8 ½" x 11" paper for each child
➡ Extra paper for more paper airplanes if needed
➡ Colored markers
➡ Copies of Commander's orders for each child
⇨ Pencils
⇨ Half sheets of paper, marker, pins or tape

INSTRUCTIONS

1. Ask children to pretend they are Star Fleet Captains on a mission. You, the adult, are the Star Fleet Commander and you are going to lay out the Commander's orders and strategy for the mission. (When children play pretend, they get more into their feelings and it's easier for them to express love and care.)

2. Pass out paper to each child. Tell them you want them to make their very best flying crafts or spaceships.

3. Demonstrate how to make a paper airplane, as some children won't know. (See instructions for making an "aerodynamic" plane on next page.) Rub creases well so folds stay in place.

Making A Paper Airplane

A. Fold the left hand top corner of an 8½" x 11" piece of paper down along dotted line. Rub crease well so paper stays folded.

B. Fold the right corner down using the dotted line as a guide.

C. Next, fold down the top corner.

D. Turn edge of folded corner under edge so it is even with the edge.

E. Fold in both left and right sides along the dotted line. Next, fold entire pattern in half at the center along the dotted lines. Rub crease well so folds stay in place.

F. Your pattern should now be neatly folded in half. Now fold each side out along the dotted line (approximately ⅝" from the center fold). This will make a small fold for holding the plane.

G. Hold paper airplane between thumb and rest of fingers and give a toss. Watch the graceful loops and turns.

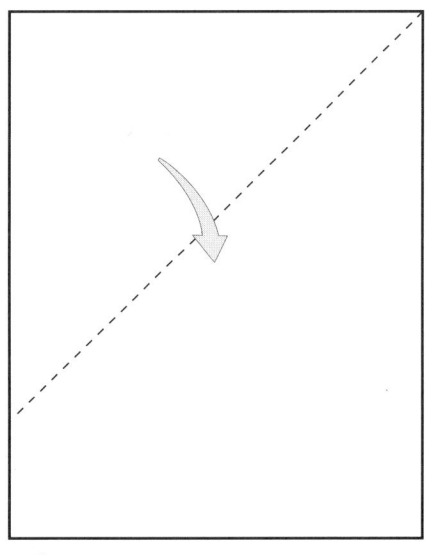

A. Fold Left Corner Down and to the Right

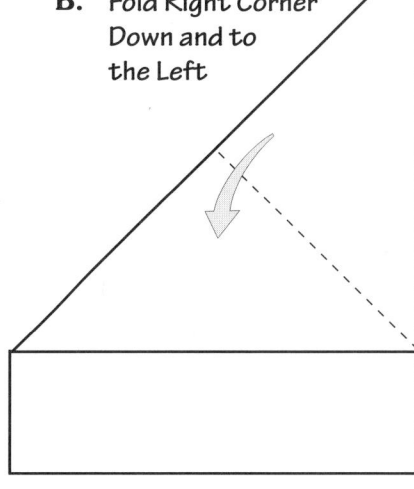

B. Fold Right Corner Down and to the Left

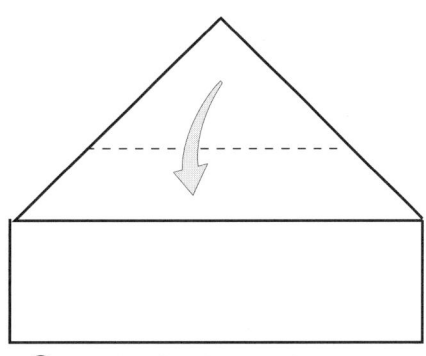

C. Fold Top Corner Down

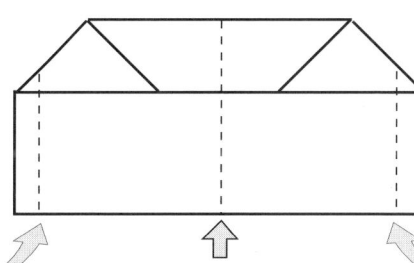
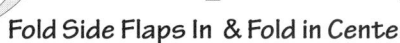

D. Fold Flap Under and Tuck In

E. Fold Side Flaps In & Fold in Center

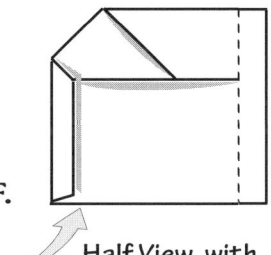

F. Half View with outer edge folded in

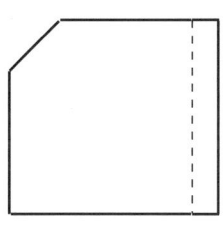

View of backside after folding in half

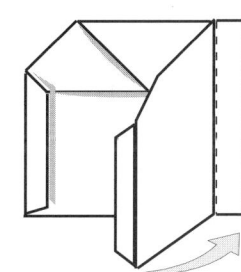

Fold Out from Dotted line (5/8" from Center fold)

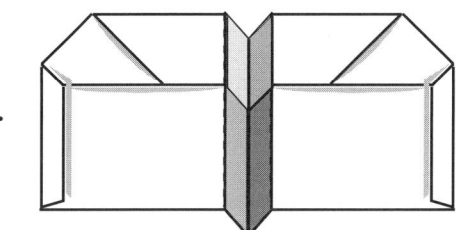

G.

4. Read the Commander's orders for the mission to the children. Give each child a copy of the Commander's Orders and post a copy on the wall.

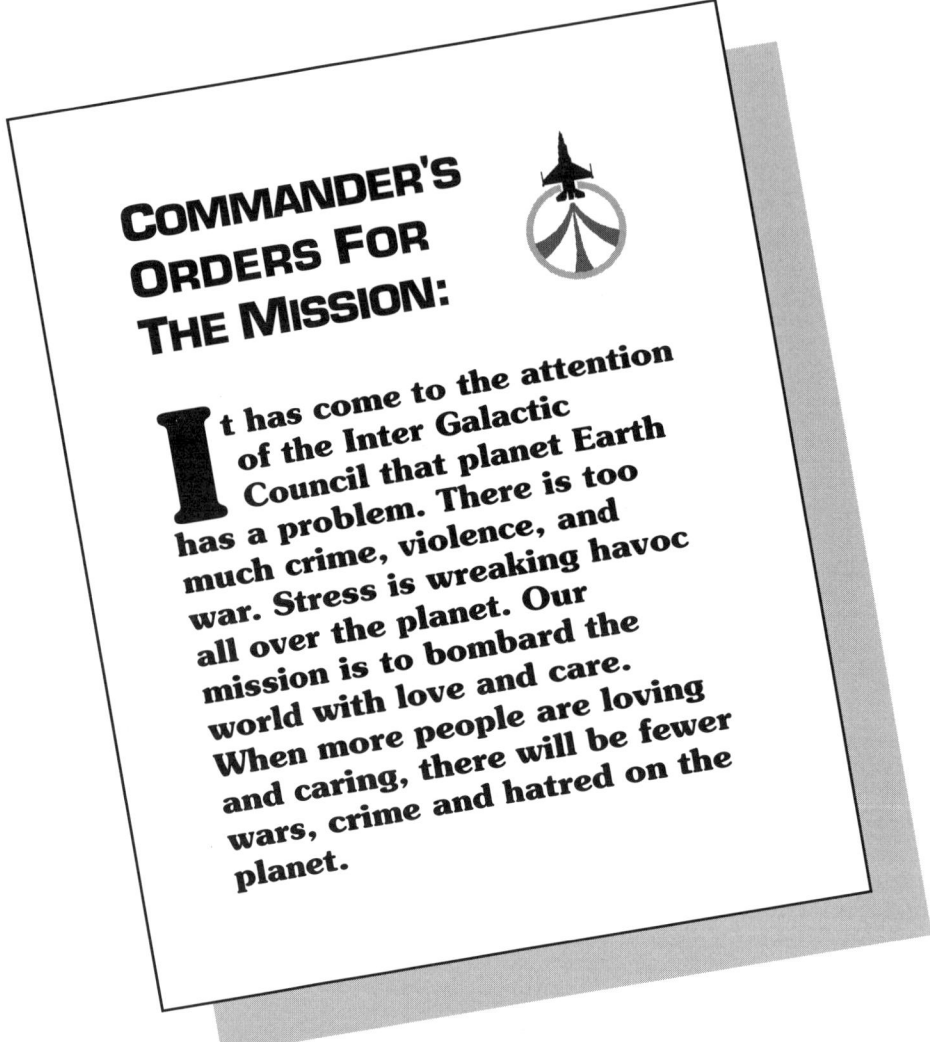

COMMANDER'S ORDERS FOR THE MISSION:

It has come to the attention of the Inter Galactic Council that planet Earth has a problem. There is too much crime, violence, and war. Stress is wreaking havoc all over the planet. Our mission is to bombard the world with love and care. When more people are loving and caring, there will be fewer wars, crime and hatred on the planet.

5. Next, read the mission strategy to the children and ask them if they have any questions.

Mission Strategy

- Each Star Fleet Captain shall make two spacecraft (one to use and a spare in case the first one becomes immobilized). Each craft shall bear the markings, SEND LOVE. (Consider having some of your best airplane makers create additional craft in case some don't fly so well and their makers get discouraged.)

- This is a secret mission. It must be done quietly. Any loud discussion or arguing in sending or receiving craft will result in failure of the mission. Those involved in unnecessary noise will be removed from the mission and must sit quietly while they are grounded. If a craft lands on the ground between two people, the two must FREEZE-FRAME before anyone tries to pick it up. The mission is to quietly send love to planet Earth and to everyone and everything on the planet. This includes all people of all races and nationalities, the rainforest, the oceans, the ozone layer, the animals, the rivers, etc. Any questions are to be referred to the Commander.

- Before sending your craft, you must take thirty seconds to fill it with love. Think of a global issue you care about and put that into your craft. **Examples:** Victims of war, starving children, people out of work, the homeless, gang violence, animals becoming extinct, smog over cities, polluted rivers, and whatever is current news.

  After you have launched your craft, you must wait QUIETLY until you receive one. Then you should wait at least thirty seconds before filling that one with love and sending it out again.

- Since each of you is a Star Fleet Captain, you are responsible for making sure the entire planet is covered with LOVE, so don't send two craft to the same place. Make sure everyone (or the whole world) is receiving love. THAT IS THE MISSION! (Tell the children that each person represents a different country, continent, issue, etc. depending on the size of your group.)

- The mission should be completed in about twenty to thirty minutes. The Star Fleet Commander times the mission. When it is over, all Captains report back to Star Fleet Commander for a debriefing.

- Ask the Captains if they feel the mission was a success. Did they really put LOVE into their crafts before sending them? Were they conscious of sending the craft to different people and not always to the same person? Ask the children how sending love can help the planet. If the game was a success, plan to do it again the following week or in several weeks. (If played too often, it could become over-stimulating. The balance and sincerity would be lost and you could wind up with a lot of noise and paper airplanes.)

VARIATIONS

1. Identify and make a list of global issues with the children prior to the mission. Captains use pencils to write on the craft who or what issue will be sent love and care. Whoever receives the craft reads what was written, sends their love and care, then crosses off that issue and writes down another issue before sending the craft to the next person.

2. Write each issue on a separate half sheet of paper using a bold marker. Assign each child an issue and pin or tape the paper to his/her chest. When sending love to that issue, the craft is directed toward that particular child.

Comments from children in a second and third grade class at a U.S. naval submarine base: "I liked the game because you could help people by "sending love." "It was fun because we could make airplanes when ordinarily we can't. Planes flew everywhere!" "I liked the game because we got to stop wars, violence, and crime." Overall the kids liked the fact that the "mission" had a story they could go by and a common goal to work toward. They were very involved in the game.

Cut And Paste My World

PURPOSE

This creative activity helps adults and children understand how they perceive themselves and also how others perceive them. Teens, especially, are so focused on developing a sense of identity, they often don't stop to reflect on how they perceive themselves. Nor do they know how adults perceive them. By creating a self-portrait collage from a variety of magazine pictures, symbols, and logos, then sharing the results, a wonderful communication emerges. When we look at ourselves through our own and each other's eyes, we widen our perspective and find a deeper bond with others.

AGES
8-16

TIME
1 hour or longer (or do in two sessions)

PLAYERS
Adult and two or more children

LOCATION
Indoors (at a table)

EQUIPMENT
➡ Oversized white paper, glue
➡ Assortment of magazines
➡ Scissors for each player
⇨ Favorite pictures brought by players

INSTRUCTIONS

1. Discuss the purpose of this game. Both adult(s) and teen(s) are to make a self-portrait collage that represents "the real you" using pictures from a variety of magazines.

2. Look through the magazines and cut out images that best represent who you are. Pictures of clothing, nature shots, animals, movie stars, logos, ads, etc., can contribute to the art piece. Glue them on white paper to make a collage.

3. When finished, take turns sharing the collages with each other. Explain the meaning of the artwork, especially what the individual pictures represent to you.

4. Have each person comment on whether the self-portrait matches the way they see that person.

VARIATIONS

1. Follow the instructions above, but this time create a portrait collage of another person present. Sometimes children find this easier than a self-portrait.

2. Each player brings a picture of a friend, a favorite personality, or someone they deeply admire and places it on the table one at a time. After each picture is placed on the table, everyone else goes deep in the heart to see why that special person was chosen and what qualities are admired. Everyone shares their heart perceptions in turn. Only after everyone has shared does the person who selected the picture explain the reasons behind the choice.

Care Versus Overcare

PURPOSE

As the teen years unfold, a tendency toward "overcaring" begins to manifest amidst peer pressure and a sometimes shaky development of self-concept. Concerns about appearance, friends, social status, grades, drugs, violence, and parents can initiate thought loops of insecurity or anxiety that condition a teen's mental and emotional outlook on life. As overcares grow, true care for oneself and others declines. This activity explores what teens care about, what they overcare about, and some solutions to the challenges of overcare.

AGES

12-19

TIME

45 minutes or longer

PLAYERS

Adult and three or more children

LOCATION

Indoors

EQUIPMENT

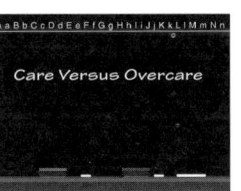

➡ Greaseboard or chalkboard with appropriate markers

➡ Webster's or American Heritage Dictionary

➡ Pencil and paper for each team

➡ *Speed of Balance* tape, tape recorder

INSTRUCTIONS

1. The adult begins by asking the group what they think the word "care" means. Write answers on a greaseboard or chalkboard. Then introduce the definition of care from *Webster's Dictionary* or *American Heritage Dictionary*. It will be similar to this: "A burdensome sense of responsibility, mental suffering, grief, worry, anxiety." Ask the group why their answers are so different (and they usually are). Discuss how the dictionary definition of care is really overcare, and that we as a society care so much about things sometimes that we deplete our energy and feel a lot of anxiety.

2. Next, have the group break up into smaller groups of two to four players and discuss the following:
   a. their areas of care
   b. their areas of overcare.
   Have one player from the group write down all the input on a piece of paper.

3. Bring the larger group back together and have one person from each smaller group share what they wrote about their areas of care and their areas of overcare. The adult writes down the answers for both categories on the greaseboard or chalkboard, putting a check mark by answers that have previously been mentioned.

Review which answers were the most common and ask the larger group to explain the following:

a. Why are the three top areas of care so important?

b. Why are the three top areas of overcare so important?

4. Afterwards, have the same small groups regroup and practice the CUT-THRU tool (see page 22) on their areas of overcare. Optional: Play *Speed of Balance* while the group is practicing the CUT-THRU tool. Ask them to write down their heart intelligent answers on how to deal with these challenges, then discuss with each other.

5. Bring the larger group together again to share the results of their small group discussions.

VARIATIONS

1. Divide the group into boys and girls. Ask each group to make a list of what their overcares are, then a list of what they think the overcares of the other group (the opposite sex) are. Compare boy overcares versus girl overcares. Which overcares do they have in common and which are different? Ask them which overcares they learned from parents? school? society? other?

   Examples: A ninth-grade classroom divided into groups of boys and girls to make their list of overcares as follows:

What the Boys Said Are *Boy Overcares*

Height	Hair	Self-judgment	Parents	Gray hair
Clothes	Eating right	Girls	Baldness	Voice
Success	Fitting in	School	Future	Money
Masculinity	Being wrong	Not being an idiot	Genital size	Prostrate cancer
Sports	Face	Weight		

What the Boys Said Are *Girl Overcares*

Weight	School	Being stupid	Fitting in	Love
Height	Chest size	Clothes	Skin	Overeating
Boys	Food	Monthly period	Phone	What guys think
Makeup	Eyes	Health	Money	of them

What the Girls Said Are *Girl Overcares*

Appearance	Men's perception	School	Perfectionist	Peer pressure
Normality	Hair comparisons	Grades	Children	Clothes
Being a rebel	Rape	Health	Parents	Weight
Competition	Security	Getting in trouble	Being judged	First impressions
Virginity	Being accepted	Career	Popularity	
Marriage	Friend's situations	Relationships	HIV/AIDS	

What the Girls Said Are *Boy Overcares*

Sports	Popularity	Looking good	Testosterone	Competition
Being cool	Reputation	Unemotional	Car	Facial hair
Freedom	Impressing	Parents	Stereo	Comparisons
Girls	everyone	Vulnerability	Girls	Acting like nothing
Machismo	Sex	Status	Looks	matters

Common Categories of Boy and Girl Overcares

Relationships	School	Status	Clothes	Peer acceptance
Parents	Weight	Hair	Appearance issues	issues

---

2. As a group project, survey fifty adults on their top five overcares and tally the results. Compare adult overcares with teen overcares. Which are the same and which are different? Discuss why. Consider having the teens teach the CUT-THRU tool to appropriate adults and see what answers the adults come up with.

3. Break into small groups of two to three players and make a list of ways that each player could "self-care" for themselves to avoid further stress and anxiety.

Guess What I'm Feeling?

PURPOSE

The teen years are characterized by a wide range of intense feelings and emotions. By learning to identify and acknowledge feelings, teens gain self-understanding and increase their ability to care. When combined with the tool CUT-THRU, teens discover the difference between real care and overcare. "Guess What I'm Feeling?" uses charades as a fun and instructional way to identify feelings. Participants act out (pantomime) a specific feeling in front of other teens without any verbal cues or props. The audience tries to guess the feeling. What results is a lot of fun and a broader understanding of the realm of emotions and feelings.

AGES

12-19

TIME

45 minutes or longer

PLAYERS

Adult and three or more children

LOCATION

Indoors

EQUIPMENT

➤ *Slips of paper or index cards, pencils*

➤ *Bowl or box*

➤ *Greaseboard or chalkboard with appropriate markers.*

➤ *(Optional) music and tape player*

INSTRUCTIONS

1. Have teens call out a list of typical feelings. Write them on a greaseboard or chalkboard. As they call them out, a volunteer also writes each feeling on a separate slip of paper or index card and places them in a bowl. The quantity of feelings listed should outnumber the players in case extras are needed.

    Examples: happy, sad, worried, loving, frustrated, romantic, nervous, excited, bored, mad, ecstatic, appreciative, joyful, upset, jealous, surprised, proud, peaceful, caring, overcaring, inspired.

2. Have each player pick one of the slips of paper. Each player then silently acts out that feeling in front of the group. The other players try to guess the feeling. (If you have a large group or limited time, decide in advance how many players will act out a feeling. Save enough time for Steps 3 and 4.)

3. Afterwards, introduce the CUT-THRU tool on page 22, first reading the introduction to the tool to help them understand what overcare is. Discuss examples of overcare from their own lives.

4. Write the steps of the CUT-THRU tool on the board, simplifying the words as needed. Talk about how applying the CUT-THRU tool to a disturbed feeling helps you change the feeling, see a new perspective, and choose a more effective response to a situation.

Have them pick a problem that makes them feel overcaring, angry, sad, jealous, worried, upset, etc. and try going through each step. Ask them to see if they can change the feeling and find a new perspective. If they can't think of a problem, have them practice the tool anyway, so they'll know how to use it when they need it. As an option, put on soothing music in the background as the teens practice the steps. The last three songs of the album *Speed of Balance* (music that was intentionally designed to facilitate emotional balance and the practice of the CUT-THRU tool) are ideal for this activity.

5. Discuss the results.

VARIATIONS

1. Divide the group into teams and have one team member act out a feeling while other team members try to guess the feeling.

2. Have the group write down typical situations that evoke feelings on slips of paper or index cards. A player acts out both the situation and the feeling and the audience tries to guess both.

Examples:

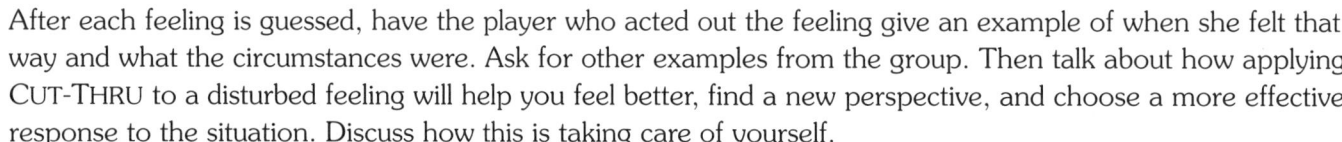

• You studied hard for a test and felt disappointment in the poor test results.

• After watching a wonderful movie, you felt happy.

• A friend is mean to you and you feel sad.

• Someone loans you some money for lunch and you feel grateful.

• An old friend calls you and you feel surprise.

• You're moping around because there's nothing fun to do. You feel bored.

After each feeling is guessed, have the player who acted out the feeling give an example of when she felt that way and what the circumstances were. Ask for other examples from the group. Then talk about how applying CUT-THRU to a disturbed feeling will help you feel better, find a new perspective, and choose a more effective response to the situation. Discuss how this is taking care of yourself.

3. Have teens pantomime a situation and subsequent disturbed feeling, then do a CUT-THRU and act out the new feeling and how they would handle the situation differently.

4. Have teens write a poem about a feeling and recite the poem before the rest of the class.

Here are samples of poems from junior high students who played this variation:

LOVE	ANGER
Love looks like a fluffy teddy bear	Looks like red and black colors in your eyes
Love tastes like sweet candy	Sounds like a gun
Love smells like Calvin Klein™	Tastes like stomach acid
Love sounds like slow jams	Smells like burning
Love feels like a great life spirit	Feels like uncomfortableness

CHAPTER
6

"Listen
Deep"

Deep Heart Listening Song

PURPOSE

This song is a fun way to introduce "deep heart listening" to younger children. It's also a creative way for children to perceive "listening." Children form listening habits at an early age. By explaining the lines of the song and the hand movements that go with them, you can help children learn how to listen better. Sing the song often for fun and sing it as a reminder when children are not listening to you.

AGES
2-8

TIME
10 minutes or longer

PLAYERS
Adult and one or more children

LOCATION
Indoors or outdoors

EQUIPMENT
➡ (optional) piano, guitar, or other musical instrument
⇨ (optional) Buddy Bubbles tape

INSTRUCTIONS

The "Deep Heart Listening Song" is sung to the tune of the popular children's square dance song "Turkey in the Straw." If you want to listen to it, it's on the *Buddy Bubbles: Magical Games for a Child's Heart* tape. You can also come up with your own tune.

1. Tell the children they're going to learn the "Deep Heart Listening Song." Talk about the purpose and the lyrics of the song, then sing the lines slowly, showing them what to do. "When you stop and FREEZE," means stop and freeze your body. "And you listen well," means cross your hands on your heart so you can listen better and "You will always hear what there is to tell." "Put a heart on your ear and an ear on your heart" means bring your hands from your heart to your ears and cup them on your ears so that "When you really listen, you become real smart." Sing the lines again and have the children do the hand movements with you.

2. Then sing the last four lines to the children. Ask older children, "Why does deep heart listening help your friends and family and why does it make your mommy or daddy so proud of you?" Discuss.

3. Now, have the children sing along and do the hand movements with you.

When you stop and Freeze and you lis-ten well you'll be sure to hear what there is to tell Put a heart on your ear and an ear in your heart when you real-ly start to lis-ten you be-come real smart Deep heart lis-tening ev-ery day Deep heart lis-tening That's the way To help your friends and fam-ily too and to make you feel so proud of you.

Making Going To Sleep Easier

PURPOSE

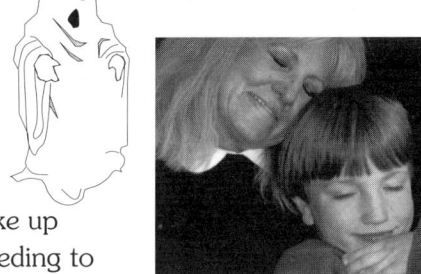

Some children have a difficult time falling asleep and others wake up during the night hearing noises, crying, having a bad dream, needing to go to the bathroom, wanting a glass of water, etc. Falling back to sleep can be scary if a child hears things go bump in the night, sees a strange shadow, or can't shake a nightmare. This listening activity can help comfort children who are unsettled or afraid at bedtime. After a few days of playing this game, children will fall asleep more easily and feel more peaceful throughout the night. This activity originated from a mother whose daughter frequently woke up crying. Because the mother enjoys nature, her sincere appreciation and sensitivity to the sounds of the night conveyed a peaceful feeling to her daughter.

AGES
2-8

TIME
10 minutes

PLAYERS
Parent and child

LOCATION
On the child's bed

EQUIPMENT
⇨ <u>Buddy Bubbles</u> tape, tape recorder

INSTRUCTIONS

1. Before your child goes to sleep, hold her to your heart and as you breathe, focus in your soft heart and feel as though you are breathing love to her. Have the child breathe love with you. Tell her everything is all right. Then listen to the many sounds of the night together and name what they are.

   Examples: A car in the distance, the wind blowing the leaves in the tree tops, the bark of a dog, people talking, the call of a night bird, the refrigerator motor kicking on or off, the rustling of the child's sheets, even the sound of the child's own breathing. Listening to and identifying the sounds you hear helps make the night feel ordinary and safe.

2. If your child wakes up feeling insecure, thinks she heard or saw something scary, or had a nightmare, take a few minutes to comfort her by holding the child to your heart and breathing love again. Reassure her that everything is all right.

3. After the child has calmed down, suggest that you again listen to the many sounds of the night together and say what they are.

4. When she sees that everything is okay, let her know she can sleep peacefully and fall back to sleep quickly by pretending she is floating on a cloud in her soft heart or imagining rainbows over her that are protecting her. Then if something wakes her again, she can remember her rainbows and know she'll be all right. She can feel safe and go right back to a peaceful place.

VARIATION

Turn on the tape *Buddy Bubbles: Magical Games for a Child's Heart* so your child can learn how to find the "soft heart" and sleep easier.

Put On Your Heart Ears

PURPOSE

Trying to get children to stop and sincerely listen to you when they are absorbed in activity or distracted by their surroundings can be challenging. This fun game helps children learn to quickly shift gears into a listening mode when someone is trying to get their attention. It also helps them learn how to listen deeply. "Put On Your Heart Ears" becomes a simple code that parents or teachers use to let children know, "It's time to deep heart listen now!"

AGES
3-7

TIME
10 minutes

PLAYERS
Adult and one or more children

LOCATION
Indoors

EQUIPMENT
⇨ Paper or felt
⇨ Crayons, scissors, tape
⇨ Yarn
⇨ Large, blunt needles

INSTRUCTIONS

1. When you want children to listen deep, tell them you are going to say a special code called, "FREEZE-FRAME — Put On Your Heart Ears." To teach a child this code, first pause and call "FREEZE-FRAME." Then instruct the child that this means, "I need to tell you something important. I want you to stop whatever you are doing, get in your heart, look me in the eye, and listen to what I will say." (If children are not yet familiar with FREEZE-FRAME, give them simple instructions. You can tell them that when you FREEZE-FRAME, you freeze whatever you are doing and let all of your thoughts and feelings come to your heart, then think of someone or something you love. Put your hand on your heart to help you. Explain that when you are feeling love, it's easier to listen.)

2. When you have the child's attention say, **"Now I want you to put on your heart ears."** Using your index finger of both hands, pretend to draw a heart on both ears and ask the child to do the same.

3. **"Now put an ear on your heart."** (Using your index finger of one hand, pretend to draw an ear on your heart and ask the child to do the same.)

4. "Are you ready to hear what I have to tell you?" If the child is not focused, tell him that he needs to try again, because you don't think his heart ears are on yet.

5. Calling "FREEZE-FRAME — Put On Your Heart Ears" and doing the finger movements becomes the special code you use whenever you want your child to sincerely stop whatever he is doing and deep heart listen.

VARIATIONS

1. It is fun for children to make hearts and tape them on their ears as they are learning this game. You can also make an ear to tape on their heart. Use paper, crayons, scissors, and tape to help children make hearts and ears. Play a game where they practice "Heart on Ear" and wear their hearts and ears until it is clear that they understand the game.

2. You can also use felt to make heart ears (felt is soft and molds well to the ear). Cut a center from the bottom of each felt heart so children can wear them on their ears. The heart ears fit over the top of a child's ears and won't fall off. Felt ears can be decorated with creative stitches using yarn and large blunt creative stitchery needles. Children will love to save their felt ears and use them over and over again as they learn to deep heart listen.

Heart Ears Pattern (actual size)

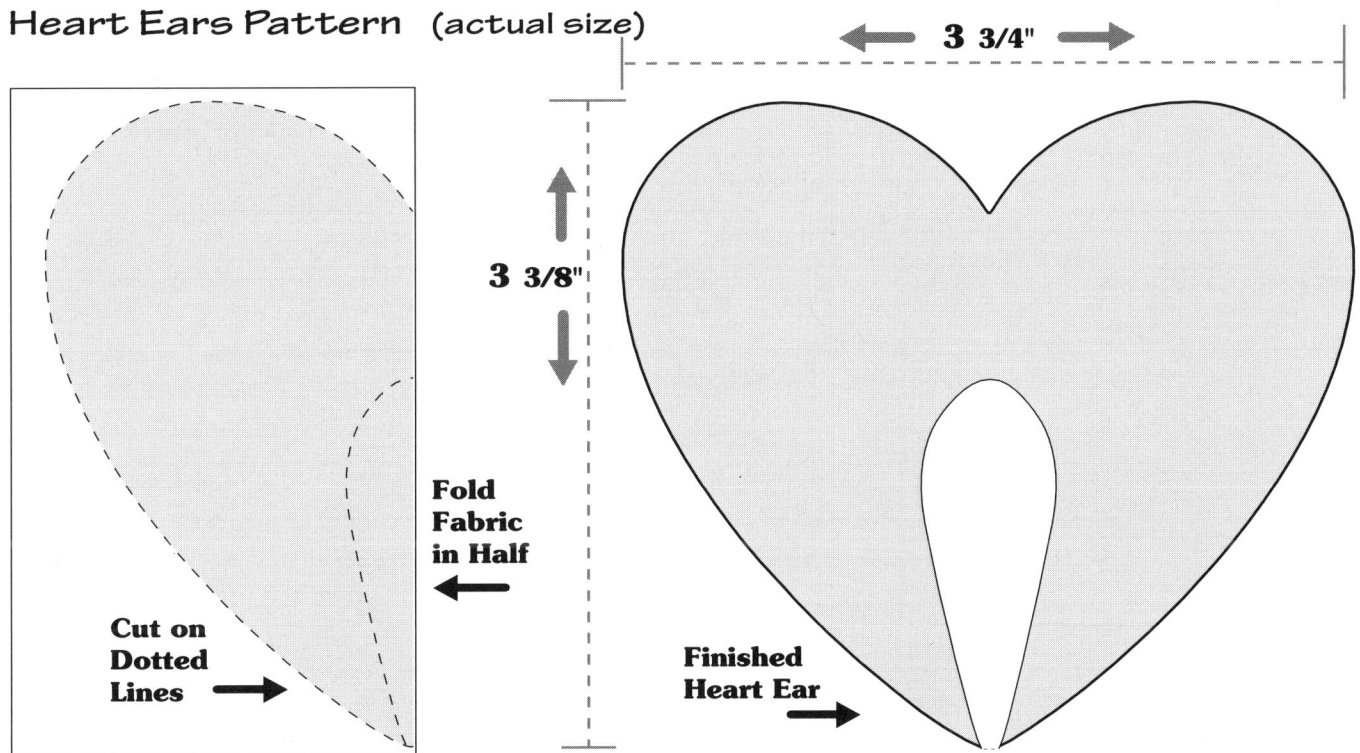

3. Once children have made their heart ears, have them practice deep heart listening with their ears on. With more than one child, have them work in pairs. Have one child speak while the other deeply listens. The child listening repeats back what the first child has shared, then reverse roles. Children love doing this activity with their heart ears on. This activity can be done each day for a week or two to help children really learn to listen to one another and to you. Each day, have them share a new topic with one another. Make the topics simple, such as what is your favorite toy, animal, place to go, or person who makes you feel good inside.

EXAMPLE

Several teachers commented that this activity is such an excellent "attention getter" that they use it daily. One teacher commented, "Children love wearing their heart ears. It's great for clean-up time and to switch learning activities. It gives children something constructive to do with their hands while I am giving instructions. Many times it is hard for them to keep their hands to themselves while trying to be quiet and sit still. I only had to go over the instructions twice, as the children were very eager to learn this game."

Touch The Earth

PURPOSE

"Touch the Earth" is a simple, fun exercise that children enjoy because it is both physically and mentally challenging. Similar to the game "Simon Says," the supervising adult or older child gives instructions to the players on specific physical positions to follow. After an initial slow start, the positions begin to change quickly and only the most alert listeners can follow the rapid and sometimes deliberately confusing instructions. The result is a lot of heartfelt laughter, excitement, and robust physical exercise.

AGES
3-10

TIME
10 minutes

PLAYERS
Adult and one or more children

LOCATION
Indoors or outdoors (where there is space for each player to spread out their arms)

EQUIPMENT
None

INSTRUCTIONS

1. Demonstrate the five different physical positions in "Touch the Earth." Begin with a normal standing position with legs together and arms to the side. "Touch the Sky" is raising one's arms and hands in the air as high as possible. "Touch a Tree" is extending one's arms sideways parallel to the floor. "Touch the Mountains" is placing one's hands on the hips. "Touch the Earth" is lowering the arms to the floor with the back as straight as possible. And finally, "Over the Waterfall" is extending the arms over the head with the back in an arched position.

2. Explain to the players that "Touch the Earth" is like "Simon Says" except that there are two parts to the game. In the first part, the leader calls out a position and moves into that position. Everyone in turn follows the movement of the leader. Tell the players that the speed of the instructions may vary and could get too fast for some to keep up.

Touch the Sky   **Touch a Tree**   **Touch the Mountains**   **Touch the Earth**   **Over the Waterfall**

3. The second part of this activity becomes much more challenging. Tell children under five that it's okay to stop and watch. The older children will listen to and follow the leader's verbal instructions only, ignoring whatever physical positions the leader demonstrates. In other words, the leader might call out, "Touch the Sky" but be in a "Touch the Tree" position. The players should be in the "Touch the Sky" position, ignoring the "Touch the Tree" position. The leader again varies the speed of instructions.

"Uh Oh!"

PURPOSE

"Uh Oh!" builds sincere listening among children. The game challenges children to focus in the heart and be good listeners. It's guaranteed to develop memorization skills through linear heart/mind listening. Through a deeper heart focus, you care so intently that you actually can remember more. Children learn that, yes, they want their own ideas heard, but they also want to hear their friend's ideas.

AGES
4-10

TIME
15 minutes or longer

PLAYERS
Adult and five or more children (If more than nine, divide into two groups.)

LOCATION
Indoors or outdoors

EQUIPMENT
➡ Stopwatch or watch with a second hand
➡ 6 poker chips for each player
➡ Large box

INSTRUCTIONS

1. Everyone sits in a circle.

2. The gamemaster lays out the purpose, talks about sincere listening, and explains that listening from the heart helps you care more and remember more. Remind children that to listen from the heart you have to focus your attention in your heart and feel your care. You can put your hand on your heart to help you focus. Have everyone practice as you explain the following rules.

3. A topic will be chosen which will require a one or two word answer from each player in sequence, but only after they repeat the answer given by previous player(s) on the subject. Children ages four and five only have to repeat one previous player's answer before they give their own answer. Children ages six and seven have to repeat two previous players' answers. Children eight and over have to repeat four previous players' answers (This can only be done if there are at least five players in the game).

4. Each player is given six poker chips. As each player's turn comes up, they have two or three seconds (by the watch) to recall all the previous answers. The leader decides the number of seconds according to age and number of children. Make it challenging but possible. If too slow, it won't be fun. If too fast, it will be too hard. After the player recalls all the previous answers within the set time, he goes deep in the heart and adds his own answer.

117

5. When a player recalls accurately and adds a new answer, the turn moves to the next player. If a player is not alert and forgets any part, a group chorus of "Uh Oh!" erupts from the other players and the player who missed has to put one of his poker chips in the box. Rehearse the group chorus of "Uh Oh" beforehand so it comes across as a fun heart expression and not as a put down. Remind children as needed. Play continues until all players have participated in the round. Then another topic is selected with the same format. The second rotation begins with the second player, the third rotation begins with the third player, etc. When a player is out of poker chips, he is out of the game.

6. The gamemaster sets a time limit or decides at the start of the game the number of rounds that will be played. The players with the most chips left at the end of the game are the winners.

7. As children get skilled at the game, the gamemaster can increase the number of previous players' answers they have to remember.

Suggested Topics

Name a favorite song   Name a favorite food   Name a favorite subject in school

Name a favorite sport   Name something that's fun for you

Name something that makes you happy   Name your favorite holiday

Name a favorite book   Name a favorite musical instrument

Name a favorite animal   Name someone or something you care for

Name something that makes you unhappy   Name something that makes you laugh.

VARIATION

Leaders can integrate current school subjects or popular subjects into the game topics.

Awareness Walk

PURPOSE

This game helps children slow down, go deep in the heart to listen, and become more aware of their surroundings. Through heart-focused observation and listening, children increase their sensitivity, care, and appreciation of the environment. Special attention is placed on the senses of sight, hearing, and smell.

AGES

5-12

TIME

20 minutes or longer

PLAYERS

Adult and two to eight children

LOCATION

Outdoors (where there is attractive landscape and, if possible, some wildlife)

EQUIPMENT

⇨ Blindfolds for pairs of children
⇨ Pencil, paper, and something hard to write on

INSTRUCTIONS

1. Before taking the children for an outdoor walk, discuss the game rules. Ask the children to focus in the heart and deep heart listen so that they hear and understand all the rules.

2. The goal is for them to be very conscious of what is going on around them while they walk. Be aware of sounds, smells, and various things to look at. Give the children some examples to be aware of: the sound of leaves crunching under their feet, an animal scurrying away, horns honking from cars nearby, etc. They might smell a scent from a flower or smell a fire burning nearby, or observe a bird cocking its head watching them walk, an unusually shaped tree, tiny wildflowers hidden in the grass, etc. Suggest that they be silent and stay in a "soft heart" in order to stay focused.

3. They will walk for several minutes, then the adult will call out, "Deep Heart Listen." At that point, everyone stops, closes their eyes, remembers to focus in the heart, and is silent. Each person asks themselves, "What did I sincerely hear?" After a few moments, tell everyone to open their eyes. Ask one of the children to tell everything they heard, saw, or smelled. After the first child has finished, have other children add to the list.

4. Continue walking, then stopping and softly listening, until all the children have had an opportunity to speak first. Talk about how you can name more things by being softer, quieter, and more observant.

VARIATIONS

1. Use blindfolds. An older child who is not blindfolded holds the hand of a blindfolded child and leads him as they walk, making sure he is safe and doesn't trip or hurt himself. Only the blindfolded child tells what he heard or smelled.

2. Take pencil and paper and work together as a group to compile a list of things seen, smelled, or heard.

Duplication

PURPOSE

"Duplication" is a creative game for children to develop deep listening and clear communication skills. A child draws a simple sketch, then describes what was drawn to a partner, who then tries to replicate the sketch without seeing it. The child communicating learns to give instructions simply and clearly so his partner can understand and duplicate them. The partner learns to listen from a deep heart focus to accurately receive, understand, and follow instructions.

AGES
5-18

TIME
20 minutes

PLAYERS
Two or more children

LOCATION
Indoors with table space for each pair

EQUIPMENT
➡ Paper, pencil, crayons, or colored markers
➡ Cardboard partitions or a hardbound 8½" by 11" book that will stand upright for every pair
⇨ Pattern blocks or Legos™

INSTRUCTIONS

1. Divide the group into pairs.

2. Each person draws a simple sketch on plain, white paper, keeping the drawing hidden from their partner's view. The drawing can be a simple geometrical shape, a symbol, a nature scene, or still life.

3. Keeping all drawings concealed, have each player pair off with a partner. Place the partitions between each pair.

4. Have one player from each pair describe their drawing to the other. No peeking! The communicator will have to frame her words very simply and clearly to convey exactly how her partner is to duplicate the drawing. The communicator might have to give directions in steps.

   Example: "Draw a square with one inch sides, two inches from the left hand corner of the paper." When the listener says he is finished, the communicator explains the next step, "Draw a dot right in the middle of the square," etc.

5. After the listener has finished drawing the sketch, have the pair compare results between the original drawing and the duplicate. Each pair should look at the accuracy of the duplicate drawing and discuss the reasons for success or failure in the communication process. Then switch roles.

VARIATIONS

1. Have the listener repeat back what the communicator says at each step to check the accuracy of what he heard. If he heard inaccurately, the communicator rephrases the communication and the listener repeats back until both are in agreement.

2. If your partner duplicated the drawing easily, repeat the game and increase the complexity of your drawing to challenge your communication skills and your partner's listening skills. If your partner did not get the duplication right, repeat the game and simplify your drawing so your partner is more likely to get it right.

3. Have the players build patterns with pattern blocks or three dimensional figures with Legos™ instead of drawing a picture.

Rainsticks

PURPOSE

Rainsticks are soothing noisemakers used by people living in rainforest areas. Listening to the natural sounds of water, like a waterfall or a stream, is very relaxing and helps people naturally get into their hearts. Listening to a Rainstick is similar to putting your ear up to a seashell and hearing the ocean waves or listening to the pitter-patter of a mild rain. You have to listen deep to hear the hidden sound. In making a Rainstick, children gain a deeper understanding of another culture. In listening to the Rainstick, they gain a deeper appreciation for nature and its wondrous sounds — plus they feel proud of their unique creation.

AGES

8-18

TIME

3 hours (divided into several time periods)

PLAYERS

Adult and one or more children

LOCATION

Indoors or outdoors (with a table where painting, design work, and drying can take place without disturbance)

EQUIPMENT

➡ Paper tube for each player, (36" x 2" diameter) for beginners or bamboo stick for the more advanced

➡ A piece of colored craft paper, wallpaper, or fabric (7 $\frac{1}{2}$" x 36") for each player

➡ Pencil and drawing paper

➡ Paint, markers, or crayons

➡ Paint brush

➡ String, yarn, beads, feathers, jute, or other decorative materials

➡ Scissors

➡ Glue (quick drying is the best)

➡ 2 strips of poster board (2 $\frac{1}{2}$" x 36")

➡ Ruler, heavy books or bobby pins

➡ Colored cloth tape or mailing tube caps

➡ 1 cup rice (different grains make different sounds: wild rice, basmati rice, short grain rice, long grain rice, lentils, or couscous) or small seashell pieces can be used.

These listed materials are designed to create a full size rainstick — 3' in length with a 2" diameter. If you want to create rainsticks in a different size, measure out your paper tube, craft paper, and poster board accordingly.

INSTRUCTIONS

1. Begin by bringing in a Rainstick and demonstrate its sound. Allow the children to gently handle the Rainstick while introducing them to the project. To introduce Rainstick designs, review magazines and books that have pictures of the jungle or rainforest. Recommended titles: *At Home in the Rainforest* by Diane Willow and Laura Jacques; *Why Save the Rain Forest?* by Donald Silver; *Welcome to the Green House* by Jane Yolen; and *Usborne's Rainforest Wildlife*. These books have beautiful illustrations. Children can create a jungle scene or make the entire design be a plant, animal, or insect. Designs can also be made with brightly colored textile patterns or decorated with beads, feathers, dried leaves, shells, string, yarn, or other materials. Children begin the creative process by drawing a sample Rainstick design on a piece of drawing paper.

2. Construction begins with children drawing their final design on a 36" x 7$\frac{1}{2}$" piece of colored craft paper, wallpaper, or fabric. Use paint, markers, crayons, or other materials gathered to decorate the design.

Assembling the Rainstick

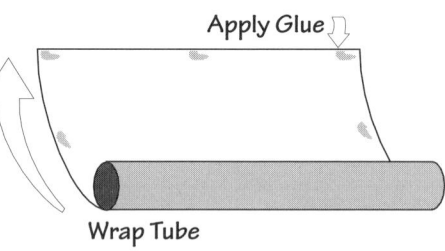

Apply Glue

Wrap Tube

1. Cover the paper tube with the recently-made art work. To do this, place the craft paper lengthwise on the table with the plain side up. Put dabs of glue at the top, middle, and along the bottom edge of the craft paper. Press the paper tube down along the edge of the paper to secure the paper to the tube. Wait a moment or two to let the glue set. Press down on the tube a couple of times to make sure it holds to the paper.

2. Roll the paper tube forward. Smooth out the surface of the paper as you are rolling. Put glue along the entire length of the edge of the paper and fold it over the starting seam. Smooth down the paper carefully and make sure the seam is closed. Any paper extending over the ends of the tube can be cut off or tucked into the tube.

3. Cut two strips of poster board $2^1/_2$" x 36" each, and put glue in a fine line down the center of one strip. Put the two pieces of poster board on top of each other and glue them together. Put the strips under a weight (e.g. several books) or clip them together with bobby pins until the glue is dry.

Apply Glue

Glue

Cut   Folds

4. When glue is dry, cut 1" slits at 1" intervals along the length of the poster board on both sides of the strip. Fold back the 1" paper flaps in opposite directions to create a paper core with four spokes (see illustration).

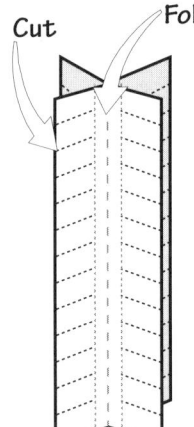

5. Shape the paper core to look like the illustration by pinching the ends and rolling the paper tabs inward. Crush the tabs gently along the length of the core and twist core slightly so it will fit into the tube.

6. Insert the paper core into the tube and rotate it several times as it goes in to create a spiral. You may have to adjust the flaps of paper to get them into the tube.

Twist

7. Close one end of the tube by making an X with cloth tape. Use two or three pieces of tape to make sure there are no holes. Mailing caps with the same inside diameter as your tube can also be used.

8. Insert the rice or other grains into the tube. Now test your Rainstick for sound. Use your hand to close the open end of the paper tube. Tip the tube over several times to verify that the rice is filtering through the core. To make adjustments, twist the ends of the core in opposite directions .

Rice

9. To complete the project, close up the remaining open end of the tube.

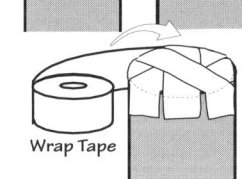

Wrap Tape

Ways To Use The Rainstick

Examples: A listening exercise to identify the different sounds it makes. Comparing the sounds of one player's Rainstick to another player's Rainstick. A musical instrument to dance to. A relaxation game where each player turns their own Rainstick quietly and imagines sitting next to a waterfall to go more deeply into their heart as they listen. A relaxation game where one player turns his Rainstick slowly while everyone else listens and relaxes in the heart.

The Intuitive Listening Game

PURPOSE

Most children (and adults) have been in conversations where they felt they weren't being heard. Maybe their words were heard but not their feelings or real meaning. When people of any age feel heard, they connect with their hearts. In this game, players learn to listen from the heart and practice intuitive listening skills in pairs. Then they test their skill in a fun, role-playing game.

AGES
12-19

TIME
30 minutes each phase

PLAYERS
Four or more children

LOCATION
Indoors (on chairs or on the floor)

EQUIPMENT
None

INSTRUCTIONS

1. Talk to the players about listening. Ask the following questions, "Do you feel heard when you express yourself?" "Do you feel heard by some people but not by others?" "Are you are a good listener?" "Do you intuitively understand people even when their words don't say what they mean?" Discuss some of the problems that get in the way of good listening.

2. Explain that the purpose of "The Intuitive Listening Game" is to learn intuitive listening skills that encourage a deeper heart understanding of another person. There are two phases to this activity.

Phase I

1. Pair everyone up. One person will speak about one of the suggested themes (for not more than one minute) while the other person listens deeply from the heart. The listener will listen for three important levels of communication and "mirror" back what the speaker communicated at each level. The speaker will then tell the listener whether he "got it right" or help him if he did not. To hear all three levels, the listener has to intuitively listen from the heart. When the speaker feels the listener got it right, they switch roles.

   a. Word Level — what is actually said
   b. Feeling Level — the feeling behind the words
   c. Essence Level — the real meaning

   Example of Listener Mirroring at Three Levels:

   Word Level — "What I heard you say is that one of the biggest risks you took last year was when you stayed out past your curfew with some friends and you could have been grounded.

123

There was a movie you really wanted to go to the next day and you didn't want to miss it. But you were having so much fun, you didn't want to leave the party. When you got home, your parents had already gone to bed so they never knew you were late."

Feeling Level — "You were really scared, then you were really relieved when it all worked out."

Essence Level — "You saw it was a big risk, but it worked out. It might not have worked out and you would have had to miss the movie."

Suggested Themes

- What is one of the funniest things that happened to you last year?

- What is one of the most frightening things that happened to you last year and how did you overcome the fear?

- What is one of the most important lessons you learned last year?

- What was one of the biggest risks you took last year?

- Name one goal you would like to achieve.

- Name one thing that most people don't know about you.

2. After each player has had a turn being a listener and a speaker, talk about how everyone did. Which level was the most difficult to mirror back correctly? Talk about situations at home, at school, or with friends, where "Intuitive Listening" would be helpful.

3. Play the game one more time with another theme. Ask the children if it was easier the second time.

Phase II

Divide the group into smaller groups. Phase II begins with each small group creating a short role play where the players create and rehearse a conversation involving the three levels of communication. Afterwards, they act out their mini-drama in front of the larger group. The larger group tries to identify the three levels of communication in at least one of the main characters.

Mini-Drama Example:

Parent: Why didn't you clean up like I asked you? I'm tired of having to remind you to clean up your messes. Maybe I need to take away some of your privileges.

Daughter: But mom, you don't understand. I have a lot going on right now. How would you like to be taking six classes, after school sports, and then try to have a social life? It's real hard.

Parent: That's no excuse. You could at least take care of the small messes that you create.

Larger group identifies the three levels of communication in the parent:

Word Level of Parent: Why didn't you clean up like I asked you? I'm tired of having to remind you to clean up your messes. Maybe I need to take away some of your privileges.

Feeling Level of Parent: Angry, frustrated, disappointed

Essence Level of Parent: Loves daughter and wants her to be responsible. Tired of reminding daughter. Tired of excuses. Might remove privileges to get her to clean up her stuff.

Music Generations

PURPOSE

It's hard to believe there was a time when clothing and music were handed down from generation to generation. Nowadays, a grand canyon can exist between parents and teens in these two areas. A fun way to bridge that gap is to use the medium of music to help both the adult and teen understand the values and preferences of the other. Through sincere listening, a mutual understanding can take place. While agreement on musical taste might not be achieved, there will be less judgment and more actual communication.

AGES
12-19

TIME
20 minutes or longer

PLAYERS
Adult and one or more teens

LOCATION
Indoors (where there are no distractions)

EQUIPMENT
➡ CD or tape player
➡ CD or tape of each person's favorite music
➪ Favorite clothes

INSTRUCTIONS

1. Introduce the teen to the purpose of the activity — to develop more understanding of each other through the medium of music.

   Discuss the three levels of deep listening:

   Word level: listening to the words being spoken
   Feeling level: listening to the feeling behind the words
   Essence level: listening to the deeper meaning

2. Adult and teen each pick one of their favorite songs and find a comfortable place to listen to the music.

3. Take turns listening to each other's song, practicing deep heart listening. After the song is over, talk about what the artist is trying to communicate. Go through the three levels listed above. Try to come to some conclusion together. Then reverse roles.

EXAMPLE

One mother of a teenager commented, "I think this is a great way to start to bridge the communication gap, because once my fourteen-year-old daughter felt heard; she felt cared for. We listened to hers first, then she was very receptive to mine. We did come to some conclusions together. After we did this exercise, it opened up much more communication between us."

VARIATION

Enjoy a similar activity with clothes. Both adult and teen dress up in their favorite style of clothes. Discuss the choices and meaning behind the respective clothing styles, trying to arrive at a common conclusion.

CHAPTER
7

"Communicate
As You
Go"

Heart Sonics

PURPOSE

Have you ever noticed how people's voices can sound different when they are enjoying something from their heart? You might walk by two children who are playing together and ask, "Are you having fun?" The response might well be a melodic, "Uhhhh Huhhhhhhh!" Similarly, an adult walking toward a beautiful sunset that glows on a lake may express spontaneous appreciation by saying, "Mmmmmmmm." It's as if the heart is humming its own song. The purpose of this activity is to help children recognize and creatively voice heartfelt appreciation and love.

AGES
4-7

TIME
10 minutes or longer

PLAYERS
Adult and one or more children

LOCATION
Indoors or outdoors

EQUIPMENT
➡ Pencil and paper

EXAMPLES

**Fun Things and their
Heart Sonics Responses:**

• Cuddling your doll or favorite stuffed animal — **Mmmmmm**

• Petting a puppy — **Aawwwww**

• Relaxing in a hot bath — **Ahhhhhhhh**

• Giving a big bear hug —**Ooooooohh**

• Getting tickled — **Teeeeheeee**

• Eating ice cream — **Yummmmm**

• Swinging on a swing — **Weeeeeeee**

• Playing in the park — **Yessssssss**

• Winning a game — **Yaaayyyyyy**

INSTRUCTIONS

1. Think of things your child enjoys, such as favorite foods, places, times, people, pets. If playing with a number of children, try to find something that each child appreciates. Write their favorite items on a piece of paper.

2. Explain "Heart Sonics."
Tell the children that when we are truly happy or thankful, our heart is singing and we sometimes express it through different heartfelt sounds.

When we pet a kitty, we might purr too, "Mmmmm." A list of favorite items will be read and when a child hears something he likes, he is to show enjoyment by humming "Ummmmm" or making another soft heart sound.

3. Listen carefully to the children's sonics and you will be able to tell the things that they sincerely love and appreciate. Ask them to be aware of the sound of their voice. Point out sonics that are pleasant and from the heart.

4. As children play this game, they become more conscious of when they are acting and speaking from the heart. You will begin to notice the difference between true heart sonics and sonics that come from a "happy head." If the children become too loud and boisterous, you should stop the game and explain that you aren't hearing heart songs now, only head noise. This helps young children begin to differentiate between the head and heart.

Happy Heart Song

PURPOSE

Helping young children express their hearts in song and melody is a wonderful way for them to feel appreciation and love. People of any age often find it easier to express their feelings in music.

AGES
4-7

TIME
5 minutes

PLAYERS
Adult and one or more children

LOCATION
Indoors or outdoors

EQUIPMENT
➡ (Optional) piano, guitar, or other musical instrument

INSTRUCTIONS

Sing the "Happy Heart Song" together. When singing this song, extend the ending sonic. Make it soft and melodic. Make up more verses and sonics as you go along.

Happy Heart Song

Sung to the tune of
"If You're Happy And You Know It Clap Your Hands"

If you feel good in your heart say, 'Uh Huhhhhh'
If you feel good in your heart say, 'Uh Huhhhhh'
If you feel good and you know it
then your voice will surely show it.
If you feel good in your heart say, 'Uh Huhhhhh'

If you really love your Mommy say, 'Oleyyy'
If you really love your Mommy say, 'Oleyyy'
If you love her and you know it
then your voice is sure to show it
If you really love your Mommy say, 'Oleyyy'

If you're thankful for your home say, 'Hoorayyy'
If you're thankful for your home say, 'Hoorayyy'
If you're thankful and you know it
then you're voice is sure to show it
If you're thankful and you know it say, 'Hoorayyy'

If you're thankful for your food say, "Yumm, Yummmm"
If you're thankful for your food say, "Yumm, Yummmm"
If you're thankful and you know it
Then your voice is sure to show it
If you're thankful for your food say, "Yumm, Yummmm"

VARIATION

Have children make up more verses that express positive feelings.

Finger Poems

PURPOSE

"Finger Poems" are delightful, little exercises that combine finger movements with thematic poems. As children learn the rhythm of each poem, they can begin to manipulate their fingers, capturing the spirit of the theme. Once learned, children will want to repeat "Finger Poems" over and over. Parents and teachers can create poems that speak to the heartfelt needs of each child.

AGES
4-8

TIME
10 minutes or longer

PLAYERS
Adult and one more more children

LOCATION
Indoors or outdoors

EQUIPMENT
None

INSTRUCTIONS

1. Before involving children in "Finger Poems," practice a few rounds with the poems yourself to learn the finger movements.

2. Demonstrate a "Finger Poem" to the children, then ask them to participate.

3. Repeat "Finger Poems" regularly until children know the words and finger movements by heart. Eventually, they will improvise movements and also musical themes to go with the poems.

I Hear My Heart Speaking Today

Do I hear my heart speaking today?
Place left palm flat against middle of chest with right hand cupped to right ear.

Is there something it wants to say?
Place left palm flat against middle of chest with right hand gesturing out from heart several times.

Why yes, if I listen real closely
Place right hand and left hand against right and left ears in a cupped position.

To the good feelings inside of me.
Place both hands next to area around the heart and make circular motions.

I have things that I love and care for.
Place both hands next to area around the heart and continue making circular motions.

People, places, toys, and a lot more.
For people, make fingers of right hand move up and down in sequence like playing the piano; next, for places, move the left hand like the waves of the ocean; for toys, move right hand up and down; and for a lot more, extend both hands outward away from the body.

I hear my heart speaking today.
Place left palm flat against middle of chest with right hand cupped to right ear.

Love the Earth

1 **Love the earth,**
With both hands, make a circle the size of a basketball and gently sway the hands back and forth in opposite directions.

4 **Thanks for the people,**
Rapidly point with both index fingers to imaginary people on the ground.

2 **Thanks for my home,**
Bend the fingers of both hands so that the tips form a 'V' shape with the palms acting like the sides of the house.

5 **Thanks for the trees,**
Make the fingers stand up like trees.

3 **Thanks for the animals,**
Make the fingers walk like animal steps.

6 **Thanks for my life,**
Point fingers upward with arms spread apart and slightly bent. Move fingers as though there is spirit in them.

The Eensy Weensy Spider

The Eensy Weensy Spider
Touch right hand little finger to left hand thumb, then right hand thumb to left hand little finger

Went up the water spout.
Keep alternating opposite thumb and little finger touching as you slowly raise arms to eye level

Down came the rain and washed the spider out.
Wave both hands up and down with palms open

Out came the sunshine and dried up all the rain.
Bring backs of two hands together then open wide and make a big sun

And the Eensy Weensy Spider went up the spout again.
Again alternate thumb and little finger touching to walk spider up the spout

Hickory, Dickory Dock — from Mother Goose

Hickory, Dickory Dock
Place the elbow of the right arm in the left palm. The arm is upright and swings back and forth.

The mouse ran up the clock.
Fingers of the left hand run up the right arm.

The clock struck one,
Raise the index finger of the right hand.

The mouse ran down,
The fingers of the left hand run down the right arm and right elbow rests in the left palm.

Hickory, Dickory Dock!
The elbow of the right arm remains in the left palm. The arm is upright and swings back and forth.

Remember the Day

 The day is almost over, It is time to go to bed. *Place left hand under the blanket of the right hand.*

 Before you close your eyes, *Cover eyes with both hands except for little peepholes*

 Tell me about your day. Did you have fun times? Was their joy in your heart? *With right hand, make a hand movement like a blender near the center of the chest*

 **And if you were sad,** *Place hands against the sides of both cheeks and press firmly enough to create a wrinkled face.*

Tell me about that too.

Dinner Table

Dinner is almost ready, It's time to wash up.
Rub hands against one another as though washing one's hands.

I'll be with my family
Interlock fingers together.

With the table set up.
Extend arms out, admiring the food and the table setting

Give thanks for the food,
Place right palm against the center of the chest.

Give love to the cook,
Place left palm against the center of the chest.

Let us eat a good meal,
Cup the left hand like a mouth with the left thumb as the lower jaw. Bring the right hand into the mouth of the left hand and move the fingers and thumb of the left hand up and down as it eats food

And feel full in our hearts
Place both hands overlapped across the center of the chest.

Calm Down
(for children who are prone to anger)

**Calm, calm down
Relax into the ground**
Stretch hands above and in front of the head and like leaves falling off a tree, let the hands zig zag down to shoulder height

Just relax, everything is OK
Place both hands overlapped across the center of the chest.

Don't get angry stomping all around
Make wild finger movements with right hand with left hand remaining in chest area

Be in your heart and breathe deep
Place both hands overlapped across the center of the chest.

And peace will be found

VARIATIONS

1. Select a favorite poem and create accompanying finger movements.

2. Create your own poem and accompanying finger movements with the children.

Talking Stick Game

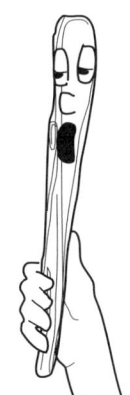

PURPOSE

A "Talking Stick" can facilitate communication, listening, and conflict resolution. By allowing only the person who is holding the Talking Stick to speak, children learn fundamental skills for cooperative communication. Once children are calm and understand the rules, this game fosters speaking your truth and sincere listening.

AGES

6-14

TIME

20 minutes or longer

PLAYERS

Adult and two or more children

LOCATION

Indoors or outdoors

EQUIPMENT

➡ A smooth rod or broom handle (around 2' long) for each person

➡ Paint brushes and paint or colored markers that won't rub off when handled; stickers or other decorative items

INSTRUCTIONS

1. Each child paints and decorates his own Talking Stick. Create a safe place to store all the Talking Sticks.

2. Bring out a Talking Stick when you want to have a group or family talk on an important topic or to resolve a conflict. Only one Talking Stick is used during a group talk. The person whose Talking Stick is used gets to speak first. At the next group talk, bring out someone else's Talking Stick and that person will get to speak first.

3. Tell the children they will each have an opportunity to talk, but they may only speak one at time so that they can be heard by everyone. Having the Talking Stick in your possession indicates it's your turn to speak. If someone else wants to talk, they may raise their hand, indicating they want to speak next. Remind the children that while the stick bearer is talking, they are to listen closely and try to understand what is being said. No one is to interrupt while the person holding the stick is talking.

4. To begin, the first speaker holds the selected Talking Stick while everyone silently sends heart to each other for thirty seconds. Then the stick bearer speaks his truth.

5. When the stick bearer is finished talking, the stick is passed to the next child and so forth, until everyone has had a turn speaking.

6. When the discussion is complete, have the children go to their hearts and ask what they learned. If it was a conflict resolution, ask them what they could do differently to prevent a recurrence of the situation. Suggest to the participants that they come up with a solution that all can agree on. Continue to pass the Talking Stick until a solution is reached.

7. When the game is over, have the child put his stick back in the designated storage place.

EXAMPLES

A parent of three children, ages three, seven and ten said, "The Talking Stick helped solve some problems between my seven and ten-year-old boys. Focusing on the talking stick and having an agreement to take turns and listen allowed them to resolve their conflicts. It even opened me up to listen better. My sons really came around. I'm impressed."

Heart Burst

PURPOSE

"Heart Burst" helps children gain a deeper understanding of the intelligence of the heart through free-association. Each child draws a topic from a box of topics that speak about ways to live more from the heart. They have thirty seconds to talk freely and sincerely about their topic. Because of the short time limit, spontaneity is unleashed allowing the wisdom of their heart to emerge.

AGES
7-16

TIME
15 minutes or longer

PLAYERS
Adult and one or more children

LOCATION
Indoors or outdoors

EQUIPMENT
➡ Paper, pencils, scissors
➡ Box or container
➡ Stopwatch, watch with second hand, or glass timer
➡ Chalkboard or greaseboard, chalk or markers

INSTRUCTIONS

1. Cut up small pieces of paper and write one topic on each piece of paper. Have at least twice as many topics as there are children. Choose topics which will encourage children to dwell on the qualities of the heart.

2. Fold and place the topics in a container from which each child, in sequence, draws a topic.

3. After drawing their topic, each child has one minute to relate what she knows or feels about the topic. Another player or adult should keep track of the thirty second time limit.

4. After each child has had a turn, discuss as a group. Other children can add their ideas about each topic.

TOPIC EXAMPLES

• Things I appreciate about_____(someone they know).

• Things I appreciate about myself.

• Ways to get in your heart.

• When is a good time to send heart to others?

• If someone makes fun of you, how would you react from the head and how would you react from the heart?

• How do you help a brother, sister, or friend who is out of their heart?

• How do you pick gifts for people?

• How to make going to bed on time fun.

• How to make cleaning your room fun.

VARIATIONS

1. Divide a large class into seven groups of four or more students. Have each group draw a topic from the container. Each group has two minutes to write their group answers to the topic. When they finish, have the groups silently trade topics, then take two more minutes to write answers to the new topic. When all groups are finished, a scribe from each group writes his group's answers on a greaseboard and compares them with the other group who had the same topic.

   Example: A junior high school teacher wrote, "This variation to the game 'Heart Burst' was very popular with my students. The fun competition motivated each group to pour themselves into this activity."

   Here are two of the topics his junior high class picked:

   • Reasons to FREEZE-FRAME — stress, parents, homework, school projects, tests, put-downs, money, sickness, loneliness

   • If someone makes fun of you, how would you react from the head and how would you react from the heart?
   Head: violence, yell, spit, die of humiliation, get angry, frustration, tension
   Heart: ignore, FREEZE-FRAME, communicate to teacher, relax, forgive and forget, learn to love, laugh

2. Have the children stop mid-game and talk in-depth about a topic that interests them.

EXAMPLE

An elementary school teacher played "Heart Burst" on a rainy day with twenty children. After three children had shared about three different topics, the next child talked about how he helps his little sister when she's out of her heart. This spawned a spontaneous discussion among the children on different ways they help family and friends who are upset. The discussion was so sincere and creative that the teacher spent the entire period letting the children talk about ways they can help people who are out of their heart rather than continuing on with more topics.

How Do You Respond?

PURPOSE

It's important to learn to speak our truth when we want to express a need or when someone does or says something that we feel is not right. How we communicate often determines whether we will be heard, ignored, or yelled at. Learning to speak from the heart can ease some of the stress buildup in challenging situations. This activity teaches assertive communication skills that can help prevent and resolve difficult situations or conflicts.

AGES
10-19

TIME
45 minutes or longer

PLAYERS
Adult and three or more children

LOCATION
Indoors

EQUIPMENT
➡ 3" x 5" cards (2 per player)
➡ Pencils

INSTRUCTIONS

1. Discuss the purpose of this activity with the children and then read the following to them: When we want to express a need or when someone does or says something that we feel is not right, unfair, or unreasonable, we basically have three choices in how we respond.

   • We can attack with anger, blame, or frustration. This usually makes the other person mad or feel hurt and doesn't help resolve anything.

   • We can assert ourselves, stating clearly from the heart our position without unfairly offending the other person. This way seems the most effective.

   • We can passively respond, ignore, let go, or retreat from a conflict or problem because we don't want to make any waves. Sometimes this way is helpful and sometimes it is not.

2. Ask the group how they would respond (attack, assert, or be passive) in the following situations:

   • Your brother took extra helpings of ice cream, leaving you with a small portion.

   • A friend wants to go to a movie that you don't want to see.

   • You have been standing in line for a long time and someone tries to push ahead of you.

   • A classmate teases you everyday as you pass each other in the hall.

   • Your parent gets frustrated with you about how much time you watch television, your lack of responsibility at doing chores, or disappointing school grades.

- You got a bad grade on the Math test. Someone says to you, "Are you really that stupid?"

- Someone has spread a false rumor about you. You run into the person in the hallway.

- An older student threatens you during lunch time.

3. Have players each describe two situations in their lives on 3" x 5" cards (one situation per card) where they need(ed) to speak up and say what they feel is right.

4. Have players meet in small groups of three or more and read one or both of their situations to each other. Discuss and brainstorm as a small group the most appropriate, heartfelt response to help resolve the situation. Each player write down the best response to their situation on the back of their 3" x 5" card.

5. Each small group pick one of the situations to role play for the larger group and create a successful ending.

6. Role play, then discuss.

EXAMPLES

- Someone borrowed two of my books and had them for over a month. I was frustrated because I really wanted to read them. How do you respond? "It's really taking a long time for me to get the books back. Can I get them back soon because I want to read them?"

- A guy wanted to get the best seat on the bus and was threatening anyone who took this seat. How do you respond? "Try to be calm and say, 'Go ahead.'"

- We played a pickup game of basketball and our team lost. A guy on the winning team laughed at me and made fun of me. How do you respond? "Let it go and don't care. Tell him in a sincere way, 'Hey man, you won that game. No big deal. I didn't play that great. Maybe next time.'"

VARIATION

Have players from one group read their challenging situations, mix up all their 3" x 5" cards, then read all the "how do you respond" answers to a second group. Have the second group try to match the answers to the situations. Then the groups reverse roles.

To Tell The Truth

PURPOSE

This game is a creative way to encourge children to practice their deep listening skills as well as share how they have used the Heart Tools. Through questions and listening, the group tries to determine which one of the three players is telling the truth about a personal story and which two are bluffing.

AGES

10 -19

TIME

30 minutes or longer

PLAYERS

Adult and six or more children

LOCATION

Indoors

EQUIPMENT

➡ Paper and pencils for everyone

INSTRUCTIONS

1. Have players write a short one or two paragraph story recalling a time when they either had to: a) FREEZE-FRAME, b) practice "Oops, No Big Deal," c) care for someone in need of care, or d) find something to appreciate in order to not let something else bother them.

2. Collect the papers and secretly select one story.

3. Choose three players from the group, including the author of the selected story, and instruct all three to leave the room for several minutes. Away from the group, they will read the selected story together, acquainting themselves fully with any necessary details before reentering the room. The objective of each one of the players is to convince the remaining group that they wrote the story, even though two of them will be pretending to be the authors.

4. Next, the supervising adult reads the selected writing to the entire group.

5. The group now asks ten questions to any of the three players who are standing shoulder to shoulder in front of the group. A player in the group may pass if he cannot think of a question. After ten questions have been asked, the game stops.

6. A poll is taken to determine who believes player A, player B, or player C wrote the story.

7. The real author remains standing while the two pretenders sit down. Those who guessed the real author are the winners.

8. Discuss as a group what clues or information tipped off the accurate selection of the mystery author or what misperceptions led one astray.

VARIATION

Teachers can vary this activity by asking students to write stories on the character of a historical figure, a literary character, or a current events topic.

Campfire Talks

PURPOSE

As a night campfire blazes, a group of teens sit on logs around the fire, enjoying each other's company. They are talking about important events in their lives, sharing feelings, memories, hopes, and stories. The atmosphere is one of camaraderie and fun. To hold a campfire talk, or capture that feeling in another setting, is a wonderful, secure, and encouraging way to get teenagers to talk about what is meaningful to them. Whether the setting is an outdoor fire, a dimly-lit classroom, or a cozy living room, the aim of "Campfire Talks" is to create an environment where every teen can sincerely express what is real in their heart. These discussions can be helpful in reducing feelings of isolation and receiving compassion and understanding from peers.

AGES
12-19

TIME
30 minutes or longer

PLAYERS
Adult and four or more children

LOCATION
Outdoors (around a fire) or indoors (in a dimly lit room)

EQUIPMENT
➡ Logs, matches, kindling, and newspaper for campfire or fireplace

➡ Candles or kerosene lamps and matches if no fireplace

INSTRUCTIONS

1. Prepare the atmosphere by organizing an outdoor campfire, indoor fireplace, or dimming the lights and bringing in candles or a kerosene lamp for indoor discussion. Arrange seating comfortably, preferably in a circle.

2. Set a theme for discussion (see topic examples below). As the adult gamemaster, be conscious of modeling the behavior and tone you are seeking to create. Be open and understanding. Share how everyone has their ups and downs and no one is spared from feeling some stress. Share some of your own stresses, life events, hopes, or experiences. Encourage everyone to participate but allow for non-participation if someone doesn't feel comfortable talking.

TOPIC EXAMPLES

• Share a stressful event from the past that you finally overcame. How did you do it? Did listening to your heart help you overcome the stress?

• What is your biggest problem now? How are you handling it?

• What were some of your fears when you were young? What are they now?

• What were some of your dreams when you were young? What are they now?

• When you were younger, who were your heroes? Who are your heroes today?

• Did you ever get in trouble for lying? What would have happened if you had told the truth?

• What was one of the most embarrassing things that ever happened to you? What embarrasses you now?

• What are two things you once were but no longer are? What are two things you will be but are not yet?

• Who is the happiest person you know? What makes that person happy?

• What is one of the nicest things someone did for you (or you did for someone)?

CHAPTER
8

Balance In The Heart

Message Mobiles

PURPOSE

Making mobiles is a wonderful way to teach children about balance and values. Mobiles are collections of objects attached by string or wire to a ceiling, light fixture, or large doorway. Because they are carefully balanced and hung where air currents circulate, mobiles can move freely in space. As air currents change, you have to continuously adjust the mobile's balance. It's the same with people. People have to continuously adjust their balance to flow with the changing currents of life. By adding meaningful messages, either visual or written, children are more likely to enjoy the mobiles and use them as a reminder.

AGES
3-12 (Adult can make mobile for infant or toddler)

TIME
1 hour or longer (may take 2 sessions)

PLAYERS
Adult and one or more children

LOCATION
Indoors

EQUIPMENT
→ Different colored poster board, oak board, construction paper, lightweight or corrugated cardboard, or felt

→ White paper for mobile templates

→ Scissors or mat knife, pliers

→ Glue, paste, or scotch tape

→ Markers or crayons

→ Theme pictures

→ 7" dowels - 3 per child

→ Black carpet thread or clear nylon fishing line

→ Cup hook or anchor screw for hanging mobile

→ (Optional) black spray paint for painting dowels

→ (Optional) camera, film

INSTRUCTIONS

1. Select an appropriate theme that enhances values (see suggested themes). Select location (if made at home) to hang the mobile where your child can easily see it.

2. Create a template from paper (heart shape, circle, rectangle, long rectangular strip, etc.) and cut out shapes from the colored poster board (oak board, construction paper, cardboard, or colored fabric-like felt) to be hung on the mobile.

3. Write, draw, color, glue, or tape theme pictures, images, or words on mobile shapes.

4. (Optional) Paint dowels with black paint and let dry.

5. Begin putting mobile together by using black carpet thread or nylon fishing line to attach two mobile shapes to the main dowel and three mobile shapes to the other two dowels.

Decide thread lengths according to position and size of mobile shapes. (See sample on page 144) Attach thread either by gluing or knotting thread through small holes in mobile shapes. Attach the two completed dowels to the main dowel. Knot all threads two or three times and clip loose ends off.

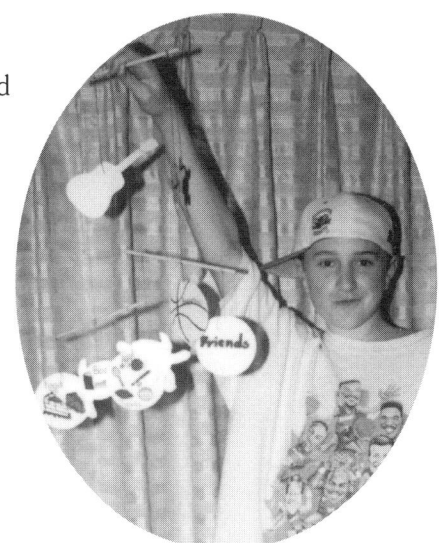

6. Attach a 30" piece of thread to the main dowel (tied three times securely around dowel) to serve as the attachment to the ceiling hook.

7. Slide the threads along the dowels until all dowels are horizontal and mobile shapes are balanced. Make sure they swing freely. Finding balance is largely a matter of trial and error. It may take a couple of times so be patient.

8. Hang the mobile up.

9. Spend some quality time reviewing the themes on the mobile with your child. If you are a teacher, request that the child and parent review the theme together. Message Mobiles can be great catalysts for heartfelt discussions on balance and learning to continuously adjust your balance to flow through life's changes or spending quiet moments together looking at the mobile messages and feeling love, care, or appreciation.

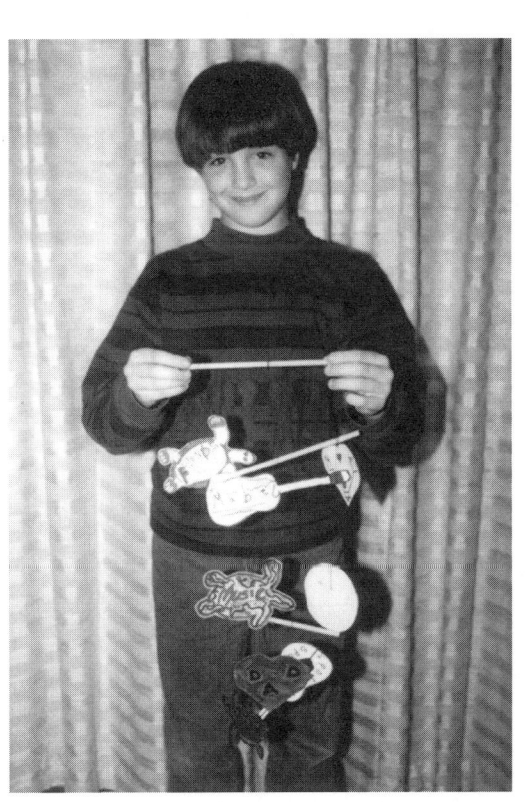

SUGGESTED VALUE THEMES FOR MOBILES

- Family picture mobile — photos of family members, relatives, pets, family events, close friends, etc. Use bright colored poster board to mount pictures. Larger pictures improve visibility. Great for infants and toddlers.

- Appreciation mobile — people and things that the child appreciates

- Heart Tools: FREEZE-FRAME, appreciation, forgiveness, HEART LOCK-IN, send love, stay in your heart, deep heart listen, speak your truth, balance, etc.

- Reminder mobile — I love you, brush your teeth, wake up time, weekend chores, reminder tools to help overcome specific stresses, keep your balance, etc.

- Objects from places that bring up positive feelings (beach, park, desert, campground, sandbox, field, etc.)

Message Mobile

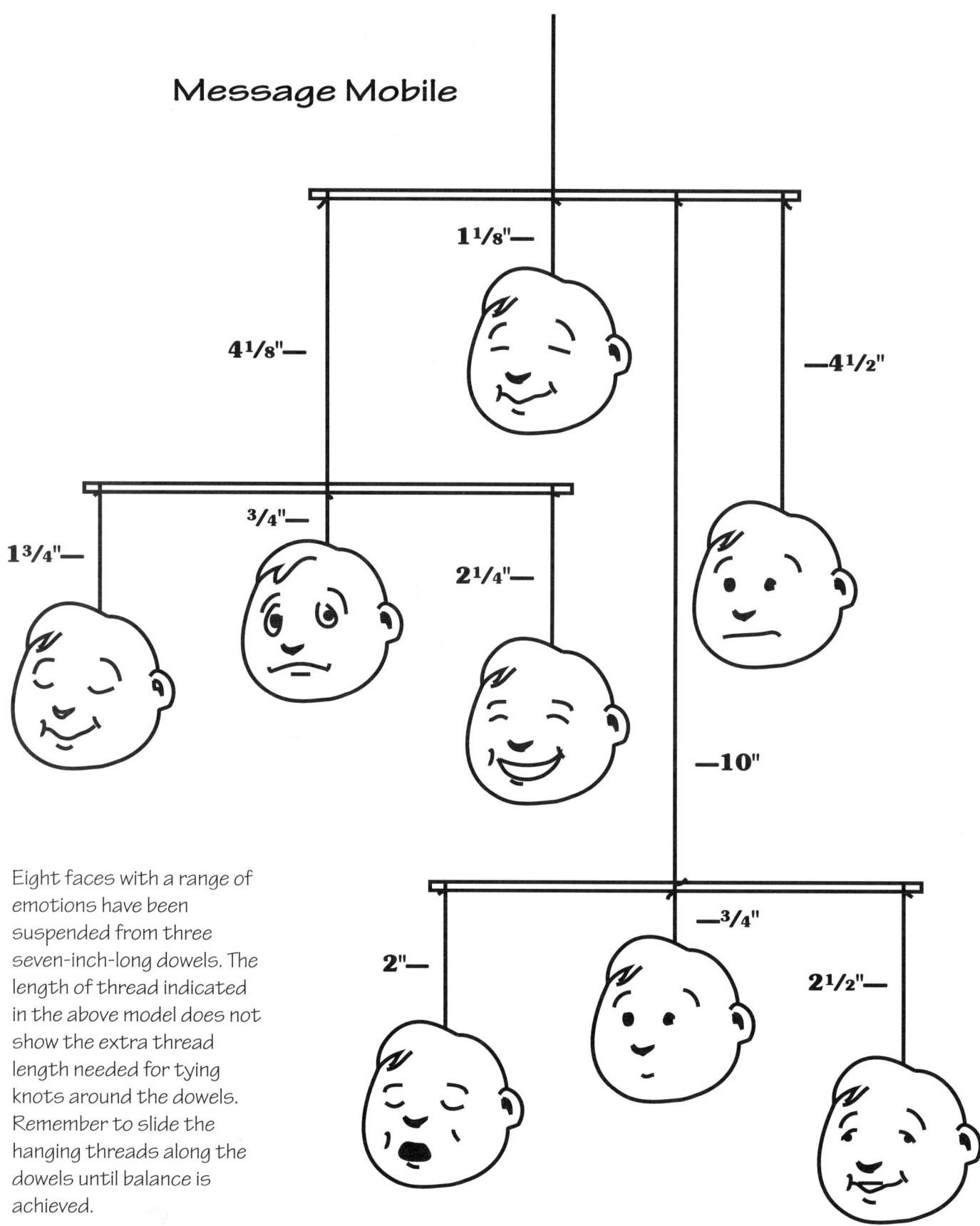

1 1/8"—

4 1/8"—

—4 1/2"

3/4"—

1 3/4"—

2 1/4"—

—10"

2"—

—3/4"

2 1/2"—

Eight faces with a range of emotions have been suspended from three seven-inch-long dowels. The length of thread indicated in the above model does not show the extra thread length needed for tying knots around the dowels. Remember to slide the hanging threads along the dowels until balance is achieved.

Movement, Balance, and Fun

PURPOSE

Playing this series of movement activities helps young children develop hand-eye coordination and physical balance at the same time. They also learn the importance of maintaining emotional and mental balance while playing with other children.

AGES
3-7

TIME
30 minutes

PLAYERS
Two or more children (a small group is better)

LOCATION
Indoors or outdoors

EQUIPMENT
➡ Bright-colored object to indicate a goal or destination (e.g., orange cone, orange laundry detergent container)
➡ Two plastic eggs, two paper plates
➡ A medium-sized sponge ball
➡ Two marbles, two large spoons
➡ Two blindfolds
➡ Two trays, two plastic or paper cups, and a pitcher of water

INSTRUCTIONS

1. Before beginning the activities, have all the children FREEZE-FRAME for ten seconds. (Tell them: Let all of your thoughts drift down to your heart like a leaf falling off a tree, then think of someone or something you love and send love to them.)

2. Remind the children to stay in their soft hearts while playing balancing games. They will want to move quickly, but remind them that going a little slower and staying balanced sometimes gets you there faster. If you lose your balance or make a mistake, it's okay. Just say, "Oops, No Big Deal" and FREEZE-FRAME again to go back to your heart.

3. During each activity, it is important to express appreciation to children who are playing in a balanced way. This not only makes the child feel good, but helps establish a pattern of balanced behavior for all the children.

Activity 1—Paper Plate and Egg. Ask the children to count off 1,2,1,2, etc. and have the 1's form a line, with the 2's forming another line to make two teams. Hand a paper plate and plastic egg to the first 1's and 2's in each line and tell them that they are to carry the egg about ten feet to and around a specific object or goal and back to the starting line. Their next teammate in line will then be handed the paper plate and egg and continue the game. See which team comes in first. Explain that sending love to the egg will make it easier to carry without dropping. If a child drops the egg, remind him to FREEZE-FRAME, pick up the egg, and continue on as planned. If you see a child who is out of control, remind her to go to a soft heart for balance, then move a little slower to help her get to her destination faster.

Activity 2—Pass Around the Circle. Have the children form a circle with enough space between them to move around comfortably. Hand a medium-sized sponge ball to one child and explain the game, saying, "When I say go, pass the ball around the circle to your right." Make sure young children understand the difference between right and left. As the children pass the ball around the circle, vary the directions by adding comments like, to the left, to the right, faster, slower, under your legs. If a child drops the ball, he must pick it up, run around the circle to his starting place in the circle and begin again.

Activity 3—Spoon and Marble. (For children 5 and older). Divide the group into two teams and have them form two separate lines. One player at a time from each team will be carrying a marble in a big spoon to and around a specific object or goal and then back to the starting line. Then the next players in line step up. This activity progresses from simple to more complex.

- Walk to the goal, carrying a marble on a spoon.

- Run to the goal, carrying a marble on a spoon.

- Blindfolded, walk to the goal carrying a marble on a spoon.

- Interlace fingers and hold them palms down away from the chest. Balance the marble on top of the hands and try to walk, change directions, and turn without letting the marble all off.

Activity 4—Tray and Cup of Water. (For children 5 and older, outdoors only). Divide the group into two teams and have them form two separate lines. One player at a time from each team will be carrying a tray with a cup of water to and around a specific object or goal and then back to the starting line. Have the pitcher of water available in case of spilled cups. Refill at point of impact and encourage child to continue.

Creating To Your Heart's Content

PURPOSE

A time-honored activity that gives children a chance to focus while stimulating creative expression is turning them loose with paper, felt pens, and other art materials. Raising balanced children requires a balance of structured and unstructured play. Given the opportunity, many children relish the experience of exploring their imaginations and inventing what is important to them. Expect a lot of talking, laughing, and short periods of intense concentration as they draw and create to their heart's content. Asking the children to explain their creations helps integrate verbal expression into the artistic process.

AGES
3-10

TIME
15 minutes or longer

PLAYERS
One or more children

LOCATION
Indoors or outdoors (with adequate table space)

EQUIPMENT
➡ Plastic or paper table cloth
➡ Paper, felt pens, crayons, scissors, tape, glue, hole punchers, sticky dots, or other creative materials
⇨ Music (background only—try Heart Zones or Speed of Balance)
⇨ Oversize paper
⇨ Video recorder and tape

INSTRUCTIONS

1. Cover the table with protective plastic or paper and set out the art materials.

2. Tell the children they will have a free drawing and creative arts time. Show them the types of material available for use. Tell them they have a time limit and at what time they need to be finished. (Set the time limit according to the age of the children, so they maintain the creative sparkle and fun and stay attentive.) Tell them to begin and create to their heart's content.

3. When time is up, ask each child to explain her creation. The adult should not comment on the skill level of the final product, just appreciate the creative expression and effort.

4. Ask children to help clean up by placing all tools in a central place, throwing away trash, etc.

VARIATIONS

1. Play music in the background (try Heart Zones or Speed of Balance) to add a pleasant or upbeat atmosphere.

2. Have children create in pairs or groups, using oversize paper.

3. Have children act out the subject matter of their creative work.

4. Have children dictate to you a short one or two sentence story line that describes their creative work. Attach it to their piece.

5. Videotape the creative expression time and explanation period, then have the children watch the videotape.

Prime Time

PURPOSE

How does a busy parent balance a loving, supportive parent-child relationship with a packed daily schedule? By establishing a routine of "Prime Time." Prime Times are those short moments each day where parent and child bond and reinforce their primary relationship of love. They are times to check in, share stories of the day, be quiet together in the heart, and maintain a quality connection despite a busy, hectic lifestyle. Here's an effective Prime Time program.

AGES
4-18

TIME
5 minutes or longer

PLAYERS
Adult and one child

LOCATION
Indoors

EQUIPMENT
None

INSTRUCTIONS

1. Together, parent and child decide on a convenient Prime Time to meet once per day and connect. Even if the length of time is only a few minutes, make a commitment to follow through each day. As a reminder, post the meeting time on a centrally located place like the refrigerator, bulletin board, or a visible wall space. When the scheduled time conflicts with other time demands, make sure you reschedule another time so that continuity is maintained.

2. Establish a guideline that sincere listening without interruptions will take place during any Prime Time conversation. The parent should especially model quality listening from the heart.

3. During Prime Time, use the following activities or ideas as triggers to build or enhance your heart connection. Over time, new ideas will spring from your intuition which knows what activity is appropriate for the circumstances and mood of your child.

PRIME TIME ACTIVITIES

- Do a two minute HEART LOCK-IN, sending love and appreciation to each other.
- Each person in turn talks about the highlights of their day — what went well and what was challenging.
- Give each other a long hug.
- Share qualities that you appreciate about each other.
- When either of you is stressed-out or had a hard day, have the other person just listen with compassion, and then mirror back the words and feelings. Sincere listening is caring in action.
- Each of you share five things that you appreciate about your life.
- Read a favorite story together or make up one together.
- Learn the words of an inspiring, short poem that becomes a regular ritual to recite together.
- Post a picture of the two of you together in your regular meeting place as a reminder of the love that you feel for each other.
- Be quiet for a few moments and send heart together to someone that needs love or compassion.
- Go deep into your hearts and make a heart wish of something that you would like to happen in your respective lives. Share the results together.

Balance

Ooops! No Big Deal!

PURPOSE

Balance is a multi-faceted and learned skill that begins in earnest with an infant's first efforts at walking and develops throughout life. In the learning process, lack of motorskill coordination or mistakes in judgment inevitably occur. Focusing in the heart builds mental and emotional balancing skills that play a crucial part in detecting the body's sense of balance and developing balanced attitudes. Children build confidence as they learn how to move forward when faced with disappointment or frustration. Tools like FREEZE-FRAME and "Oops, No Big Deal" teach children to focus on a point of inner balance during life's ups and downs and calmly pick themselves up and go on when they lose balance.

AGES

5-14

TIME

20 minutes or longer

PLAYERS

Adult and two or more children

LOCATION

Indoors (on carpeted area) or outdoors (on grassy area)

EQUIPMENT

➡ A spoon and plastic egg for each player

➡ One (5' long) 2"x 4" piece of wood (balance beam)

➡ Two small 4"x4" blocks (for balance beam supports)

➡ Beach balls and tennis or golf balls for each pair of children

➡ One 2' or 3' long dowel or stick for each player (the thicker and heavier the better, at least $5/16$" diameter)

INSTRUCTIONS

1. Explain to the children that they are going to participate in a number of fun activities that will require balance. By listening to the heart, they will be better able to stay calm and focused. Just as a baby will fall down, then get back up again when learning to walk, we need to do the same when we make mistakes or lose our balance. Tools like FREEZE-FRAME and "Oops, No Big Deal" can help us deal with any disappointment or frustration. Also, emphasize the importance of safety "spotting" in some of the activities where players need to be closely watched and followed by other players to prevent a fall.

2. Ask the children to do a short FREEZE-FRAME with their focus on the heart. This act will establish a focus point for all the activities that follow. Remind them to practice FREEZE-FRAME and "Oops, No Big Deal" if they lose their balance or patience.

3. When the activities are finished, ask the children whether they were able to keep their focus on their heart. Discuss how practicing FREEZE-FRAME and "Oops, No Big Deal" when mistakes were made helped them.

149

Activity 1 - Age 5 and up

Have the children balance their weight on their right foot with the left leg lifted in the air. Request that the children focus their attention on their heart while balancing. After fifteen seconds, switch legs.

Activity 2 - Age 5 and up

Have children place a spoon in their mouth and carry a plastic egg across the balance beam. Emphasize the element of fun along with balance.

Activity 3 - Age 6 and up

Set up the balance beam by placing the five-foot-long, 2"x4" board on the support blocks. Have children hop on one leg across the beam. With young children, hold their hand as they hop until they find their own balance. Use spotters as necessary to prevent a fall.

Activity 4 - Age 6 and up

Provide a blown up beach ball for each pair of children and have them place the ball between their two foreheads. Have the children practice walking across a flat area without letting the ball drop. If their skill level warrants a more difficult challenge, ask them to walk across the balance beam without letting the ball drop. (One child will walk backwards while the other walks forwards.) Use spotters because of the awkward foot movements required. This activity can also be done on a flat surface in a race format.

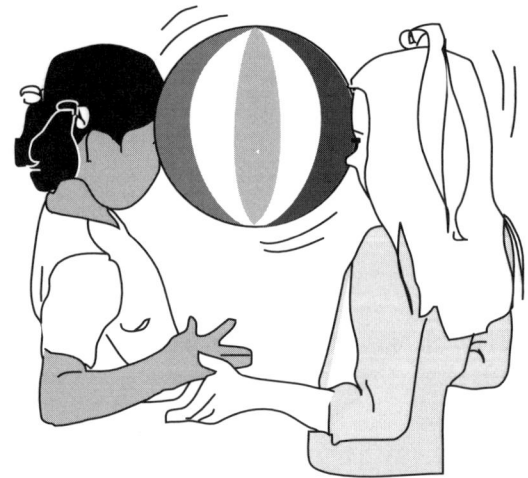

Activity 5 - Age 8 and up

Have two children walk across the balance beam, each gripping the ends of two dowels (like they are carrying a stretcher between them), with either a tennis ball or golf ball resting between their two dowels. (One child will walk backwards while the other child walks forwards.) The goal is to walk to the end of the balance beam while trying to keep the ball from rolling off the dowels. Add more balls if appropriate. Remind them to keep their focus in the heart.

Activity 6 - Age 9 and up

Provide each child with a dowel, emphasizing that these sticks are for a balancing game and are not to be used for sword-fighting or hitting. The goal of this activity is to balance the dowel for five to ten seconds (or less depending on age) with one end in the palm of one hand and the other facing the sky. Demonstrate the activity first. Tell children how you are focusing your attention in the heart, then balancing the dowel.

Heart Tool Hopscotch

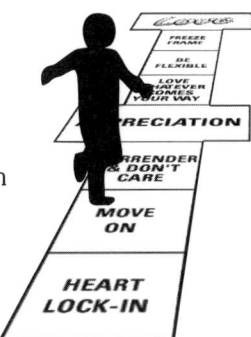

PURPOSE

Staying balanced while hopping on one foot can be a challenge for anyone. When children feel overcare or frustration in playing games, it's even harder to maintain balance or play their best. Consciously focusing in the heart makes it easier to stay balanced — mentally, emotionally, and physically. "Heart Tool Hopscotch" teaches children how to balance in the heart while playing hopscotch.

AGES
6-11

TIME
10 minutes

PLAYERS
Two to four children per hopscotch pattern

LOCATION
Outdoors (preferably on concrete)

EQUIPMENT
➡ White chalk for drawing the hopscotch pattern on concrete
➡ Colored chalk for writing words
➡ A flat stone for tossing

INSTRUCTIONS

1. Create the hopscotch pattern using the hopscotch diagram on page 152. The first three blocks should be eighteen-inch squares, joined together to form a column. The first square is labeled, "HEART LOCK-IN," the second square, "Move On," the third, "Surrender and Don't Care." The fourth block should be about three feet wide and eighteen inches long and labeled Appreciation. The fifth, sixth and seventh blocks should be eighteen inches square and labeled, "Love Whatever Comes Your Way," "Be Flexible," and FREEZE-FRAME. The final block or finish line should be about the same size as the fourth block and labeled "Love."

2. Explain to players that it's easier to stay balanced on one foot when you stay in your heart. The game starts with the "HEART LOCK-IN" block, so ask each person to lock-in their hearts for ten seconds before beginning the game. Also ask them to practice each tool they land on. The tools written in each square are important reminders that in order to have fun one must stay in the heart.

3. The beginning player starts behind the "HEART LOCK-IN" block, tosses the stone into a block, then hops on one foot until reaching the block in which the stone landed. Any throws that land outside of the pattern are to be thrown over again. The fourth block "Appreciation" and the final block "Love" are the only blocks in which the player can put both feet down. If the stone lands in any other block, the player must retrieve the stone while standing on one foot and toss it into another block. Should the player lose balance and put both feet down, he must start over.

4. Each player gets three tosses of the stone to make it to the finish line. It's a good idea to try to hit the Love block as soon as possible and go straight to the finish. Remind the children to not become discouraged or frustrated if they have to start over. Ask them to use the tool that was written in the square where they "Oopsed" to help them stay in their hearts.

5. The winner is the first player who makes it to the finish line with the fewest number of tosses.

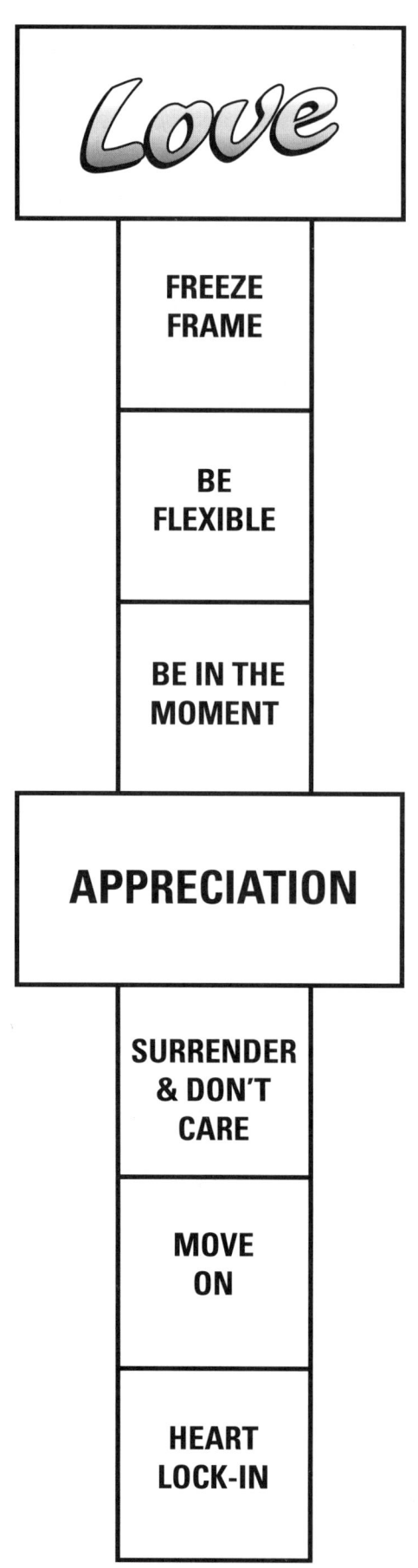

Balance Your Account Card Game

PURPOSE

This game helps children understand the power of the Heart Tools. It shows them how to create assets (positive experiences) and balance out deficits (stressful experiences). The deficit cards give examples of being "out of the heart" and suggest an asset card that can help children get "back in the heart." Playing life skills games in a fun environment helps children practice and prepare for challenging situations before they happen. Learning sinks in deeper and they are better equipped to handle real life challenges with heart intelligence.

AGES

7-14

TIME

20 minutes or longer

PLAYERS

Two to six children (per deck of cards)

LOCATION

Indoors or outdoors

EQUIPMENT

➡ Table or flat surface

➡ Cardstock cut into 52 playing cards 2 ¼" x 3 ½" each

➡ scissors

➡ (optional) Two different colored pens

➡ (optional) Pencil and paper

INSTRUCTIONS

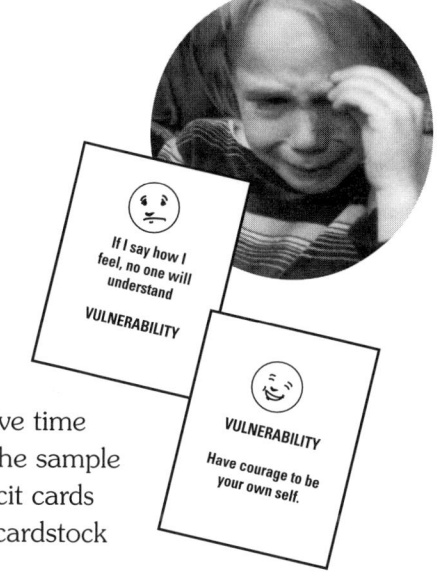

1. Prepare the deck of cards. Having the children create their own asset and deficit cards is a wonderful activity. If you don't have time to do this, photocopy the sample pages of asset and deficit cards (pages 155-160) onto cardstock and cut up the cards.

2. To make their own cards, help children make a list of 26 common deficits that they experience. Use examples from typical school, family, friend, or household situations. (See sample pages of deficit and asset cards for examples.) Create 26 deficit statements from the children's list and choose a Heart Tool to go with each one. Write one deficit and the accompanying tool on each card until you have 26 deficit cards. To create the asset cards, copy each tool you wrote on a deficit card onto a new, blank card along with a short explanation of that tool until you have 26 asset cards. Print clearly as this will become your permanent deck of cards. To distinguish between asset and deficit cards, draw an asset picture about each tool using the same colored pen on all asset cards. Then draw a deficit picture using the other colored pen on all deficit cards.

THE GAME

1. Playing this game is similar to the memory game, "Concentration."

2. After shuffling the cards, place all 52 cards with the type facing down.

3. Play begins clockwise starting with player to left of dealer.

4. Starting player turns one of the cards over face up, then turns over another card trying to match the correct asset card with the correct deficit card.

   Example: Starting player turns up the deficit card, "I don't want to go to their house for dinner." The player then turns up another card. If the second card is the asset card "Surrender and Don't Care," it's a match! The player then takes both cards (asset and deficit) and may try to match cards again.

5. If the player doesn't find matching cards, the play moves onto the next player in sequence.

6. The winner is the person who has the most matching pairs of asset and deficit cards at the end of the game.

VARIATION

Play the game similar to the card game, "Go Fish" or "Old Maid." Each player is dealt five cards. Starting player reads one of her own deficit or asset cards and then asks another player if she has the matching card. If selected player gives requested card, the asking player immediately puts down matching cards (both asset and deficit) and now may ask for another card from the same or another player. If player being asked doesn't have the requested card, she tells the asking player, "Go to the Bank." Asking player then picks up a card from the draw pile and play proceeds to the next player. If all draw cards are taken from the pile, play continues until one of the players has won by balancing all their asset and deficit cards with no remaining cards in their hand.

**USE THE
TOOLS**

To change a tire you
need a tire tool. To
change a situation you
need a Heart Tool.

ENJOY NATURE

Take time to
appreciate the
flowers, trees,
and all of nature.

VULNERABILITY

Have courage to be
your own self.

REMEMBER

Remember
to go to your heart
to find the answer.

**TALK TO
A BUDDY**

Share the situation
with a friend. A
buddy can often help.

FREEZE-FRAME

Stop! Put your
thoughts on pause and
go to your heart.

**SPEAK
YOUR TRUTH**

Say the things
you really feel
from your heart.

HEART LOCK-IN

Take 5 minutes
in your day to
go to your heart
and feel love.

**DEEP HEART
LISTENING**

Let your heart listen.
That way you hear
a person's deeper
heart and not just
someone's words.

PRACTICE CUT-THRU TO FEEL BETTER

Stir the worried feeling in your heart to find new ways to help.

BE IN THE MOMENT

Do your best and don't waste time worrying about the future or the past.

BALANCE

Not too slow, Not too fast, Not too much, Not too little.

MOVE ON

Go on! Do what you need to do.

GO TO YOUR HEART

The heart is the best place to stay when you're upset.

BE LOVING

Everyone needs some love and care.

BE FLEXIBLE

Things will be OK. Be willing to accept changes you weren't expecting.

FAIR HEART

Ask your heart what's fair for everyone.

LOVE THE PEOPLE

Love everyone. There's a jewel in everybody.

BE POSITIVE

Choose the heart.
Look for the
best in life.

**BE RESPONSIBLE
FOR YOURSELF**

It's up to you
to use the tools.

**GO TO
NEUTRAL**

Don't judge.
Keep your energy
from going down
the drain.

APPRECIATION

Stop fussing!
See if you can
find something
to appreciate.

**LOVE
YOURSELF**

Remember the
good you do.
Someone else sees it.
Why not you?

BE CASUAL

Not too loud,
not too soft.
Not overly excited,
not too serious.

PLAY

Ask your heart
to show you
what's fun to do.

**SURRENDER
AND
DON'T CARE**

Go to your heart and
let go. Maybe something
good will happen.

**Why
do I feel
so miserable?**

USE THE TOOLS

**I need a break
from all this
homework.**

ENJOY NATURE

**If I say how I
feel, no one will
understand.**

VULNERABILITY

**Why do I
have to wash
the dishes?**

REMEMBER

**I just can't stop
thinking about
what happened
today.**

TALK TO A BUDDY

**I'm so angry!
You always
blame me!**

FREEZE-FRAME

**If I tell them
what I really feel,
they won't like me.**

SPEAK YOUR TRUTH

**I'm not
happy today.**

HEART LOCK-IN

**What he said
is dumb.**

**DEEP HEART
LISTENING**

**I'm worried
about my cat.**

**PRACTICE CUT-THRU
TO FEEL BETTER**

**I can't stop
worrying about
the test.**

**BE IN
THE MOMENT**

**I ate too much
candy. My
stomach aches.**

BALANCE

**I don't want
to do my
homework.**

MOVE ON

**That really
made me mad!**

**GO TO
YOUR HEART**

**That new kid
bothers me.**

BE LOVING

**I'm not moving
out of my room
for a guest.**

BE FLEXIBLE

**Maybe if I cut
in line, no one
will notice.**

FAIR HEART

**I don't like people
from other countries.**

LOVE THE PEOPLE

I'm not
having any fun
today.

**BE
POSITIVE**

I don't want
to Freeze-Frame.

**BE RESPONSIBLE
FOR YOURSELF**

I think
she is a jerk.

GO TO NEUTRAL

I hate this food.

APPRECIATION

I'm not good
at anything

LOVE YOURSELF

I'm so excited I
could scream
for joy!

BE CASUAL

I'm bored
right now.

PLAY

I don't want to go
to their house
for dinner.

**SURRENDER AND
DON'T CARE**

No Man's Land

PURPOSE

"No Man's Land" is a challenging activity that develops balance, coordination, and cooperation. It helps children learn to not overcare or lose confidence when they make a mistake by practicing the tool "Oops, No Big Deal" and going back to the heart to rebalance. It also builds teamwork skills and is loads of fun.

AGES

8-18

TIME

15 minutes or longer

PLAYERS

Adult and three to ten children

LOCATION

Outdoors (preferably on a grassy lawn)

EQUIPMENT

➡ Walking planks—Two sanded 4' (or longer) 2"x 4" boards

➡ Resting stations — Five sanded 3' (or longer) 4" x4" boards

➡ One blindfold for every player

⇨ Stopwatch or watch with second hand

⇨ Paper and pencil

INSTRUCTIONS

1. Create a path from the Old Land (starting line) to the New Land (final destination) by placing the ends of the first walking plank on two resting stations. Next, lay down a third resting station and lay one end of the second walking plank on the third resting station and the other end on the second resting station. Try to create an irregular or curved path between resting stations. (See diagram on page 162) Place the fourth resting station approximately four feet away from the third station with no plank in between. Do the same thing with the fifth resting station. In order to reach the final destination (fifth resting station), players will have to complete the path by moving one of the planks to the empty space between the third and fourth and then between the fourth and fifth resting stations. This will take teamwork and coordination while players stand on planks.

2. The object of the game is to walk on the planks safely from one resting station to the next until all players have reached the final destination. Falling off a plank into the hot, volcanic lava below makes a player lose their sight (become blindfolded). Each blindfolded player climbs back on the plank they fell from and continues walking the planks with coaching from team members who are not blindfolded and are watching them from resting stations. Team members give verbal instructions or hold the blindfolded player's hand if they are on the same plank.

Because there may be fewer planks than players, players must cooperatively share the use of the planks. A player cannot move backwards. Emphasize that mistakes might be made and to call out and practice the tool "Oops, No Big Deal." The game is over when all players have reached the final destination or if all players have fallen off and been blindfolded.

3. Debrief afterwards and discuss what helped and what didn't.

VARIATIONS

1. Time the group. This can be an incentive to do better in future runs.

2. Divide the group into teams and record best times for each teams.

3. Have the group come up with more variations that encourage fun teamwork, such as everyone holding hands as they walk the planks, walking the planks backwards, etc.

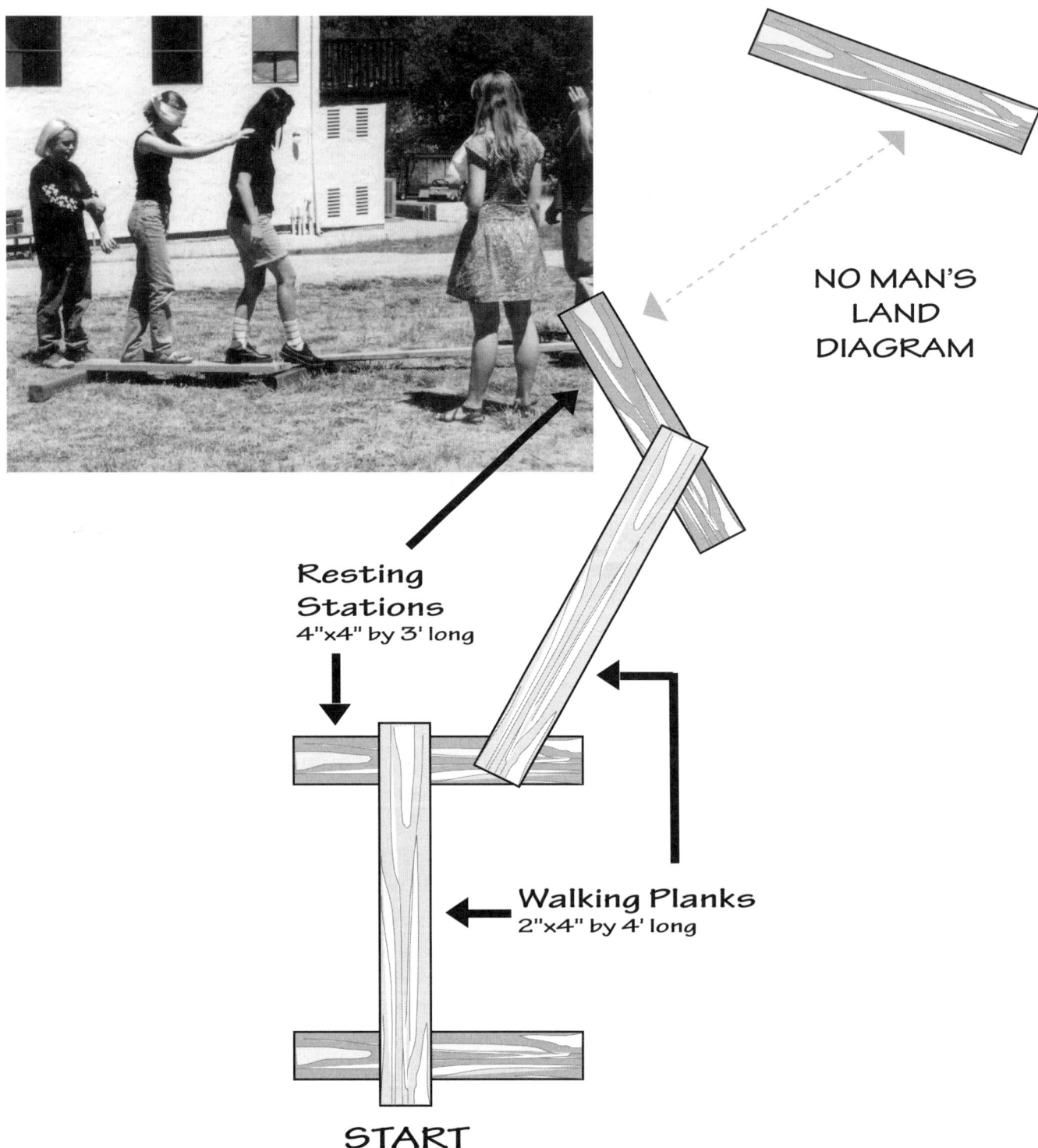

NO MAN'S
LAND
DIAGRAM

Resting
Stations
4"x4" by 3' long

Walking Planks
2"x4" by 4' long

START

The Balance Sheet

PURPOSE

Communication between adults and teens can easily downgrade into the proverbial "ships passing in the night." While there is a common household, there is often no shared language or culture. It's essential that dialogue remain open for family bonding to be sustained. The "Balance Sheet" is a helpful tool to revitalize communication and keep abreast of the day-to-day lives of teens and adults. Because teens respond best to frank communication, this activity is an excellent means to accomplish that goal.

AGES
12-19

TIME
20 minutes or longer

PLAYERS
Adult and one or more children

LOCATION
Indoors (with a flat surface to write on)

EQUIPMENT
➡ Clear cup with water
➡ Pencil and paper for each player
⇨ *Heart Zones* or *Speed of Balance* tape, tape recorder

INSTRUCTIONS

1. Find a suitable time when adult(s) and teen(s) can sit down together, preferably at the end of the day. Initiate the discussion by holding up a cup full of water as a metaphor for how we start the day full of energy. As the day rolls along, stressful issues, events, or conflicts will put little holes in the cup, draining the cup of water (energy). At the same time, positive events, conversations, and accomplishments will add energy to the cup. Where do we stand at the end of a day? Have we emptied our water cup because of excess stress? Or have we maintained our enthusiasm and sense of balance by responding positively to life's events?

2. Hand out a sheet of paper to each player. Instruct them to write Balance Sheet on top of the paper and draw a line down the middle. Label the left column "assets." Label the right column "deficits." Have each player write down the positive events, conversations, and interactions of the day under their assets column.

To trigger the memory of how the day went, retrace your day from waking up, going to school, work or other activities, coming home, etc. Do the same with the deficits column, recording, in a few words, those issues, conversations, and events that were negative or drained energy. (See sample on page 164).

3. After completing both columns, write down a conclusion about your day. Was it energizing and satisfying? Was it stressful and draining? Was the amount of stress greater than the amount of quality experiences? Where could you have reduced your stress and added more satisfaction?

4. Complete the activity by each person sharing the story of their day. Deep heart listen to each other and appreciate the sincerity of communication.

5. Discuss how often you would like to do the "Balance Sheet" together. Some families do it daily, others prefer doing it weekly.

VARIATIONS

1. Consider doing a Balance Sheet of the past week rather than the past day.

2. Use the Balance Sheet as a tool for evaluating pros and cons of different projects, vacation choices, problems, vacation choices,problems, reconciling conflicting opinions on a subject, etc.

3. Play *Heart Zones* or *Speed of Balance* in the background as the players fill out their Balance Sheets.

Balance Sheet

Assets	Deficits
Play basketball	Washing too
Eat stuffed pork chops	many dishes
Read	Taking out the
Sleep	greasy garbage
Seeing my friends	Not playing basketball
Seeing my parents	Getting impatient
My team wins	with people
Going to movies with	Losing a game
my friends	Allergies

Conclusion — It was a good day. I am glad to see that I had more assets than deficits. The assets make me feel great and help me relax. If I had more deficits, I definitely would feel out of balance. Bad things don't take away the good things so much unless they counter each other out. Then I would have to deal with them.

164

CHAPTER
9

Expanding Perception

Learning To Perceive

PURPOSE

Helping toddlers learn to perceive when they are "in the heart" or "out of the heart" helps them understand how to respond effectively to situations. It builds a foundation of inner security and emotional intelligence that will assist children throughout life. The "Terrible Twos" is when toddlers begin to explore what it means to be assertive. They will often say "no" when they mean "yes" but want to test your reaction. Two-year-olds are easily frustrated and there can be temper tantrums or other exaggerated behavior. They are beginning to perceive opposites such as, big/little, hot/cold, short/long, like/don't like, happy/sad. By helping your toddler identify how he feels when he is "in the heart" versus "out of the heart," he can make better assessments. He learns that when he feels frustrated, angry or sad, it's because he is "out of the heart." When he feels loving and happy, he is "in the heart." This game teaches children age two to four how to shift back to the heart to perceive differently and make better choices.

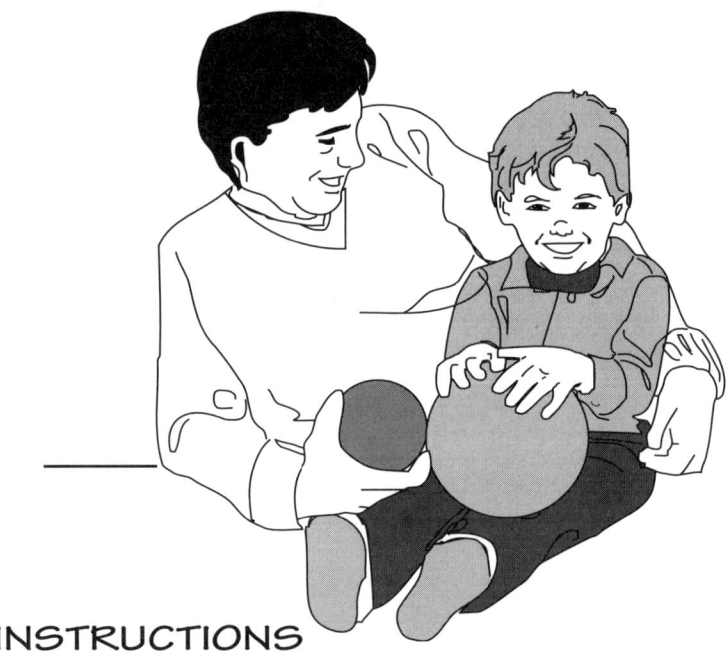

AGES

2-4

TIME

20 minutes

PLAYERS

Adult and one to three children

LOCATION

Indoors

EQUIPMENT

➡ A small hand mirror

➡ Crayons, scissors, and materials to illustrate opposites

⇨ Materials for making puppets

⇨ Buddy Bubbles tape, tape recorder

INSTRUCTIONS

1. Familiarize your child with opposites.
   Here are some examples:

   • Show a large ball for "big," then a small ball for "little."

   • Sing a song "loudly" then "softly."

   • Provide a sip of warm soup and explain it is "hot," then provide an ice cube to feel the "cold."

   • Switch a light on and off saying, "'Lights on' means light, 'lights off' means dark."

   • Provide two different lengths of string for "long" and "short."

   • "Open" a door and step "out." Come back "in" and "close" it.

2. Ask your child to show you how she looks when she is happy. Then hold up the mirror, show her how she looks and say, "When you are happy, it's because you are 'in your heart.'"

3. Ask the child to show you how she looks when she is sad or angry. Hold up the mirror again to show her how she looks and say, "This is how you look when you are 'out of your heart.'" Ask the child, "Which face feels better?" Children usually choose the happy face.

4. Make a sad or pouty face and explain, "When you are wearing this kind of face, it doesn't feel good. You feel angry or sad or want to cry or hit someone. You need to go back to your heart and become loving again." Place your hand in the area of your heart and say, "Freeze! Be very still and don't move. Freeze means it's time to send love to someone or something. That makes you happy again and helps you know what to do next." Let's practice.

5. Tell the toddler that the next time you see her out of her heart, you will bring out the mirror and ask her to play "Freeze" and get back in her heart. You will remind her to send love or pretend that she is cuddling a puppy or hugging someone. Then you will ask her what would be the best thing to do next.

6. Play games with the mirror for several days or until your child associates being happy or loving with being in the heart and angry or sad with being out of the heart. During the day, remind your child to "Freeze" and send love when she is wearing a sad or angry face. Display the mirror in a prominent place where your child can play with it easily. When your child gets angry or upset, hold up the mirror and say it's time to "Freeze." Then help your child switch to the feeling of love. After the child is happy again, show her what she looks like in the mirror and tell her she is back "in the heart" again. Then ask her what would be the best thing to do next. Appreciate her for making a better choice.

VARIATIONS

1. Help your child make and decorate happy and sad puppets, but refer to the happy puppet as "in the heart," and the unhappy puppet as "out of the heart." Have the toddler show you each puppet one at a time and you guess if the puppet is "in the heart" or "out of the heart." When the child gets angry or upset, point to the "out of the heart" puppet and say it's time to "Freeze." Then help the child switch to the feeling of love. After the child is happy again, point to the happy puppet and tell her she is back "in the heart" again.

2. Have your child listen to the tape *Buddy Bubbles: Magical Games for a Child's Heart* and sing the "Heart Magic™ Song" to see how to get back in the heart fast whenever he feels fussy, angry, or sad — "out of the heart."

167

Banquet For The Senses

PURPOSE

"Banquet For The Senses" provides a delightful opportunity for children to experience a range of sensory responses to various stimuli while blindfolded. Being blindfolded helps eliminate pre-judgments about how something smells, tastes, feels, or sounds and helps children perceive each of their senses in a new way. Note the spontaneous expressions on the children's faces.

AGES
5-13

TIME
20 minutes or longer

PLAYERS
Adult and three or more children

LOCATION
Indoors (in a quiet place)

EQUIPMENT
➡ Blindfolds for everyone
➡ Blanket or tablecloth
➡ Plates or cups to hold different objects and food
➡ 4 sources of smell (e.g., spices, flowers, colognes, soaps, foods)
➡ 4 sources of taste (e.g., orange, lemon, onion, apple, cinnamon, honey, salt, pepper)
➡ 4 sources of touch (e.g., a rough rock, smooth stone, waxy leaf, piece of cotton, fur, sponge, sandpaper, plastic, metal, velvet)
➡ 4 sources of sound (e.g., bell, wood blocks, sandpaper, whistle, gong, trickle of water poured from one bowl to another, etc.)
➡ Plenty of paper towels or napkins

INSTRUCTIONS

1. Place the different objects on plates or in cups without the children seeing them. Line them up and cover with a blanket.

2. Hand out a paper towel or napkin to each player.

3. Blindfold everyone and request quiet. No talking in the room. Remind children not to guess out loud what they think the objects are.

4. Remove the blanket and begin creating the different sounds, one by one. Allow ten seconds of sound and ten seconds of silence between sounds.

5. Pass around the different objects of smell, giving each child ten seconds to smell each object. If possible, use an adult volunteer to help pass around the objects.

6. Next, pass around the different objects of touch.

7. Then pass around the different items of taste, encouraging the players to use their napkins or paper towels if their hands get sticky.

8. Finally, ask the players to silently take off their blindfolds and be aware of the first thing that catches their eye and their attention.

9. Discuss what everyone experienced. Ask the players which sense they enjoyed the most, which one they liked the least, and which objects were easiest to identify.

VARIATION

After each sensory round (sound, smell, touch, taste), ask each child to guess what the sources were. See if the children can come to an agreement, but do not divulge the answer.

Did You Ever See?

PURPOSE

Creating puns is fun and imagining word combinations helps children see new concepts. Without imagination, the wheel would never have been invented. Had Columbus not visualized the world as round instead of flat, he may never have sailed to the new world. This activity helps children perceive the difference between the analytical mind and imagination. In trying to think of puns, the mind can get stuck on the usual meaning of a word. Heart imagination, on the other hand, can see new possibilities.

AGES
8-14

TIME
20 minutes or longer

PLAYERS
Adult and one or more children

LOCATION
Inside (at a table or desk)

EQUIPMENT
➡ Pencils and paper for each player
➡ Dictionaries (1 per 3 children)

INSTRUCTIONS

1. Read a few examples of puns (below). Have children draw pictures of what they visualize as you read.

2. Ask children to write their own puns. It may take a few minutes, but most children can quickly come up with some good ones. Encourage them to look around the room at different objects or look through a dictionary for ideas.

3. Have children share their puns. This is a great activity to spark imagination and laughter when children are restless or bored, wondering what to do on a rainy day or while riding in the car, and to enhance creative writing.

EXAMPLES

Cardboard Box
Did you ever see a cardboard box?

Barn Dance
Did you ever see a barn dance?

Diamond Ring
Did you ever hear a diamond ring?

Microwave
Did you ever see a micro wave?

Mountaineer
Did you ever see a mountain ear?

Housefly
Did you ever see a house fly?

Jelly Roll
Did you ever see a jelly roll?

Square Dance
Did you ever see a square dance?

Porch Swing
Did you ever see a porch swing?

Horsehide
Did you ever see a horse hide?

Fishbowl
Did you ever see a fish bowl?

"Oops, No Big Deal"

PURPOSE

Mistakes are made by everyone, but for adolescents mistakes can be painful or embarrassing. This game introduces a tool that can ease some of the discomfort of mistakes by offering fun and hilarious perspectives. "Oops, No Big Deal" is a tool that helps pre-teens and teenagers not judge themselves or others.

AGES
9-15

TIME
20 minutes or longer

PLAYERS
Adult and four or more children

LOCATION
Outdoors (Indoors if there's space)

EQUIPMENT
➡ Book, marble or ping pong ball, spoon, plastic egg
➡ Paper towels
➡ A book of tongue twisters
⇨ Paper and pencil

INSTRUCTIONS

1. Explain the rules of the game. There will be a series of fun activities that require some form of skill, either physical or verbal. If someone makes a mistake, the rest of the players yell out in unison, "Oops, No Big Deal." During the game, the player who made the mistake is eliminated from the game. The last player remaining wins. (Have the group practice saying, "Oops, No Big Deal" three times in unison before the game starts.)

2. The Activities. (Rotate players so everyone participates)

- Carrying a book on your head for ten feet.

- Carrying a ping pong ball or marble on your head or back for five feet.

- Carrying an egg, ping pong ball, or marble on a spoon for twenty-five feet.

- Reciting tongue twisters three times in a row without "miffing" a word.

Tongue Twister Examples:

- Six long, slim, slick, slender saplings grew in the woods.

- How much wood would a woodchuck chuck, if a woodchuck could chuck wood?

- Flexible Flossy Freeze-Framed forgiveness for flaky Frankie Floyd for forgetting french fries at the fish fry.

- Heartful Harry helped heap hoards of heart on unhappy Hannah's hurt hand.

VARIATIONS

1. Divide players into teams to compete against each other or do the different activities at the same time.

2. Have children make up their own tongue twisters of different heart tools.

3. Have children create more activities that are "mistake prone."

4. Have a discussion about mistakes and how people respond when they make mistakes, especially on school tests. Talk about how self-judging blocks clarity and rules out using our talents and energies in an enhancing way. Ask children what their self-talk is like? Do they tell themselves, "You're stupid," or "You idiot," or "My teacher (dad, mom, friend) won't like me?" Talk about how your heart intelligence can show you how to assess yourself without judging yourself when you make a mistake. Telling yourself, "Oops, No Big Deal" helps you find a balanced perspective. Then FREEZE-FRAME can show you what to do next.

5. Have children pick one area where they self-judge (school work, tests, appearance, sports, behavior, etc.) to practice "Oops, No Big Deal," then FREEZE-FRAME to find out how to improve. Have them write down their answers. Discuss the results.

Where Do You Live?

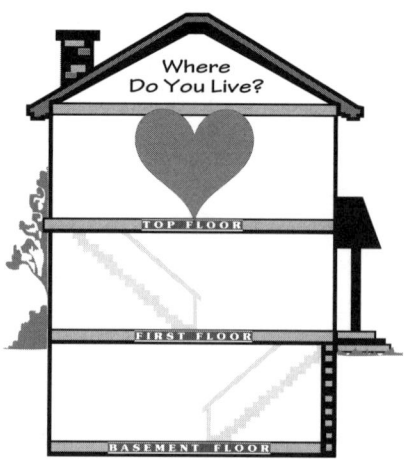

PURPOSE

This activity shows how negative judgments of ourselves or others keep us out of the heart and block solutions. Left unchecked, judgments keep replaying over and over in the mind, making us feel miserable. We may feel a negative judgment is justified because of what someone did. Justified or not, when judgmental thoughts and feelings drain our energy and rob us of our peace and fun, they are a deficit. By using the tools, we can perceive a situation with heart intelligence and find a fair assessment of why a person behaved that way. Then we can decide what we want to change in our thinking so we don't drain our energy. Using heart intelligence, we can eliminate the whisper judgments that stack up inside and find a greater understanding of ourselves, another person, or any situation.

AGES
9-18

TIME
20 minutes or longer

PLAYERS
Adult and one or more children

LOCATION
Indoors or outdoors

EQUIPMENT
➡ Colored and plain white paper, stapler
➡ Pencil for each player

INSTRUCTIONS

1. Explain that we are going to do an experiment. Each participant will keep a journal of how many times they can catch themselves negatively judging for one week. If they sincerely play the game, they will be surprised at how many judgments flash through the mind each day. Explain that everyone judges. Sometimes we do it so quickly that we are hardly aware that we even made a judgment.

2. Each player makes a journal. Give each player two pieces of colored paper for journal covers. Copy one sample page of "Where Do You Live?" house (page 174) and seven blank "Where Do You Live?" templates (page 175) for each player and explain.

THE BASEMENT is where you live when you feel angry, resentful or hurt. You blame or find fault with others or yourself and justify being judgmental and out of the heart.

THE FIRST FLOOR is where you live when you are trying not to be upset and remain neutral. Although someone might not have treated you fairly or did something that was careless, you are trying to go to the heart and find compassion and understanding as you assess the situation. However, negative judgments still come up like little whispers. You need to go deeper in your heart to see, understand, then decide what you want to change in that judgment to find a positive solution.

THE TOP FLOOR is where you live when you have a bigger view of the whole situation. You realize that you are responsible for how you feel. You stop the judgment and ask your heart intelligence how to make things better in the moment. You listen to your heart and do what it says. Sometimes your heart will tell you to sincerely speak your truth to avoid having another judgment arise. Other times, your heart will tell you to have compassion and understanding to find out why someone did what they did. If you are judging yourself, your heart intelligence might tell you to say, "Oops, No Big Deal," stay in your heart, and move on.

3. Ask participants if they can recall any judgments that put them in the basement? the first floor? the top floor? By talking about examples of judgments, we will have a better understanding of what we are looking for as we keep our journals.

4. Each participant is to keep their journal with them and write down when they make a judgment or self-judgment. Sometimes a participant will only be aware of one judgment for the day. Whenever a judgment occurs, make a note in the proper section of the house. Then do a FREEZE-FRAME and ask the heart to give you clarity so that the judgment does not reoccur. You might not get an answer immediately. If you keep going to the heart and are diligent and sincere in asking, your heart will give you a release and a solution. Don't be discouraged if the judgment comes up again and you stay on the first floor for awhile. Keep asking your heart intelligence and try not to leave any judgment unresolved. Write the answer in the top floor section.

5. Ask the participants if they would like to learn the secret to a quick elevator ride from the basement to the top floor. The secret is this: When you recognize a judgment and FREEZE-FRAME, try to drop all thoughts and breathe love from the center of your chest for twenty seconds. Breathing love puts you deeper in the heart. The answer may still not come to you right away, but it will come more quickly as you go deeper in your heart.

6. Remind participants each day to record judgments in their journals. At the end of one week, discuss results.

Where Do You Live?

Where the heart resolves a judgment by releasing stress and coming to a greater understanding.

Examples:
→ I'm overcaring and starting to judge myself. I'll CUT-THRU and send myself compassion and understanding.
→ When I sincerely listen to Steve, even though he's different, he does have interesting things to say. I'll go to my heart and care instead of judging him.
→ My parents just don't understand what it's like to be a teen. I'll try to not judge them and get mad the next time and ask to have a heart-to-heart talk instead.

TOP FLOOR

Where we try to let go of a judgment but it still comes up as a whisper judgment and resurfaces again.

Examples:
→ Maybe I'm overreacting a little bit. I'll practice CUT-THRU and send heart.
→ They don't want to listen to me, but I can't expect them to. They don't know any better.
→ I could have done the same thing they did. I need to have some compassion.
→ Sometimes I can't keep my mouth shut. Instead of judging myself for being stupid, I'll tell myself "Oops, no big deal," stay in my soft heart, and do better.

FIRST FLOOR

Where we keep our junk and hold on to stressful judgments.

Examples:
→ There she goes again (nagging me).
→ Everybody is being so mean to me. They're making fun of me.
→ John's idea was really stupid.
→ If they would just listen, they might understand what I'm saying. Forget them!
→ Why did we have to go to the arcade instead of the roller coaster? I hate the arcade.

BASEMENT FLOOR

Where Do You Live?

TOP FLOOR

FIRST FLOOR

BASEMENT FLOOR

"That's Cool, Dude"

PURPOSE

Young people often act "cool" to try to impress their peers and fit in. This behavior is often at the expense of what their heart might tell them to do and say. The object of this activity is to encourage teens to use their hearts and minds to decide what is truly "cool" behavior.

AGES
10-18

TIME
45 minutes or longer

PLAYERS
Adult and six or more children

LOCATION
Indoors

EQUIPMENT
➤ 8 ½" x 11" paper
➤ Pencil and paper for each small group
➤ Blackboard or greaseboard and two colors of chalk or markers
⇨ Heart Zones or Speed of Balance tape, tape recorder

INSTRUCTIONS

1. Review the Heart Map directions on page 49 before leading this game.

2. Instruct players that they are going to first Mind Map and then Heart Map the topic "Being Cool" in small groups of three or four. Afterwards, the small groups will share their results in the larger group. Demonstrate what mapping is by reading the Heart Map directions on page 49 as you illustrate a sample Heart Map (on another topic) using the blackboard or greaseboard. Encourage everyone to contribute freely, pointing out that there are no right or wrong answers.

2. Divide the group into small groups of three or four players according to age. Each small group needs a piece of paper, a pencil, and a scribe.

3. Have the scribe in each group draw a horizontal line across the middle of the paper. Draw a small circle in the center of the top section with the word "Cool" in the center of the circle.

4. Instruct the players to feed ideas to the scribe on what constitutes "cool" behavior. With each player's ideas, the scribe draws a line from the central circle that looks like a spoke on a wheel and writes a few descriptive words of what's been said on the line. Ideas that are similar or in the same category are written on lines that branch off the main topic line. Allow all ideas to be included, however "uncool" they may sound. Don't judge or censor anyone's ideas during this brainstorming session.

5. When everyone is done, ask all players in the smaller groups to do a one-minute FREEZE-FRAME, asking their heart what is "cool behavior."

6. After the FREEZE-FRAME, have the scribes in the small groups draw a circle in the center of the bottom section with the word "Cool" in the center of the circle. Have the small groups refocus and now do a Heart Map on what constitutes "being cool."

7. Have the small groups read both their maps and discuss differences or similarities between their Mind Map and their Heart Map.

8. Have each small group share their results before the larger group. As they speak, map their answers on the chalkboard or greaseboard. Use one color for the Mind Map and another color for the Heart Map.

9. Ask what conclusions can be derived from the larger group Heart Map. Discuss what is truly "being cool" as opposed to "appearing cool?"

VARIATIONS

1. Discuss in the days following the mapping session what new observations they have made about "cool behavior." Discuss why it's cool to "follow your heart."

2. Play *Heart Zones* or *Speed of Balance* during the FREEZE-FRAME and in the background while they are creating their Heart Maps.

Judgment Game

PURPOSE

"Judgment Game" requires players to give opinions on issues, celebrities, personalities, foods, and other age-appropriate topics. Half the fun is seeing how players will respond to other player's choices and what internal processing occurs as they deliberate. It is stated in advance that there are no right or wrong answers, there are only perceptions. Afterwards, it is important to discuss what kinds of responses, judgments, or self-judgments occurred while the players participated in the game. Players end up discussing how challenging it is to just be yourself.

AGES

10-18

TIME

15 minutes or longer

PLAYERS

Adult and six or more children

LOCATION

Indoors or outdoors (with space to form three lines)

EQUIPMENT

➜ Pencil and paper

INSTRUCTIONS

1. Create a list of twelve to fifteen names of celebrities or issues that might spark a keen response from the group. Try to avoid highly controversial issues that might leave unresolved feelings without a proper forum to resolve them. Issues or topics that have been used successfully: Madonna, Michael Jackson, Heavy Metal music, Rap music, Arnold Schwarzenegger, the current President of the United States, broccoli, milk, steak, death penalty, popular movies, or school subjects.

2. The object of the game is for each player to make a choice as you call out each name — either approving, disapproving, or unsure of a specific celebrity or issue. Three lines are formed. Approval choices form a line at one side of the room. Disapproval choices form a line at the opposite side of the room. Unsure or neutral choices form a line in the middle of the room.

3. After the game is over, ask players the following questions:
   a. Did any of you change or even consider changing your opinion once you saw other players' responses?
   b. Did anyone judge someone else for their choice?
   c. Did anyone feel embarrassed, awkward, or self-judgmental about their choice?
   d. Why is it difficult to make a choice or state your perception, especially if it runs against the flow of popular perception?

VARIATION

Use words where players have to define themselves. If they feel a word strongly represents who they are, they stand in the approval line. If they're neutral or unsure, they stand in the middle line. If the word doesn't represent them, they stand in the disapproval line.

Sample words: gentle, courageous, loud, playful, sincere, modest, analytical, emotional, energetic, physical, talkative, introspective, sensitive, mellow, imaginative, social

Self-Perceptions

PURPOSE

The adolescent blueprint propels teens to define themselves in relation to peers and society. This transitioning self-identity can be like a tailless kite in a strong wind, shifting from one trend to another without direction. The fast pace of life only magnifies the rapid fluctuations that teenagers experience. Perceiving oneself from the heart can provide a strong anchor in navigating through the winds and turns of this unsettled age. This activity offers a way for teens to view themselves with more depth and a greater sense of hope and direction.

AGES
13-19

TIME
20 minutes or longer

PLAYERS
Two or more children

LOCATION
Indoors or outdoors

EQUIPMENT
➡ Paper and pencil for each player
➡ A small mirror for each player

INSTRUCTIONS

1. Present an overview of this activity. During the teen years, there are many questions about identity. Who am I? Where do I fit in? How do I compare to my peers? What is there to do and with whom? There will be three rounds in this activity in which you will write down answers to these types of questions. Everyone will have the use of a small mirror to help them explore their perception of themselves. This is a private exercise unless you want to share with everyone afterwards. Explain that Round 1 begins with seeing obvious physical traits as well as a general sense of who you are. Round 2 goes deeper by starting off with a short FREEZE-FRAME, then exploring what you appreciate about yourself (assets) and what needs improving (deficits). Round 3 begins with another FREEZE-FRAME, then asking your heart the questions: who are you and where are you going? Viewing yourself from the heart's perspective will give you a more objective look at yourself. The FREEZE-FRAME tool will help you get out of the mind and see yourself more clearly without self-judgment.

2. Hand out a mirror, paper, and pencil to each player. In Round 1, tell them to write down their observations about themselves without judging their comments.

3. After a few minutes, start Round 2 and guide everyone in a FREEZE-FRAME. Remind them to go deeper into the heart as they further explore themselves. Then have *everyone* write down their assets and deficits.

4. In Round 3, begin with another FREEZE-FRAME. Request that they go deeper this time. Have them write down answers about who they are and where they are going.

5. Conclude the activity with a discussion of their experiences. *Ask some of the following questions:*

   • Was it easy or hard viewing yourself? Why?

   • How much of your view of yourself is determined by social status? How much of your view of yourself is determined by a true heart assessment?

   • Do your perceptions of yourself change?

EXAMPLES

14-Year-Old Girl

Round 1—I'm an 8th grade girl, with blond hair, glasses, braces, freckles, and hazel eyes. I love TV, movies, and ballet.

Round 2—Assets—nice, quiet, friendly, willing, good grades, nice ring, hair, eyes, caring family. Deficits—glasses, braces, freckles, get mad easily, fight with brother.

Round 3—I am going to finish high school then maybe go to college. Maybe I will act or be a surgeon, like on ER. It looks fun but I know there's a lot of accuracy, trauma, and hours. I want to get married too. I'll just wait and see what happens.

14-Year-Old Boy

Round 1—basketball fanatic, rapper, someone who is vain, not quiet.

Round 2—Assets—fly (not shy), likes music, lots of energy, desire of basketball and sports. Deficits—gets too personal about basketball and my body, talks too loud, too impatient.

Round 3—I'm a person in a building who most of the time is in the room where the party is. I am going into new rooms to try things differently, to expand.

14-Year-Old Boy

Round 1—A regular teenager with a hat to protect him from the world and coat to keep him warm.

Round 2—Assets—emotionally disciplined, sensitive, loves challenges and goals, semi-flexible, likes almost everyone. Deficits—Sometimes I get mad at grown ups. I shift moods everyday, can get quietly defensive and depressed. I don't have a hobby. I like to dream or think too much.

Round 3—Regular person connected to my interior intelligence. With my creative mind, I'm going to have a hard working job for five years. I'm going to sleep in a van, use water fountains to brush my teeth, and eat whatever I can. When I have saved up enough money, I will get a house in Palm Springs or North Carolina and then get a job and live peacefully as a hard working man. When or if a girl comes along, I'm going to use my heart and practice staying in my heart.

15-Year-Old Boy

Round 1—I see Peter. I see freckles, red hair, green/blue eyes, family nose, family lower lip. Red cheeks, braces, yellow teeth, zits, need to brush my hair.

Round 2—Assets—funny, nice, friendly, intelligent, strong, calm. Deficits—a bit flaky, need to be more truthful to myself and others, need more discipline.

Round 3—I am an animal, a human, another step on the evolutionary ladder. I can and will make a difference whether I like it or not. I, like everyone, wish to be more than I am. I wish to live and live well. I am not satisfied with my surroundings and find most people beneath me, although I do not judge them as people because of that. I will go on to do what I want with my life, although I do not know what that is and probably will not know until I am ready to. I will probably accept my fate, if fate it is.

Stress Survey

PURPOSE

How do people handle stress? Initially, that topic might not seem like a top ten area of interest for teens. But when they finish this activity, they will have expanded their perceptions of themselves and others. From Phase I through Phase III, teens will learn how they, their peers, their parents, and other adults respond to the pressures of modern living. They will discover how stress is increased by judging oneself, other people, or issues. This activity requires several sessions to complete.

AGES
13-19

TIME
Phase I, 40 minutes
Phases II and III, 30 minutes each

PLAYERS
Adult and two or more children

LOCATION
Indoors (Phase II survey can be done outdoors in a public place, such as a mall, supermarket, etc.)

EQUIPMENT
➜ Chalkboard, greaseboard, or flip chart with appropriate markers
➜ Paper and pencils for each player
➜ Clipboards or something hard to write on

INSTRUCTIONS

1. Explain the objectives and phases of the project. Phase I talks about how teens and adults experience and respond to stress, leading to an explanation and practice of the tool FREEZE-FRAME. Phase II is a field study where everyone completes five or more surveys with their peers, parents, and other adults. Phase III completes this activity with a tally and conclusion.

2. Begin Phase I with a discussion on the following questions:

   • What are some of the stresses that you, your peers, or adults experience? List answers on the left side of the chalkboard under "Stresses."

   • What are some of the effects of stress — mentally, emotionally, and physically — on yourself and others? List answers in the middle of the chalkboard under "Effects."

   • What are some of the solutions that you and others use to handle stress? List answers on the right side of the chalkboard under "Solutions."

   Examples:
   Stresses: who to date
   Effects: worry, stomach ache
   Solutions: eat, diet, drink, smoke, don't date

   Discuss how most solutions either:

   a. don't solve the problem or
   b. come after the stressful experience has had its effect

   Illustrate how FREEZE-FRAME intervenes when a stress is happening by writing the word "FREEZE-FRAME" between the categories of "Stresses" and "Effects."

3. Now do a FREEZE-FRAME with the players and have them experience the benefit. Ask them to FREEZE-FRAME one of their stresses (not their most difficult one). Ask them to practice FREEZE-FRAME on two more stresses before the next time the group assembles so they can talk more about it before beginning Phase II. The next time the group meets, discuss the results of their FREEZE-FRAME practice.

4. Phase II is the field study where the teens will ask five of their peers, parents, and other adults the three questions listed in #2 above. In order to tally the results of the survey, the group must come up with four likely multiple choice answers for each question and a blank for "other" that the respondent can fill in. Help them prepare the multiple choice answers. After the group has completed their multiple choice answers, type and photocopy at least five questionnaires for each teen to use for the survey. Help teens decide where to do their survey. (If they choose a store, remind them to get permission from the manager.)

5. Phase III tallies the results of all the questionnaires. This can be done by either a small group of individuals or by the whole group. You can use a bar graph for the most common answers or calculate percentages for the different categories of answers.

6. Discuss results and ask for any conclusions from the group. What did they learn? Do you think that as a society we handle stress well? Do you or your peers know how to handle stress well? Why do people have so much stress? Can you see how a tool like FREEZE-FRAME helps people deal more effectively with stress?

VARIATIONS

1. Categorize the questions into "teen stress" and "adult stress." Compare the answers, seeing what was common and what was different.

2. Consider publishing the results in a school or local newspaper.

3. Survey other topics, like communication issues, peer pressure, choices, etc. Have the group come up with the questions.

EXAMPLE

Report from a teenager following the stress survey activity:

"My buddy and I went to the mall. At first I was nervous. People said they didn't have time but then I got the hang of it. It felt like a game. We were on a mission and we didn't care what people thought after awhile because we were having fun. I wasn't surprised by the adult results. I knew work would be the ultimate stress. Adults get up early, work all day, come home late and then yell at their kids, husband, or wife. Adults get stressed over what all Americans get stressed over: work and money. That's the American Dream! Most adults try to relax, blow it off, or exercise. Personally, I think FREEZE-FRAME could work well with anyone. It can stop the stress in the moment. Teen's number one solution to stress is drugs and that's not surprising because they definitely make people relax. But that solution works only momentarily, like going on a vacation. You always have to come back to reality and deal with it."

Stress Survey of Teens
Taken by Two 14-Year-Olds at a Local Mall

Teen Stresses

1. Relationships   5
2. Family   10
3. Mean people   3
4. Drugs   4
5. School   11
6. Money   6
7. Work   5
8. Time   3
9. Friendships   2

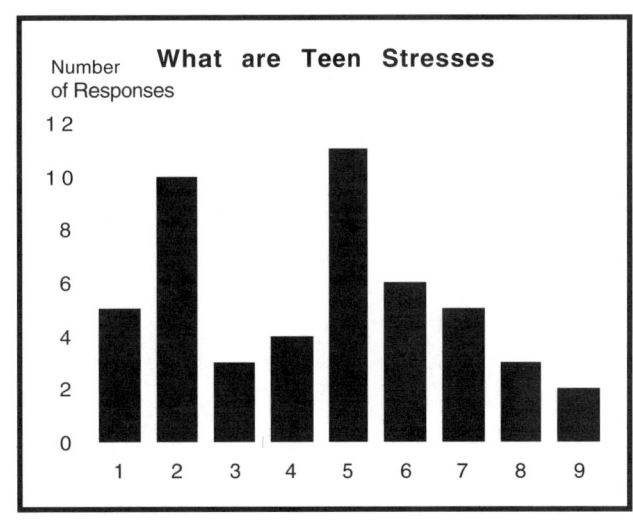

Teen Effects

1. Get angry   16
2. Physical pain   3
3. Depressed   11
4. Fatigued   10
5. Nervous   7
6. Bored   6
7. Lose sleep   4
8. None   4

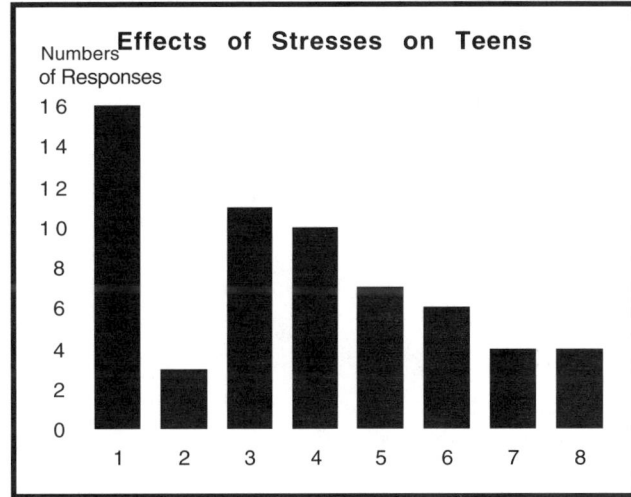

Teen Solutions

1. Meditate/pray   2
2. Buddy talk   5
3. Exercise/Sports   8
4. Get mad   5
5. Drugs   12
6. Relax   10
7. Forget about it   9
8. Try to change   3
9. Music   7
10. Relationships   4

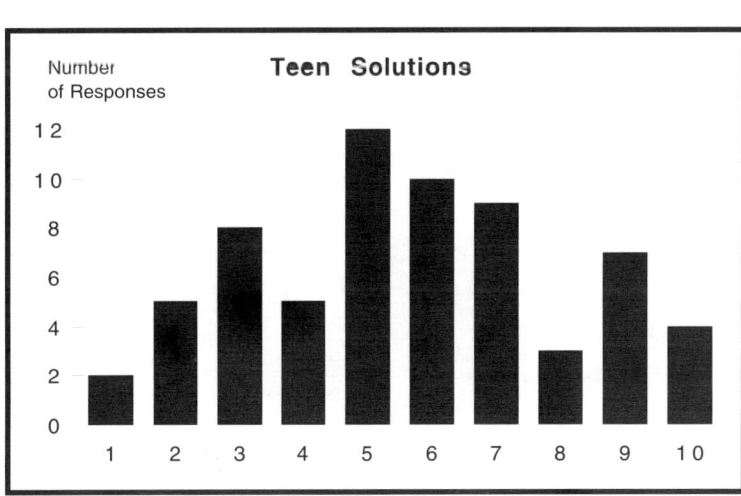

Stress Survey of Adults
Taken by Two 14-Year-Olds at a Local Mall

Adult Stress

1.	Kids	11
2.	Work	32
3.	Traffic	12
4.	Boss	5
5.	Not enough time	10
6.	Government	13
7.	Money	24
8.	Relationships	15

Adult Effects

1.	Angry/irritable	25
2.	Tired	21
3.	Tense	6
4.	Physical pain	21
5.	Confusion	2
6.	Depressed	12
7.	Nervous	11
8.	Worry	8
9.	Eat more	4
10.	Can't sleep	7
11.	Doesn't bother me	2

Adult Solutions

1.	Meditate/Prayer	14
2.	Talk about it	8
3.	Exercise/Sports	45
4.	Get mad	1
5.	Drugs and alcohol	9
6.	Relax	17
7.	Reflect and step back	23
8.	New circumstances	8
9.	Healthy diet	2
10.	Watch movies	2
11.	Enjoy nature	7
12.	Music	4
13.	Eat	2

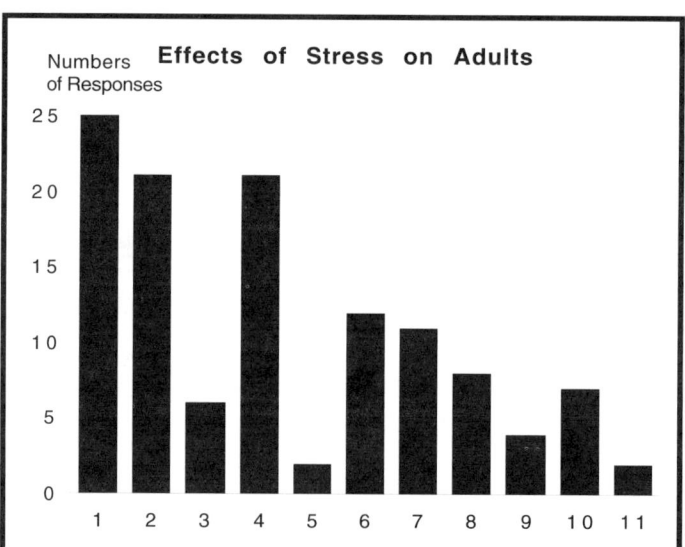

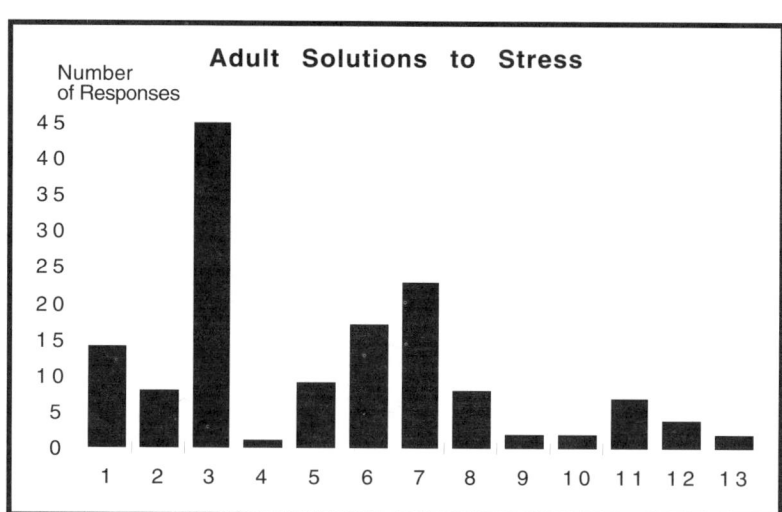

CHAPTER
10

Empowering
Teamwork

FREEZE-FRAME March

PURPOSE

Music is a fun way for children to express their spirits and lift their hearts. Enjoying music together is a great alternative to family TV watching. This activity combines a simplified version of the tool FREEZE-FRAME with marching music and requires active listening and self-control to succeed. Families and groups learn to move and play as a team. Whether you play "FREEZE-FRAME March" in the home or classroom, a lot of fun will be generated for all players.

AGES

2-8 (younger children will enjoy following along)

TIME

10 minutes

PLAYERS

Adult and three or more children

LOCATION

Indoors or outdoors with room to move in a circle

EQUIPMENT

➜ Tape or CD Player
➜ Marching music with a fun beat. (An excellent marching piece is "Heart March" on the album Speed of Balance by Doc Lew Childre. "Heart March" has a wonderful rhythm for this game and can be played repeatedly.)

INSTRUCTIONS

1. The gamemaster instructs the players that everyone is going to march to music in a circle, following the movements and lead of the gamemaster. When the music stops, everyone will do a short FREEZE-FRAME. Once the music starts up again, the marching will continue. If an adult is not available to stop and start the music, appoint a helper from the group to push the pause button two or three times during a song.

2. Demonstrate a few movements that the players will be performing: marching steps, clapping hands, etc. Demonstrate the FREEZE-FRAME position as well.

3. Ask everyone to stand in a circle, turn on the music, and begin. Encourage everyone to join in the march.

4. When the helper pauses the music, everyone freezes in the FREEZE-FRAME position. The gamemaster announces that when the music starts up again, everyone is to place one hand on their heart and send love or appreciation to the person in front of them as they march. When you announce, "Let's go, send out your love," the helper starts the music and the march continues.

VARIATIONS

1. Each time the music stops, the gamemaster calls out who to send love to next — the person marching behind you, one child in particular, your parents, the whole world, etc.

2. The gamemaster asks the children to follow the person in front of them and leads the children in different formations around the room, snaking around furniture, holding hands and forming a figure eight, etc. Older children will have fun following new dance steps and movements.

3. Have different family members take turns being the gamemaster, giving the instructions, and leading the movements.

Picture Puzzle

PURPOSE

Younger children tend to play alongside each other rather than actually playing together. The object of this activity is to learn to play together in harmony as a family or in the classroom. Finding a common interest is important in teamwork. In this game, a small group of children create their own special place together, such as a farm, fairground, zoo, beach, park, school, airport, city, etc. Choose a place that is likely to be familiar to all the children.

AGES
3-5

TIME
20 minutes or longer

PLAYERS
Adult and one to three children

LOCATION
Indoors (at a large table)

EQUIPMENT
➡ Picture book(s) of buildings, animals, etc. typically found in the location you decide to illustrate for your picture puzzle
➡ Pencil and paper
➡ A large piece of poster board
➡ Colored markers or crayons
➡ Scissors or mat knife
⇨ Several large pieces of butcher paper or poster board taped together to form a work area big enough for all children to participate
⇨ Several cans of play dough or modeling clay.
⇨ (Optional) Washable paints, brushes, paper or old sheets spread on the floor, and a smock for each child

INSTRUCTIONS

1. Decide on a picture puzzle theme, such as a zoo, farm, playground, amusement park, airport, school, beach, etc. Ask your children if they have ever visited such a place and ask them to share their experiences.

2. Show children pictures of the puzzle theme from a picture book.

3. Have the children help you make a list of a few items to draw in the picture puzzle (buildings, people, animals, objects, etc.).

4. Using a large piece of poster board, draw an outline of the picture and the different items that the children identified. The picture should be designed in pencil, then traced with a colored marker.

5. Assign each child an item in the puzzle to color in, using crayons or markers.

6. Cut the finished picture into puzzle pieces.

7. Have the children put the puzzle back together. Verbally appreciate their teamwork and the picture you all have created together.

VARIATION

Build a model. On several large pieces of butcher paper or poster board taped together, draw a picture outline of the chosen theme (farm, airport, zoo, etc.)

- Tell the children they are going to build a model. Show children pictures from a picture book to help them design their model. For example, if they are going to create a farm, try to find pictures that show the entire body of each animal. Before the children create their clay models, they must first draw and color (or paint) different items that belong in the picture (e.g. a barn for cows, a chicken coop for chickens).

- Divide the group into teams and hand out materials for drawing, coloring, or painting the picture theme. Help each team decide what part of the theme they are going to draw, color, or paint.

- After the artwork is completed, hand out clay or play dough for the creation of the animals or other objects that fit in the picture. Each child will create one clay model for their team. Have the picture book available to help. Be prepared for unique-looking objects but discourage criticism among the children.

- Afterwards, point out to the children what they have created by working together. Consider inviting parents or friends to visit the finished model and have the children speak about their unique creations.

Clap To The Beat

PURPOSE

Music is a universal language that has the capacity to capture the hearts of children from every culture. In this simple activity, the adult creates a simple beat that children accompany with clapping or (if available) shakers, sticks, and other noisemakers. Once a rhythmic beat is established, then lyrics can be created and added by the children. What results is an entertaining and creative time enjoyed by everyone, even if there are no musical experts present.

AGES

6-15

TIME

15 minutes or longer

PLAYERS

Adult and one or more children

LOCATION

Indoors or outdoors

EQUIPMENT

➜ Pencil and paper for each group

➜ (Optional): Shakers, sticks, noisemakers

INSTRUCTIONS

1. Demonstrate a simple rhythm by clapping to the beat.
   Example: simple rhythms in numbers of beats or claps

   • Clap — clap — clap — clap, repeat
   • Clap — clap/clap — Clap — clap/clap, repeat
   • Clap — clap — clap — clap/clap, repeat

2. The children clap along to the selected rhythm. When they have the beat right, try other rhythms.

3. Form everyone into small groups, pairing younger children with older children. Hand out a pencil and paper to each group. Each group is to write simple lyrics that the rest of the family can accompany with rhythmic clapping. Emphasize that the lyrics are to be clean and heart-inspired — celebrating fun. Humor is encouraged but no put downs are allowed. Ask the groups to practice saying their lyrics to the beat.

5. Have each group stand up and demonstrate their clapping rhythm. Then have them perform their lyrics while everyone else claps along.

Example:
Clapping beat: "Clap — clap — clap — clap"
Lyrics:

We want a party with good things to eat,
Games we can play with and lots of good treats.
Laughing and smiling we'll stay up real late,
Telling funny stories that make us feel great.

VARIATION

A father came up with the following variation. The father clapped a rhythmic beat on his eight-year-old son's knee and the son duplicated the beat on his father's knee. Then the son changed the beat on his father's knee and the father followed along. The process continued for ten minutes with both son and father spontaneously creating and duplicating some very sophisticated beats. A very special father-son communication emerged.

Go For It

PURPOSE

This fast-paced activity encourages both individual and team strategy, physical agility, and the use of FREEZE-FRAME. Expect occasional confusion and hilarity when opposing players vie for the same ball. Encourage respect for each other while strategizing and having fun. "Go For It" is an excellent game to play with a mixed age group, whether in a family, neighborhood, or school, and builds team spirit.

AGES
7-14

TIME
20 minutes or longer

PLAYERS
Adult and six or more children

LOCATION
Outdoors (or in a gymnasium)

EQUIPMENT
➡ 2 tennis-sized balls
➡ 2 strips of rope or 4 cones for boundary lines
➡ Whistle

INSTRUCTIONS

1. Create team boundary lines approximately thirty feet apart. Place two balls about ten feet apart in the center of the playing area between team boundaries.

2. Divide children into two teams, numbering the players according to size and ability so their match ups on the opposing team are as fair as possible.

3. Explain the object of the game and the rules. Each team stands at their boundary line. The gamemaster will call a number then blow the whistle. When the whistle blows, the numbered player from each team tries to successfully grab at least one of the two balls and then run back to the team boundary without being tagged by the other player. For every ball brought home, a point is scored. If a player with a ball is tagged by the opposing player, the tagged player is out and can't score a point. The opposing player who makes the tag either already has a ball in hand or can grab the remaining free ball but is not allowed to grab or claim credit for the ball the tagged player is carrying. Discourage any players from "hovering" or lingering around a player who is about to grab a ball as opposed to both players sincerely trying to grab a ball themselves.

4. After each round, the gamemaster announces the score then calls out the next number and blows the whistle again. Play continues until everyone has had a turn. FREEZE-FRAME "time outs" should be called to strategize and assess how the team effort is working, especially at the midway point.

5. Prior to the game, have each team do a short FREEZE-FRAME on what strategies to use.

Ask questions like:

   a. Which one of the two balls is best to grab? (Players are allowed to move laterally along their endline to get closer to one of the balls in the middle.)

   b. If an opposing player goes for the same ball, what is the best strategy to use in response? Go for the other ball or try to compete with the opposing player for the same ball?

   c. If frustration arises, what is the best response to handle disappointment? Encourage all team players to speak up and practice sincere listening to build the team spirit.

6. Each team is allowed two FREEZE-FRAME time-outs to reformulate their strategies. Allow two minutes for each time-out. After the game, have the group do another FREEZE-FRAME then discuss what was fun, challenging, or an effective strategy.

VARIATION

In a Round Robin type of format, send as many as three players out from each team at the same time. If a ball is grabbed, it can be thrown to another teammate in bounds and then that teammate can step over their team boundary for a point. If a ball is dropped or poorly thrown, the point is lost. The same rules of tagging apply.

Heart Tools Skit Game

PURPOSE

Drawing on children's creativity and imagination, this activity reinforces the use of the tools in a family or classroom through play-acting, pantomime, and skits. It provides great fun and can been used to entertain the family instead of watching TV on occasion. The game begins with a short, impromptu skit which depicts someone getting out of their heart, then Freeze-Framing, and finally using a secret tool (drawn from the tool card pile) to get back in their heart. Points are scored when the tools are correctly guessed by the observers. Whether played by individuals or teams, the enjoyment, laughter, and increased understanding of the tools makes everyone a winner.

AGES

7-18 (Children under 7 can play if teamed with teen or adult)

TIME

20 minutes or longer

PLAYERS

Adult and two or more children

LOCATION

Indoors

EQUIPMENT

➡ Heart Tool asset cards from "Balance Your Account" card game (pages 155-160)
➡ Paper and pencil
➡ A coin
⇨ Make up, dress clothes, props, lighting

RULES

1. Decide whether the group will play as individuals or in teams. Base your decision on familiarity with the tools as well as age and number of players. Children under seven need to be on a team with an older child or adult.

2. Select the Heart Tool cards (on page 155-160) from the list on page 193 to create a deck.

3. Individuals (or teams) take turns acting out skits that depict someone being out of their heart, then using a tool to go back to their heart. The tool to be used is drawn from the Heart Tool card pile.

4. The object of the game is to score the most points. In order to score a point, the team or individual watching the skit has to correctly guess which Heart Tool is being acted out without the name of the tool being mentioned. Pick a player to keep score.

1. Basic Heart Tool Cards for teams with children six and younger:
- Be Loving
- Appreciation
- HEART LOCK-IN
- Be Positive
- Talk to a Buddy
- Deep Heart Listening

2. Heart Tool Cards for children seven and older (include list 1 also):
- Speak Your Truth
- FREEZE-FRAME
- Enjoy Nature
- Go to Neutral
- Practice CUT-THRU to feel better
- Be Flexible
- Be Casual
- Move On
- Surrender and Don't Care
- Fair Heart
- Be Responsible for yourself

INSTRUCTIONS

1. Flip a coin to decide which individual or team gives the first skit.

2. Shuffle the Heart Tool cards. Each individual or team draws from the top of the deck to see which tool to use in their skit.

3. Each individual or team has ten minutes to create a short, impromptu skit which depicts someone getting out of the heart, Freeze-Framing, then using the tool drawn to get back in the heart.

4. After each skit is given, the opposing teams try to guess the tool. For every correct guess, a point is scored.

5. After all individuals or teams have given their skits, tally up the points and see who is the winner.

EXAMPLE

One team drew the card "Appreciation." Three children, ages five, eight and nine, created the following skit about a mother giving her two children each a new toy.

Mother: "I just went to the store and bought a new toy for each of you."

Children (together): "Oh boy," and they each grab a toy away from the mother and start playing with it.

Boy: "I like your toy better. It's bigger. I want that toy," and starts to grab it away.

Girl: "No, you can't have it, that's my toy."

Mother: "Stop fighting or I will take both toys away." The children both stop and FREEZE-FRAME.

Girl: "Thank you mom, for my new toy."

Boy: "I have lots of toys. It's okay if her toy is nicer. Thank you mom for buying me this toy."

End of skit—The two opposing teams in the audience both accurately guessed the tool: "Appreciation."

VARIATION

Bring makeup, dress-up clothes, props, and lights to enhance the acting.

The Maze

PURPOSE

"The Maze" is a team game that requires careful observation and draws on all players to help decipher a hidden path. Using a large maze of squares as a playing field, a gamemaster secretly creates a hidden path which the players, one by one, must try to guess and weave their way through. No talking is permitted, although nonverbal methods of communication may be used. Eventually, after numerous attempts and use of the tools FREEZE-FRAME and "Oops, No Big Deal" to relieve frustration, a player figures out the hidden path and the other players follow suit.

AGES
7-18

TIME
30 minutes or longer

PLAYERS
Adult and four or more children

LOCATION
Indoors (a large space) or outdoors (on grass or paved surface)

EQUIPMENT
➡ Masking tape is the easiest and most commonly used material to create a maze.

Other options are listed.

➡ For indoor use—100' roll of masking tape
➡ For use on pavement—two pieces of white chalk
➡ For use on grass surfaces—100' coil of rope, hammer, 4 metal or wooden stakes, a knife to cut the rope, and 50 twist ties (commonly used to tie plastic trash bags together). This option is the most difficult to make but can be used over and over again
➡ Paper and pencil
➡ Tape measure
➡ A small bell or other noisemaker
⇨ Stopwatch or watch with a second hand

INSTRUCTIONS

1. Create a maze of five rows with five squares (one foot long) in each row. (See maze diagram on page 196) If all players are older than twelve, consider expanding to six squares in six rows.

   a. If using tape, measure and tear off six, five-foot-long pieces of tape and place them on the ground exactly one foot apart with lengths evenly matched up. Complete the maze by measuring and tearing off six more, five-foot-long pieces and placing them exactly one foot apart and perpendicular to the other pieces. This will create a maze of twenty-five squares. When creating a six-foot-square maze, use seven, six-foot-long pieces of tape lengthwise and seven pieces widthwise. If using tape on carpet, turn and tape up ends so tape is easy to peel off afterwards.

   b. If using chalk, use the same measurements as tape.

   c. If using rope, measure and cut a twenty-one-long foot piece of rope. Form a square by coiling the rope around stakes that are hammered into the ground five feet apart in four corners. Knot loose ends together and cut excess rope with a knife. Next, cut eight 5' 3" long pieces of rope. Using two twist ties per knot, place and attach four of pieces perpendicular to two sides of the existing 5' x 5' square, spacing them one foot apart. Place and attach the remaining four pieces by weaving them over and under the other four pieces. Tie together all loose pieces of rope with two twist ties for strength, including those places where the ropes intersect to form squares. Cut excess rope with a knife. Roll up maze after use and store.

2. The gamemaster copies the maze diagram onto a piece of copy paper, then secretly draws an invisible path that can take players through the maze. Match the difficulty of the path to the age level of the players. See sample paths on page 196. Clearly note on paper the beginning square that players must locate and how they must proceed from square to square until they locate the last square from which to exit.

3. The goal of the game is to get all players to successfully identify and walk through the invisible path in the maze. The gamemaster will feed back to the individual players whether their choice of a square is correct and on the path or not. As long as a player continues walking on correct squares, he can continue. Once he steps on a square that is not part of the invisible path, he must stop and go to the back of the line where other players are waiting to enter. No talking is permitted among players, although nonverbal methods of communication may be used. If a player steps on a line or talks, his turn is over and he must go to the back of the line. Players who correctly exit through the path should non-verbally help those players who have not finished.

4. Players enter the maze one at a time by guessing the starting square in the first row. They may not stand or enter along the finish side nor stand behind the gamemaster (who stands behind the finish line) or peek at his paper. After the first player enters the maze, look to the gamemaster to see if you picked the entry square on the invisible path. The gamemaster will say "GO AHEAD" if it is on the path, or ring a bell if the square is not on the path. Do the same for each square. As long as you continue guessing correct squares, you can proceed through the maze. When you step onto an incorrect square, you must turn around and try to exit the maze the same way you entered it. At that point another player will enter the maze. All players need to carefully observe and remember which squares are correct and which are not. When the entire path has been navigated, then up to three players can follow on the maze at the same time so everyone can get through quicker. If one of those three makes a mistake, however, all three must exit and start again.

5. The gamemaster asks, "Are there any questions?"

6. After all questions have been answered, the gamemaster says, "You have one minute to talk amongst yourselves to devise non-verbal communication strategies."

7. The gamemaster announces (after one minute), "Let the game begin in silence. No more talking."

8. After the game is over, have everyone discuss how they experienced the game. Was it challenging, frustrating, fun? Did they have to FREEZE-FRAME at all? Or tell themselves, "Oops, No Big Deal?" What was the group dynamic? Were some people more involved than others? What kind of nonverbal communications were used? What other kinds of nonverbal communication could be used in the future?

VARIATION

Time the event, beginning with the start of the game and ending when the last person has successfully navigated through the invisible path. Consider penalizing the group a minute every time someone talks. Add a minute to the total time period for every penalty.

Maze Diagram for Gamemaster to Create Secret Maze Patterns

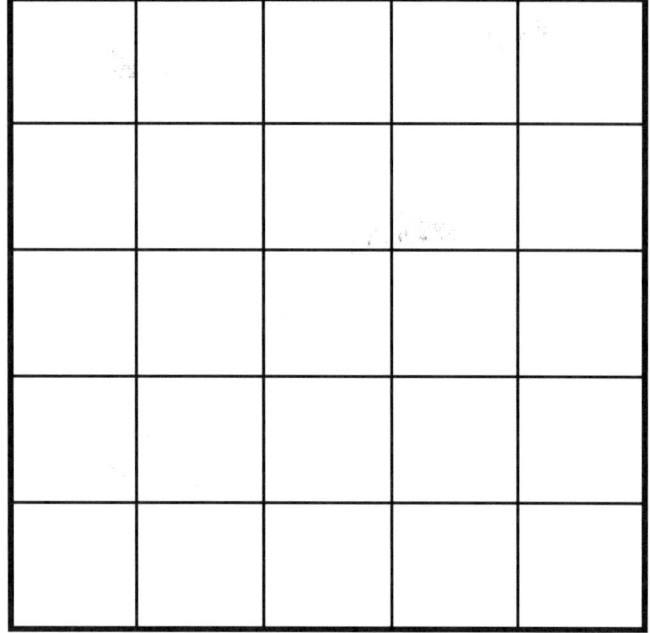

Two Examples of Maze Patterns that the Gamemaster Can Model or Improvise

ENTER

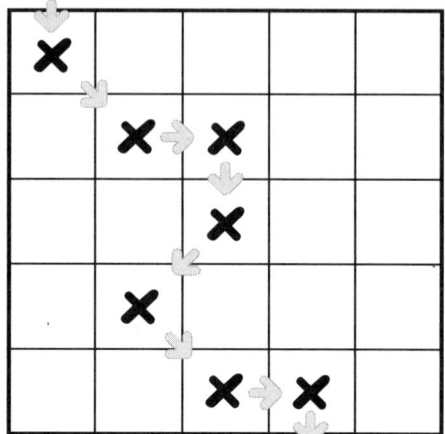

EXIT

A Sample Pattern Using 5 Rows & Columns

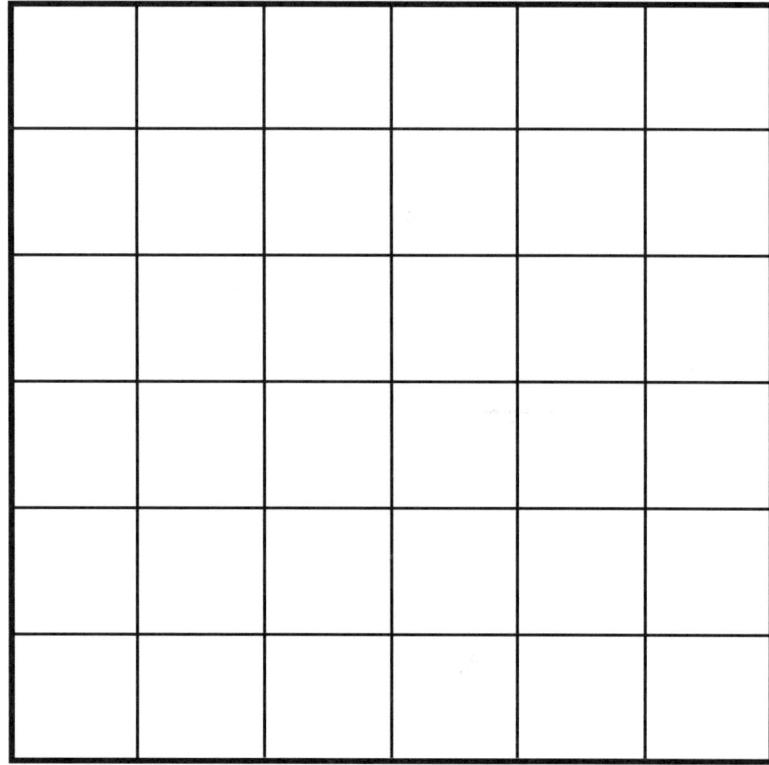

ENTER

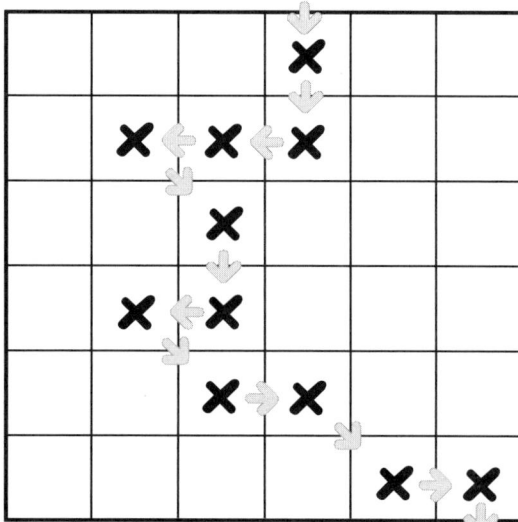

EXIT

A More Challenging Pattern Using 6 Rows & Columns

Warp Speed

PURPOSE

"Warp Speed" is designed to build coordination, cooperation, and team skills. Just as birds learn to fly in formation, sports or any team game becomes more fun as team members get in sync with each other. As children use the tools together, they can watch themselves become more coordinated, see their speeds increase, and experience a dynamic flow of team entrainment and coherence.

AGES
8-18

TIME
10 minutes or longer

PLAYERS
Five or more children

LOCATION
Indoors or outdoors (with space to form circles)

EQUIPMENT
➡ One medium-sized ball per team
➡ One stopwatch or watch with a second hand per group

INSTRUCTIONS

1. The object of the game is to pass or throw the ball around the circle as fast as possible with every player participating. Each group will be timed.

2. There are two rules:

   a. The ball must be touched by all participants.

   b. The ball must always be passed in the same order established in the first rotation.

3. Create one or more teams with approximately the same number of children with similar skill levels in each team. Designate an older child for each team (or adult) to be the gamemaster who doesn't play but keeps time.

4. When a team is ready to begin, the gamemaster starts timing. Stop timing when the ball has touched the hands of all players.

5. Whatever the scored time, the gamemaster should tell the players that they can still improve their time. Repeat the two rules once again. If there is more than one group, the gamemaster calls out the time so other groups can hear as an incentive to improve their times.

6. Suggest that teams practice Freeze-Framing before they begin, and maintain heart focus as they play in order to increase their speed and become more entrained (in sync) with each other.

7. Watch the inventiveness of each group unfold as players find creative ways to improve their times, knowing that they can always keep improving even if by a nano-second.

VARIATION

For older children, assign different patterns in which the ball must be thrown. For example, to the person across from you and one to the right; to every third person around the circle; alternating boy-boy, girl-girl, boy-boy, etc.

Blindfolded Geometry

PURPOSE

"Blindfolded Geometry" develops sensitivity to movement, cooperation skills, and teamwork. It also requires sincere listening to carefully follow the team leader's instructions. Children who are given the opportunity to be the team leader must visualize or think spatially to give effective instructions.

AGES
8-18

TIME
10 minutes or longer

PLAYERS
Adult and five or more children

LOCATION
Indoors or outdoors (on a large, flat space)

EQUIPMENT
➡ Blindfolds for each player
➡ Approximately 50 yards of standard clothesline rope

INSTRUCTIONS

1. The object of the game is to create a square (or other shape) out of the rope using all players and the full length of the rope. All players must be blindfolded and hold onto the rope. Select one of the players to be the team leader.

2. All players remain silent during the game except the team leader who, although blindfolded, will verbally instruct the other mute players to move into a square shape, circle, rectangle, diamond, or other appropriate shape.

3. When the team leader feels that the goal of creating a square (or other designated shape) is complete, he tells everyone to remove their blindfolds and determine how close they came to creating the desired shape.

4. Debrief afterwards and discuss what worked and what didn't.

5. Play the game again with a new team leader who chooses the same shape or a new shape.

Fantasy Islands

PURPOSE

Besides food, clothing, and shelter, children and adults have other basic needs like love, fun, and physical and emotional security. In this fantasy game of values and choices, each individual or team will occupy an island that specializes in a specific need. While needs are abundantly met in one area, other primary needs are missing that require fulfillment in order to live full and comfortable lives. "Fantasy Islands" is a wonderful family game that develops creativity, cooperation, and teamwork as players assess and try to meet their basic needs. Players also learn about exchanging goods and services.

AGES
12-18

TIME
30 minutes or longer

PLAYERS
Adult and four or more children

LOCATION
Indoors or outdoors

EQUIPMENT
➡ 12 index cards per island
➡ Paper and pencil for each player
⇨ Colored markers for drawings and advertisements

INSTRUCTIONS

1. Before explaining the purpose of the game, have each player personally identify six basic needs for a satisfying life. Without these needs being met, their lives would be terribly uncomfortable, malnourished, inconvenient, lonely, or boring.

   Examples: food, clothing, shelter, parents, special people, fun, health, etc. Discuss the results as a group.

2. Explain the purpose of "Fantasy Islands" and read the following. "Everyone has basic needs to satisfy in order to live healthy and fulfilling lives. In this game, each individual (or small team) occupies an island that specializes in one specific need but other basic needs are missing. Through cooperation and trading, each island can satisfy its needs by exchanging goods or services with neighboring islands. The goal is for each island to live as well as possible."

3. For teams: Divide the group into at least four teams by having the players count off 1,2,3,4... and then grouping the players according to number. If there are more than two players on every team, expand to five or six teams.

4. Each team picks a scout to gather information about the other islands' products and needs, and picks a trader who can propose exchanges with traders from other islands. If there is only one player per team, that player is both scout and trader. No talking is permitted between teams except through the trader or scout, otherwise a team can be penalized and a product taken away.

5. Each island chooses a different need category. Suggested need categories: food, fun, special people, shelter, emotions, technology, etc.

6. Each island identifies six basic products or services within their need category. Their products cannot include nor be marginally related to products that are produced on other islands. Each of the six products is written on two separate index cards for a total of twelve cards. The duplicate cards can be traded for other needs.

Examples of products or services within a need category:

Food: vegetables, bread, meat, sweets, fruit, and drinks

Fun (no technology): beach, skiing mountain, games, books, fun places to visit, zoo

Special people: parents, friends, grandparents, favorite celebrities, doctors

Emotions: joy, happiness, excitement, peace, courage, laughter

Equipment and Technology (current): computers, transportation, telephones, robots, house building, roads

7. There will be two, ten-minute rounds of trading with a five-minute evaluation period in between for each team to assess their need status. If there are more than two players per team, after the evaluation period, rotate a new scout and trader. After the second round of trading is completed, there will be a survey done by scouts to see if all islands have met their needs and are living well. If the consensus is fulfillment, have each team summarize what products their island accumulated. A third round can be added where all teams create another product (even outside their need category) to further increase their quality of life.

8. When the game is over, discuss how basic needs lead to fulfillment in regular life.

VARIATIONS

1. Do a numerical tally of the top basic needs identified by players and discuss the reasons behind those choices.

2. Have the players do a numerical survey of the top basic needs of parents and other adults. Compare and contrast these results with those of the teen players.

3. Have the players create a visual map of their islands with drawings and advertisements promoting their products.

4. Discuss the current local, state, national, or global situation and whether people's needs are being met or not, and why. Discuss solutions.

EXAMPLES

At a middle school, an ESL (English as a second language) teacher tried this game out with her students who came from many countries, including Jordan, Israel, Mexico, Poland, Pakistan, Dominican Republic, Columbia, and El Salvador. Her comment: "It went very well. The children really enjoyed this game. They especially enjoyed working in teams. Some students who normally don't socialize together were put together on the same team and they worked together real well. That surprised me. They chose the categories of food, fun, emotions, equipment, technology, and special people. Each category had a different colored index card. After two rounds of trading, the children concluded that we need each other's help in order to be fulfilled. This is an activity we will do again."

Comments from a fourteen-year-old: "It was fun because we were all doing it together in teamwork. And we got to be creative in making our own world and then watching it change as different needs came up."

The Companion Book to *Teaching Children to Love*

A Parenting Manual

by Doc Lew Childre

Teaching Children to Love provides parents, educators, childcare providers, and counselors with highly effective games and activities that teach young people how to live life from the heart. For a deeper understanding of the principles presented in this book, we recommend Doc Lew Childre's *A Parenting Manual: Heart Hope for the Family.*

A Parenting Manual offers new, insightful information on how to parent yourself as well as your children and provides an in-depth understanding of the concepts that underlie the games and activities found in *Teaching Children to Love.* Doc's intention in writing *A Parenting Manual* was to help parents cope with their own as well as their children's stresses, strengthen communication, and develop heart intelligence.

"A helpful, hopeful approach to the parenting process... empowers parents by giving them tools needed to look inside themselves for strength and guidance."
David Katzner, President, The National Parenting Center

"...practical, down-to-earth guide in bringing love, compassion and empathy into all human relationships, especially with children."
Larry Dossey, M.D., Author, *Healing Words*

"This is a perfect book for all parents on this planet."
Steveanne Auerbach, Ph.D., Director,
Institute for Childhood Resources

$14.95 • 152 pages • ISBN 1-879052-32-6

Kids' Power Pak™ $49.95

Complete System for Child Development

Give your kids the opportunity to benefit from advanced learning methods and help insure a more hopeful and productive future for your family. **by Doc Lew Childre**

Effectively dealing with challenges, speaking honestly, making important life choices with wisdom and patience, loving and being loved—all of these are learned abilities that we can teach our children. That's what the *Kids' Power Pak* is about—a system designed to teach simple, practical tools to help children reach their highest potential. Through audio tapes, music, games, and exercises children learn and apply techniques like FREEZE-FRAME, the CUT-THRU tool and how to do a HEART LOCK-IN—valuable skills for young people in today's ever-changing world.

A comprehensive learning guide shows you how to use each component for maximum results and—your children will be able to listen, read, and learn from the *Kids' Power Pak* all by themselves.

The components found in this system all work together to help children develop:

- Resiliency, Discipline, and Self-Security
- Skills for Safe and Healthy Life Choices
- Improved Academic Performance
- Lasting Values and Balance
- A More Complete Intelligence

The Kids' Power Pak Includes:

Teaching Children to Love—80 games and fun activities that increase intelligence and foster emotional balance.

Buddy Bubbles—cassette tape for children 2-8 that introduces children to the magic and power of the heart. Develops positive attitudes and self-worth.

Heart Signals—an entertaining cassette tape that teaches children 8-14 the tools FREEZE-FRAME and CUT-THRU. Increases self-security and the ability to make balanced decisions.

Heart Zones—scientifically-designed music that calms as it energizes. Great for study time to enhance the learning environment.

Speed of Balance—the latest in advanced music technology. Helps to increase emotional intelligence and inner stability.

Learning Guide—complete instructions on exactly how and why to use each component along with a scientific understanding of why this system works.

Heart Zones

Doc Lew Childre
Cassette $9.95
CD $15.95

Heart Zones, Doc Lew Childre's first "designer" music release, was on *Billboard Magazine's* top sales charts for a year. This popular music leaves you feeling calm, clear, and relaxed. Put it on in a traffic jam, before an important meeting, or when you just want to tune out the mind chatter. Feel focused, undisturbed, and refreshed no matter what's going on around you. Children are very responsive to the calming effects of *Heart Zones* too. Designed to facilitate the FREEZE-FRAME technique.

Speed of Balance

Doc Lew Childre
Cassette $9.95
CD $15.95

Speed of Balance creates an energizing and uplifting feeling, making it easier for you to let go of negative thoughts and emotions. Jazz enthusiasts, classical lovers, and even rock-n-rollers find it revitalizing and entertaining.

A recent research study showed that people can raise their own levels of the anti-aging hormone DHEA by practicing the CUT-THRU technique and listening to *Speed of Balance*.

Buddy Bubbles

Deborah Rozman, Ph.D.
$9.95 • cassette tape

NEW EDITION!

*Magical Games
for a Child's Heart
—Ages 2-8*

This Fun, New Edition Introduces Young Children to Whole Brain Learning and Heart Intelligence.

This heartwarming tape features delightful games, poetry, songs, and instruction to help children develop positive attitudes and self-worth. Children are shown how to find warmth and security within their own heart and are taught "fun"damental life skills that increase intelligence through mental and emotional balance. Children learn the difference between the head and the heart, how to talk to their "Heart Buddy" to find answers and how to slow down and focus. *Buddy Bubbles* is popular with all children and is an important resource for those who care for young children who are emotionally distraught due to life circumstances beyond their understanding. A fun, easy-to-use resource for parents, child care providers, grandparents, and early childhood educators.

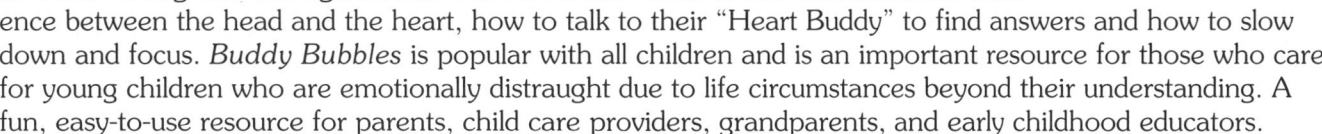

A Good Time to Listen...

- In the car—a great drive-time companion
- At home, at parties, or in the classroom
- Before sleep; calms after stimulating activities
- During special adult-child time

A Fun Way to...

- Build healthy values, self-confidence, & positive attitudes
- Enhance learning ability & creativity
- Turn frowns into giggles

The How To Book of Teen Self Discovery

Doc Lew Childre
ISBN 1-879052-36-9
$8.95 • 126 pages
Cartoon Illustrations

Find help, hope, and solutions in this book written for teens, but that talks to the teen in everyone. Offers easy tools for developing inner security and communication skills. Gives practical ways to manage emotions and reactions. Helps teens learn how to make positive choices and successfully meet the challenges of today's world.

- Approved as a textbook by the California Department of Education
- A *Reading Is Fundamental* approved selection
- Chosen for the 1996 *Read, America!* Collection

"Excellent job of introducing teenagers to their feelings—and to healthy self-esteem. An excellent tool for teenagers, adults and teachers. I recommend it highly."*— Emmett E. Miller, M.D., California Task Force to Promote Self Esteem and Personal and Social Responsibility*

Meditating With Children

Deborah Rozman, Ph.D.
ISBN 1-879052-24-5
$14.95 • 154 pages
Illustrations and Photographs
For children and adults of all ages

Written by educator and psychologist Deborah Rozman, Ph.D., contributing editor for *Teaching Children to Love*. This classic book is considered to be one of the finest books ever published on the value of concentration and centering techniques for children. Gives step-by-step lesson plans for unlocking creativity and verbal and emotional expression. Provides practical, fun methods for helping children calm and balance their energy naturally. Nonreligious in approach, this book is an excellent guide and facilitator of more harmony in all home, school, and childcare environments.

"Educators who once turned to Ritalin and other drugs for hyperactive children... are now turning to daily meditation exercises instead — with positive results."*— San Jose Mercury*

The Hidden Power of the Heart

Sara Paddison
ISBN 1-879052-35-0
$11.95 • 280 pages

This inspirational book shows how a single mother developed her heart intuition to transform her life. Sara weaves common-sense techniques into a fascinating story of triumph over insecurity and shows readers how they can do the same. Presents a profound picture of the meaning of life and the importance of bringing more love and care into daily living. Dozens of applications for bringing more fulfillment into family living.

"Sincere family feelings come from the heart...Family would include the extended family, people attracted to each other based on heart resonance, and mutual support." *— excerpted from The Hidden Power of the Heart*

FREEZE-FRAME

by Doc Lew Childre

Book
ISBN 1-879052-39-3
$9.95 • 144 pages

Audiobook
ISBN 1-879052-40-7
$16.95 • 2 stereo cassettes
3 hours • unabridged

FREEZE-FRAME is a simple power tool for managing stress in the moment — simple enough for use in the midst of hectic family situations, by both adults and children. This scientifically-based technique is presented in both *Teaching Children to Love* and *A Parenting Manual*.

- Make lasting changes that will improve your family relationships and communication
- Manage reactive emotions like frustration and anger without repressing your feelings or losing control
- Enhance decision-making abilities
- Understand what happens in your body when you're under stress and how to change for better health and more vitality
- Increase fulfillment in family living

"If you're upset, the heart feels it. What you can do in the moment to calm yourself down is called Freeze-Frame."

— Dr. Donna Willis, NBC News' The "Today" Show

FREEZE-FRAME
Inner Fitness System

Developed by Doc Lew Childre

Multimedia program includes:
- FREEZE-FRAME Learning Guide
- FREEZE-FRAME Audiobook
- Heart Zones Cassette & CD
- FREEZE-FRAME Book
- FREEZE-FRAME Video

  $99

Good health and well-being requires more than diet and exercise. The stress of the '90s has brought an awareness of the need for mental and emotional fitness as well. The FREEZE-FRAME Inner Fitness System provides you with everything you need to start you own "Inner Fitness" program. You will learn how to develop the mental and emotional "muscles" you need to renew your zest for life, boost your energy level, and achieve your goals. A $125 value.

CUT-THRU

Doc Lew Childre

Book
ISBN 1-879052-33-4
$11.95 • 160 pages

Audiobook
ISBN 1-879052-37-7
$16.95 • 2 cassettes
3 hours • slightly abridged

Learn CUT-THRU...

a simple technique that shows how to turn negative emotions into peace and clarity. Feel good whenever you want to, regardless of circumstances, by discovering what this power tool can do for you. In laboratory studies measuring CUT-THRU's effectiveness, people achieved an average 100% increase in DHEA (the anti-aging hormone) — in just 30 days!

Use CUT-THRU to...

• prevent burnout
• help balance hormones and reduce PMS
• slow the aging process

"CUT-THRU explains the crucial link between heartfelt emotions and our physical health — and then explains precisely how to apply this information in our own lives. Must reading for everyone interested in living a healthy and joy-filled life."

— Christiane Northrup, M.D., author of Women's Bodies, Women's Wisdom

Self Empowerment

Doc Lew Childre
ISBN 1-879052-34-2
$13.95 • 141 pages

A comprehensive view of today's social issues and how each individual can make a positive difference. Explains how to implement solutions to challenges everyone faces in a world of accelerating change. Doc includes wonderful anecdotes that bring his perspectives home with humor, warmth, and profound insight. Change the way you view the world, your family, and yourself.

"The first to understand the family way of dealing with people will become examples of quality relationships within businesses, social organizations, governments and at home...The earlier children understand the balance between their head and their heart, the less they will have to unlearn later in life in order to discover who they really are...Care is one of our most effective outgoing energy expenditures — it is *love* in the active modality."**—excerpted from Self Empowerment**

Women Lead With Their Hearts

A White Paper
Doc Lew Childre
$5.00 • 27 pages

Presented at the 1995 Women of Vision Conference in Washington, D.C., this brief and potent paper begins, "The empowerment of women is a global issue in the '90s." Deeply provocative, this booklet addresses the new woman of the 21st century.

"When love and self-worth permeate your system, they transform fears and insecurities into self-esteem or (spirit integration)...Women's intuition is not just an old wives' tale. It's inner power, once women know how to access it with continuity. This increases magnetic effectiveness..." **— excerpted from Women Lead With Their Hearts**

About the Institute of HeartMath Programs & Retreats

*Do something wonderful for yourself,
your family and the world. . .
Experience hope, gain real power to make
positive changes,and have the time of your life!*

You will learn:
• Tools that help you make conscious choices from the heart, build self-reliance and develop emotional flexibility and resilience

• How to make inner attitude adjustments and access heart intelligence for effective communication and discipline, including difficult children

• Vital information on the developmental stages in today's children (birth to age 19) and how their perceptual world grows at each stage

• How to revitalize and build a stronger, more caring foundation for family relationships,

• Breakthrough scientific research on the role love plays in personal intelligence, perception, and physiology

• New technology that dramatically changes the way we guide children

• How to truly care for yourself, stop the worries and decrease the impact of stress in the moment that can lead to burn-out

For more information about IHM programs and retreats, call 1-800-450-9111

For complete information on IHM training programs, contact:
INSTITUTE OF HEARTMATH
14700 West Park Avenue
Boulder Creek, CA 95006
(408) 338-8700
fax/408-338-9861
http://www.heartmath.org
E-mail: hrtmath@netcom.com

Skilled, experienced facilitators lead you on a full, in-depth learning adventure, that blends classroom instruction with personal and interactive exercises. Three-night/two-day programs, held in the beautiful redwood forests of northern California provide ample private time for learning, relaxation, recreation, and reflections. One and two-day programs can also be brought to your organization.

About the Editors

Sara Hatch Paddison, editor

Sara Paddison brings her experience as author and mother, her background in psychology and elementary education from East Carolina University, and her extensive work with Doc Lew Childre, to her editorial role for *Teaching Children to Love*. Sara is vice president of IHM, and has worked extensively with Doc Lew Childre over many years in developing the HeartMath system. She is the author of two books and editor of many more. Her book, *The Hidden Power of the Heart* (in its third printing) is the basis of IHM's Heart Empowerment® seminars. *The Hidden Power of the Heart* tells Sara's personal story of self-transformation using HeartMath tools. As editor of *Teaching Children to Love*, she is especially concerned with helping parents, educators, and counselors learn how to teach HeartMath self-management tools to children. She was also editor for *A Parenting Manual: Heart Hope for the Family*, by Doc Lew Childre.

Deborah Rozman, Ph.D., contributing editor

Psychologist, author, and IHM Executive Director, Deborah is perhaps best known for her classic books for children, educators and parents, including *Meditating With Children*. As a leader in educational psychology, she founded an innovative school specializing in creativity and intuitive development in children. Deborah develops and presents HeartMath programs throughout the U.S. and Canada and is a frequent keynote speaker. She certifies trainers in IHM seminars on Heart Empowerment, Inner Quality Management and creativity, Women's Empowerment, Empowered Parents, Teaching Children to Love. Deborah studied attitude change theory and psychology at the University of Chicago and has spent twenty years researching the psychology of consciousness. In addition to authoring five books and editing dozens of others on the psychology of human development, she is author of the cassette tapes *Buddy Bubbles: Magical Games for a Child's Heart* (for children 2-8) and *The Heart Way* (for children 6-12).

Jeffrey Goelitz, M.Ed., contributing editor

Jeffrey Goelitz is a teacher, counselor, educational consultant, and educational trainer. He is author of *The Ultimate Kid*, a whole brain learning guide for parents and teachers. Jeff travels throughout the U.S. giving "Empowered Parent" workshops and HeartMath seminars to families, teachers, and counselors. He was a featured speaker at The International Conference on Education in Stockholm, Sweden, where he trained scores of educators and youth from more than forty nations. Jeff has designed model HeartMath programs for schools and communities in crisis, including a Business Mentoring Program for at-risk teens. Currently, he serves as Director of Education at the Institute of HeartMath.

Wanda Wortman, contributing editor

Wanda Wortman, currently director of an after-school program, field-tested and refined the games and activities in *Teaching Children to Love* with children of different age groups. A mother herself, she consults with parents on strategies to help reduce stress and bring more love into the family. Wanda takes great delight in teaching children to find balance and emotional maturity through HeartMath tools and games, giving them creative support as they develop their heart intelligence.